AF605961

INSTITUTION BUILDING *in* WEAK STATES

ANDREW RADIN

INSTITUTION BUILDING *in* WEAK STATES

The PRIMACY *of* LOCAL POLITICS

GEORGETOWN UNIVERSITY PRESS / WASHINGTON, DC

Library of Congress Cataloging-in-Publication Data

Names: Radin, Andrew, author.
Title: Institution Building in Weak States : The Primacy of Local Politics / Andrew Radin.
Description: Washington, DC : Georgetown University Press, 2020. | Includes bibliographical references and index.
Identifiers: LCCN 2019038735 (print) | LCCN 2019038736 (ebook) | ISBN 9781626167940 (hardcover) | ISBN 9781626167957 (paperback) | ISBN 9781626167964 (ebook)
Subjects: LCSH: Postwar reconstruction—Case studies. | Nation-building—Case studies. | Institution building—Case studies. | Elite (Social sciences)
Classification: LCC JZ6300 .R34 2020 (print) | LCC JZ6300 (ebook) | DDC 327.1/11—dc23
LC record available at https://lccn.loc.gov/2019038735
LC ebook record available at https://lccn.loc.gov/2019038736

21 20 9 8 7 6 5 4 3 2 First printing

Cover design by Jeremy John Parker.
Interior design by BookComp, Inc.

For my father, Arthur

CONTENTS

ILLUSTRATIONS

FIGURES

TABLES

PREFACE

Improving state institutions in partner countries is an important, enduring, and challenging task for the United States and the international community. Building partner capacity is a key component of US counterterrorism strategy and US policy to deter both Russia and China. Many scholars and practitioners see institution building as essential to ensuring a sustainable peace in post-conflict societies.

A key unappreciated problem with institution building is that foreign missions often propose changes to state institutions that threaten the interests of the elites and the population within the partner country. This book explores how these proposed changes can provoke opposition that can damage the prospects for reform. I show how foreign missions in the mid-2000s in Bosnia and Herzegovina, Kosovo, Timor-Leste, and Iraq repeatedly undermined their own efforts by proposing changes to state institutions that threatened core domestic interests—namely, nationalist goals and patron-client networks. Drawing from my experience working on a RAND Corporation project in 2015, I observe the same problem in Ukraine, where Western recommendations that posed the least threat to patron-client networks ultimately made the greatest improvement to defense institutions. The book concludes that foreign reformers who proposed changes to state institutions that minimize domestic opposition while still making improvements were ultimately able to achieve the greatest progress.

This book is intended for anyone aspiring to reform state institutions in another country, including students of public policy, government officials, military officers working with foreign counterparts, and international development professionals. The book's case studies focus on reforms of central government, defense, and police institutions, but the suggestion that foreign reformers select their demands or recommendations to limit domestic opposition also applies to other state institutions. Foreign reformers are right to aspire to make partners' state institutions more effective, accountable, and law abiding, but reformers need to be selective and patient to avoid counterproductive opposition.

ACKNOWLEDGMENTS

I am grateful to everyone who agreed to be interviewed for this project. I learned a tremendous amount from foreign officials, other scholars and analysts, and, most especially, the unique perspective of local officials. I am immensely thankful that they took the time to meet with me and offer their expertise. I hope that the book is useful to my interlocutors and that anyone reading this book will appreciate the benefit of talking with researchers in the future.

I am also deeply appreciative of Roger Petersen, Barry Posen, and Fotini Christia for their encouragement, support, and honest feedback. I would also like to thank my friends and colleagues who read the work and offered comments at multiple stages, especially Brendan Green, Alec Worsnop, Austin Long, Miranda Priebe, Joseph Torigian, Joshua Itzkowitz Shifrinson, Reo Matsuzaki, David Weinberg, Jon Lindsay, Sameer Lalwani, Kristin Fabbe, Nathan Cisneros, and Paul Staniland. Phil Haun offered feedback and assistance at a final, critical stage.

Funding from the Smith Richardson Foundation was critical to getting this book published, and, ten years ago, for supporting some of the original fieldwork for this project. Research fellowships from the US Institute for Peace, the Woodrow Wilson International Center for Scholars, the University of Southern California, and the International Studies Program at the Harvard Kennedy School's Belfer Center for Science and International Affairs also made this project possible. Many individuals offered advice and suggestions on this project, and I would particularly like to thank Philippe Leroux-Martin, Louis-Alexandre Berg, Pellumb Kelmendi, Elton Skendaj, Patrick James, Jacques Hyman, Brian Rathbun, Diana O'Brien, Benjamin Graham, Steve Miller, Kelly Greenhill, Mark Waldman, Marisa Porges, Jill Goldenziel, Jonathan Markowitz, and Jenifer Keister.

I would also thank current and former colleagues from RAND who offered feedback, insight, and encouragement, including Lynn Davis, James Dobbins, Seth Jones, Chris Chivvis, Jonathan Blake, Elina Treyger, Irina Chindea, Abby Fanlo, Rachel Tecott, William Mackenzie, Rich Girven, Charlie Ries, Jack Riley,

Olga Oliker, and Astrid Stuth Cevallos. Thanks as well to Rebecca Fowler, Agnes Schaefer, John Coughlan, Denis Flieder, and Michele Platt for helping bring this project to completion.

At Georgetown University Press, my thanks to Don Jacobs for taking an interest in the project and bringing this book to fruition. I also thank Elizabeth Crowley Webber for her care in overseeing the production of the final manuscript. And I very much appreciate the comments and suggestions from Roy Licklider and one anonymous reviewer.

I also could not have done this without the love and distraction provided by my daughters, Hattie and Freya. My wife, Sara, read endless drafts at all hours, made me explain myself, and gave me the support to keep going with this project. I cannot thank her enough. My mother, Miriam, kept cheering me on through good fortune and adversity.

I would like to dedicate this book to my father, Arthur, whom we greatly miss. His encouragement, culminating in the repeating question of "Where's your book," is an important reason why this volume exists today. I was inspired by his indefatigable intellectual curiosity, passion for clarity, and distaste for jargon, even if I did not always live up to these good qualities. Months before he unexpectedly passed away, he helped to proofread and correct a final draft. My one regret is that he will not get to see the finished product.

ABBREVIATIONS

AAK	Aleanca për Ardhmërinë e Kosovës (Alliance for the Future of Kosovo)
AFBiH	Armed Forces of Bosnia and Herzegovina
ATO	Anti-Terror Operation
BiH	Bosnia and Herzegovina
C4ISR	command, control, communications, computers, intelligence, surveillance, and reconnaissance
CHoD	chief of defense
CNRT	Congresso Nacional de Reconstrução de Timor (National Congress for Timorese Reconstruction)
CPA	Coalition Provisional Authority
CPATT	Civilian Police Assistance Training Team
DRC	Defense Reform Commission
EU	European Union
EULEX	EU Rule of Law Mission
EUPM	EU Police Mission
F-FDTL	Falintil-Forcas Defensa Timor Lorosae
ICG	International Crisis Group
IEBL	inter-entity boundary line
IPS	Iraqi Police Service
ISIS	Islamic State of Iraq and Syria
JIAS	Joint Interim Administrative Structure
JNA	Jugoslovenska narodna armija (Yugoslav People's Army)
KFOR	Kosovo Force
KLA	Kosovo Liberation Army
LDK	Lidhja Demokratike e Kosovës (Democratic League of Kosovo)
MNSTC-I	Multi-National Security Training Command-Iraq
MoD	Ministry of Defense

MoI	Ministry of Interior
NATO	North Atlantic Treaty Organization
OHR	Office of the High Representative
ORHA	Office of Reconstruction and Humanitarian Assistance
OSCE	Organization for Security and Cooperation in Europe
PDK	Partia Demokratike e Kosovës (Democratic Party of Kosovo)
PfP	Partnership for Peace
PISG	Provisional Institutions of Self-Government
PNTL	Polisia Nasional Timor-Leste (National Police of Timor-Leste)
PRC	Police Restructuring Commission
PSF	Philippine Security Forces
PTT	police transition team
RS	Republika Srpska
RSNA	RS National Assembly
SAA	Stabilization and Association Agreement
SBU	Sluzhba bezpeky Ukrayiny (Security Service of Ukraine)
SCIRI	Supreme Council for the Islamic Revolution in Iraq
SDB	Strategic Defense Bulletin
SDO	State Defense Order
SDS	Srpska demokratska stranka (Serb Democratic Party)
SFOR	Stabilization Force
SNSD	Savez nezavisnih socijaldemokrata (Alliance of Independent Social Democrats)
SoI	Sons of Iraq
SRSG	special representative of the secretary-general
TAL	Transitional Administrative Law
VF	Vojska Federacije Bosne i Hercegovine (Army of the Federation of BiH)
VRS	Vojska Republike Srpske (Army of the RS)
UN	United Nations
UNMIK	UN Mission in Kosovo
UNMISET	UN Mission in Support of East Timor
UNTAET	UN Transitional Administration in East Timor

CHAPTER ONE

INTRODUCTION

In January 2015 I made my first trip to Ukraine for a RAND Corporation project to advise the Office of the President of Ukraine on security sector reform. After Russia had seized Crimea and supported separatists in eastern Ukraine, Ukraine was at war, but its defense establishment was in poor condition. Ukrainian military units were at low readiness—only six thousand soldiers of the forty-one-thousand-strong Ukrainian army were available for use.[1] Civilian volunteers provided basic logistics and formed new units outside the formal military structure. There was little coordination between the stovepiped defense and security institutions. Ukraine's large defense industrial complex was focused on exports, not on meeting the immediate needs of the military. To understand the problems facing Ukraine, our team met with a wide range of ministries and agencies responsible for security. On subsequent trips, we traveled to Kramatorsk to talk with Ukrainian personnel serving in the conflict. It was clear that major changes would be necessary to improve Ukraine's military effectiveness and achieve European and NATO standards of transparency and accountability.[2]

In my work in Ukraine, I drew from my prior work studying security sector reform in Bosnia and Herzegovina (hereafter Bosnia or BiH), Kosovo, Timor-Leste, and Iraq.[3] I had previously observed that foreign reform efforts in these societies often sought to replicate Western-style institutions. However, the elites and the mass population in these societies opposed reform when Western demands threatened domestic political priorities, and at times this opposition undermined foreign-supported reform. While some of my colleagues at RAND argued that it was most important for us to provide a model for what Ukraine's defense institutions should become, I was concerned that a backlash similar to what I observed in my previous work might occur in Ukraine. I therefore believed that we should design our recommendations with the likely sources of domestic opposition in Ukraine in mind. Our interlocutors in the government of Ukraine, however, resolved this tension by asking us to make recommendations for how the Ukrainian military could meet NATO standards, not for recommendations that were politically feasible to implement.

We proceeded by identifying problems with Ukraine's current structures and practices based on interviews with local officials and foreign advisers. We drew on models of defense institutions from countries such as the United States, France, Germany, and Australia. Perhaps our most critical recommendation was to reorganize the Ministry of Defense by subordinating the General Staff and Armed Forces of Ukraine under a civilian minister of defense. We hoped this change would strengthen civilian control, make decision-making more efficient, and encourage better coordination. We also made suggestions to improve combat support functions, such as logistics and communications, and proposed reforming Ukraine's procurement system and the state-owned defense industrial complex, Ukroboronprom.

Our report was well received by the Ukrainian government and by Western analysts. Many of our recommendations were incorporated into the Strategic Defense Bulletin (SDB) approved in June 2016. In addition to informing the SDB, Ukrainian officials told me that our report spurred discussion about reform, and Western organizations used our report as a guide and benchmark to judge progress in the Ukrainian defense establishment.[4]

Ultimately, however, as my prior research suggested, individuals and organizations within Ukraine appeared to respond to our recommendations based on the perceived impact to their interests. The minister of defense, a military officer, responded positively and publicly announced that the ministry would launch a new working group to consider our recommendations.[5] Our report generally supported his position: we recommended that the chief of the General Staff be subordinated to the minister, and we accepted that, although the minister's successor would need to be a civilian, he could be grandfathered into his current position. According to think tank reports, other individuals were less supportive, including the chief of the General Staff, perhaps in part because our recommendations would weaken their positions relative to the Ministry of Defense.[6] The report's recommendations, as I detail in chapter 6, appeared to be most implemented where they posed the least threat to the existing leadership's patron-client networks, meaning the personal connections between the leaders and subordinate officials. For example, while there was some progress implementing an e-procurement system for nonlethal supplies, major reform of the procurement system was indefinitely delayed, and there was little apparent willingness to undertake fundamental reforms of Ukraine's sprawling and opaque defense industrial complex.[7] These changes likely posed a greater threat to the political and economic interests of Ukraine's leaders.

Improving state institutions in partner countries, such as the defense institutions in Ukraine, is an important and enduring task for the United States and the international community. My experience in Ukraine points to a common but understudied problem facing foreign institution builders. To improve partner institutions, foreign reformers must propose changes to these institutions, which may be framed either as obligatory demands or as optional recommendations. These changes often threaten the interests of elites and the population within the partner country, which can lead to opposition that damages the prospects for reform. This challenge raises an important question: what types of changes should foreign missions seek in partner institutions to make the greatest progress?

My central argument in this book is that foreign institution builders achieve the greatest success when they propose changes that do not provoke domestic opposition, and that they can do so by avoiding threatening two core domestic interests—nationalist goals, such as achieving independence or ethnic autonomy, and the ruling elites' patron-client networks. I propose a "domestic opposition" theory to explain how foreign demands or recommendations that threaten these interests lead to different types of opposition. When reform threatens nationalist goals, it usually fails because of widespread public opposition, such as mass protests or boycotts by the elite. For example, in Bosnia, an effort from 2004 to 2006 to restructure the police force challenged the autonomy of the Bosnian Serbs, which led to mass protests and to Serb leaders refusing to comply with international demands for reform. The international mission was forced to compromise due to the popular opposition and as a result lost legitimacy for future reform efforts. Likewise, when reform threatens the patron-client networks of ruling elites, elites often privately oppose reform through delay tactics or co-opting state institutions. For example, in Iraq following the 2007 surge, Shia leaders blocked the recruitment of Sunnis into the police force in mixed sectarian areas, which undermined Sunnis' confidence in the government. While well-resourced foreign reformers can make some progress against elite opposition, foreigners lack the local knowledge to fully monitor and punish obstruction by domestic elites. The most successful reforms improve state institutions by avoiding threatening nationalist goals and patron-client networks. For example, in the case of the defense reforms in BiH that began in 2003, shortly before the police restructuring effort, the international community proposed incremental changes that accommodated Serb interests while still creating a unified military out of two ethnically based militaries.

To show how foreign proposals shape the outcome of reform through domestic opposition, I explore seven cases of foreign-backed reform. The main analysis considers six reform efforts undertaken by highly resourced, post-conflict missions in Bosnia, Kosovo, Timor-Leste, and Iraq. In a seventh case study, I show that similar domestic dynamics occurred in the lower resourced, non-post-conflict case of defense reform in Ukraine. Each case study uses written sources and personal interviews to explore why domestic actors opposed (or supported) reform and how their decisions influenced success. For example, in Iraq in November 2003, interviews and internal memos show how Coalition Provisional Authority (CPA) officials had to compromise for fear that a Shia walkout would delegitimize Iraq's new central governing institutions.

The book also explores two alternative theories about the success of reform that I develop from the literature on intervention. The international resources theory predicts that missions with higher resources—including a stronger mandate, more money or personnel available, and effective planning and coordination—are more likely to make greater improvements to a state institution. The path dependence theory emphasizes that state institutions are hard to change and expects that reform is also constrained by the level of development of a society and the quality of an institution before the intervention. The case studies evaluate these explanations by tracing exactly why each institution improved or declined and comparing different reform efforts (for example, military versus police reform in Bosnia) to isolate competing explanations.

In most of the cases studied in this book, domestic opposition is the most important factor determining whether reform hit a wall, made slow progress, or rapidly improved a state institution. Furthermore, it is usually more feasible for foreign interveners to change their demands or recommendations to limit domestic opposition than it is to increase international resources or avoid intervening in societies with poor preexisting institutions. Foreign reformers can achieve greater success by making demands or recommendations that avoid nationalist goals and patron-client networks while still improving a state institution. This is not to say that foreign reformers should or must accept unaccountable or ill-disciplined state institutions. Rather, foreign reformers are right to seek effective, accountable, and law-abiding institutions but need to be selective and patient in proposing changes to state institutions to accomplish these goals. Accommodating domestic interests may be disappointing, but it is a necessary tradeoff if the United States and the international community value improving partner state institutions.

WHAT IS INSTITUTION BUILDING?

This book studies foreign-supported institution building, meaning efforts by an organization outside a given society to improve a state institution within that society. These efforts are often led by foreign countries or organizations but can also be initiated by domestic actors. In describing these efforts, I adopt a frame of reference from within the target society, so I refer to the countries or international organizations pursuing institution building as foreign or international actors. I call the individuals or groups within the society domestic or local actors. I use the terms "institution building" and "reform" interchangeably.

By state institution, I mean an organization that is part of the state and provides a particular function of governance, such as the police, customs administration, education system, or central governing bodies. The book's case studies examine reform of the central government, police, and military. These three state institutions are consistently the focus of international efforts as they are believed to facilitate the maintenance of peace and to be fundamental for ensuring internal and external security, the development of democracy, and basic services.[8] Nevertheless, as discussed in the conclusion, the domestic opposition theory likely applies to efforts to reform other state institutions as well.

In studying state institutions, I consider both the people within the organization and the rules that shape their behavior. For example, defense reform may include recruiting new personnel, changing the formal structure of the military or Ministry of Defense, altering formal rules or legislation, buying new equipment, or training personnel in its use. By improving a state institution or achieving success at reform, I mean making the institution more effective, accountable, or law-abiding, as I explain below.

There is an important distinction between my definition of a state institution as a part of the state and the use of the term "institution" by many works to describe a set of widely agreed-on rules or a stable pattern of behavior. Daron Acemoglu and James Robinson, for example, describe the development of inclusive political and economic institutions, such as laws permitting anyone to open a business, as fundamental for prosperity.[9] Francis Fukuyama also identifies three basic institutions that are associated with highly developed modern democracies: the state, the rule of law, and an accountable government.[10] My usage follows the practices of many organizations that pursue institution building—the US Defense Security Cooperation Agency, for example, refers to its efforts to support military bureaucracies as "defense institution building."[11]

The state institutions studied here are closely connected to, but distinct from, the broader institutions described by scholars such as Acemoglu, Robinson, and Fukuyama. For example, a society may have a police force that is effective at fighting crime and accountable to the population, even if the overall state is weak and the government is autocratic. Or, vice versa, broad institutions within the society could be strong, but a particular state institution could be weak. Nevertheless, in general, the quality of state institutions is expected to contribute to the overall quality of the broad institutions within that society and, hence, political and economic development. The potential impact of state institutions on political and economic development points to the importance of better understanding when and how the United States and its partners can indeed build stronger state institutions abroad.

WHY STUDY INSTITUTION BUILDING?

After US-led interventions in the Balkans, Afghanistan, and Iraq, an extensive literature has developed to study these efforts, and there are growing doubts of the merits of future intervention. Still, institution building deserves further study. It is an essential component of US and international policy, and the existing literature has not offered insight into the critical question of how the choice of demands and recommendations influence reform success.

Even after the drawdowns from Iraq and Afghanistan, institution building remains an important element of US foreign policy because it is rarely practical or efficient for US organizations to address threats without the help of allied or partner organizations. Building partner capacity is a central component of the US 2017 National Security Strategy and 2018 National Defense Strategy.[12] In addition to improving the ability of partners to counter terrorism, US assistance to allies and partners can help deter adversary aggression, as in Ukraine, the Baltic states, or South Korea. In fiscal year 2019, the first year the US Department of Defense reported an aggregate statistic, it requested $3.4 billion for security cooperation.[13] Building partner capacity ultimately hinges on the ability of the United States (and collaborators) to improve state institutions in a given society. Beyond the Department of Defense, other US government organizations, government organizations in other countries, and international organizations also seek to build security or nonsecurity state institutions. In particular, international aid and development efforts often focus on building state institutions to improve accountable government, increase the delivery of services, reduce poverty, and encourage economic development.[14]

Institution building is a particularly important part of large-scale, comprehensive missions to rebuild postwar societies. Such interventions have been referred to as peace building, nation building, or state building.[15] UN transitional missions in societies such as Cambodia, Kosovo, and Timor-Leste sought to improve the police, military, and public services, as did US and allied missions in Germany, Japan, and Iraq. Some practitioners and scholars identify institution building as *the* central activity to create a sustainable peace in societies emerging from civil war.[16] In a 2001 report, then UN secretary-general Kofi Annan wrote that a sustainable peace depends on the ability of domestic institutions to resolve conflict; hence, peace mission mandates should "incorporate such elements as institution-building and the promotion of good governance and the rule of law."[17] In an influential book published in 2004, Roland Paris blames the failure of many peace-building missions in the 1990s on holding elections before strong institutions were in place. Paris recommends "institutionalization before liberalization" to correct this problem, but he does not analyze in detail when and how institution building may be achieved.[18]

Following the terrorist attacks of 2001, some analysts claimed that failed states, meaning countries with an absence of state institutions or with extremely weak ones, were unleashing "public bads," such as terrorism or refugees; they advocated for institution building to address these challenges.[19] Although contemporary US national security discourse downplays the potential for future large-scale "nation-building" missions, large US missions in societies such as Libya or Syria remain possible.[20]

Many works examining postwar intervention tend to assess success or failure at the country level, such as by observing success in Bosnia and Kosovo but failure in Iraq. By contrast, this book studies the development of state institutions, not the development of the overall country.[21] Understanding the varied success of institution building within a society offers new insight about how to adjust institution-building efforts to maximize the potential for success. It also more directly provides advice to the many professionals who work on improving one particular institution rather than the broader state. Further, changes in a particular state institution can also have a wider impact on the political development of a society. In Iraq, for example, the failure to create security institutions that were accountable to the entire population, including Sunnis, undermined the country's future stability.

This book also offers insight into a fundamental question in political science: When and how can societies achieve political development?[22] Many works are skeptical of the ability of foreign efforts to improve institutions. For example, after analyzing the potential for foreign intervention to encourage political development, Fukuyama writes, "We should thus be wary of foreigners bearing gifts of institutions."[23] But the variation in success observed in this book indicates how foreign reformers can at times contribute to political development, especially when they make demands or recommendations that improve state institutions but do not threaten core political interests. The improvements that foreign reformers achieve may not lead to radical or rapid improvements in democracy or the rule of law, but they may be an important first step that sets the stage for longer-term improvements.

DOMESTIC OPPOSITION THEORY

Foreign reformers are not on home turf. The state institutions they seek to reform are staffed by local officials, overseen by local elites, and accountable to the local population. The domestic opposition theory generalizes about the interaction between foreign reformers and these domestic actors. The theory explains how foreign demands or recommendations can threaten domestic interests, when and how domestic actors may support reform or oppose it in different ways, and how their acceptance or opposition shapes the success of reform. Many issues play a role in the domestic politics of societies experiencing foreign reform, but the theory expects two issues—nationalism and the ruling elites' patron-client networks—to be especially important in motivating domestic opposition. Chapter 2 offers more details of the domestic opposition theory and its hypotheses.

Nationalism refers to the belief that a particular group should have control of its own state.[24] Nationalism is a popular ideology in many societies, especially due to the enduring impact of violent conflict. When foreign demands or recommendations threaten the dominant nationalist goals of a major group in a society, my theory expects reform will fail. For example, in Kosovo after 2001, the United Nations adopted a policy of indefinitely delaying negotiations for independence, but independence was the dominant Albanian nationalist goal. My theory predicts that demands or recommendations threatening nationalist goals lead to widespread and recurring public opposition, as in Kosovo, where riots in 2004 occurred in response to the threat to independence. Public opposition convinces foreign actors that the population does not support their proposed reform. Foreign actors must abandon or adjust their demands, undercutting any improvement in an institution. Public opposition can also delegitimize future international efforts in a society, as occurred in Kosovo. Most foreign reformers recognize the potential for damaging opposition and adjust accordingly. Nevertheless, as in Kosovo or police restructuring in Bosnia, some foreign actors do ultimately propose demands that threaten nationalist goals and provoke large-scale protests. These cases show how the popularity of nationalism thereby ultimately constrains foreign-supported reform.

The second important domestic interest is the ruling elites' patron-client networks. In many societies, ruling elites use patron-client networks to exercise control, provide resources to supporters, and otherwise maintain their power. Patron-client networks often play an important role in the politics of societies where foreign actors pursue reform due to a history of violent conflict or limited political development. By seeking to improve state institutions, foreign reformers often make demands or recommendations that threaten these networks and thereby challenge the position of the ruling elite, as the book's opening example of defense reform in Ukraine demonstrates. Because elites' patron-client networks tend not to be popular, the theory expects that elites usually cannot rally large-scale public support. Instead, they engage in private opposition by using their networks to delay reform, extract resources, or co-opt state institutions. Private opposition is likely to be the most intense in geographic areas or components of an institution where reform poses the greatest threat to ruling elites' networks. I expect foreign actors with extensive resources to be able to mitigate private opposition by monitoring and sanctioning noncompliance, but foreign reforms facing private opposition are unlikely to achieve dramatic success due to gaps in local knowledge and the necessity of involving local officials in state institutions.

Some reforms may include demands or recommendations that threaten both nationalist goals and the ruling elites' networks. These reforms are expected to fail, most likely due to public opposition, which is more effective at resisting foreign reform. The most successful reforms are expected to be those where foreign demands or recommendations propose improvements that do not threaten nationalist goals or the ruling elites' networks. In these cases, some international resources are also necessary to achieve success. For example, in defense reform in Bosnia or the development of central government institutions in Kosovo after 2004, the use of money, advice, and conditionality was essential to build more effective, accountable, and law-abiding institutions.

EXISTING EXPLANATIONS FOR THE SUCCESS OF INSTITUTION BUILDING

While the case studies find that domestic opposition is generally the best explanation for how reform efforts unfold, other factors also matter. The literature on intervention and state building identifies international resources and preexisting conditions as two other important factors shaping the success of intervention.[25] The domestic opposition theory recognizes that international resources are sometimes important, depending on the threat to domestic interests, and emphasizes the role of patron-client networks, which are one element of the preexisting conditions of a society. Beyond these elements, the level of international resources and the path dependence of preexisting conditions offer insight for institution building. In brief here and in more detail in chapter 2, I specify the predictions of these two alternative theories. Below, I also explain how my theory builds on existing work exploring the divergent interests between foreign interveners and domestic elites.

The first theory drawn from the literature claims that greater international resources facilitate more successful interventions. This approach draws from statistical works on peace building, policy works on nation building and failed states, and critiques of bureaucratic and organizational politics in peace operations.[26] Works in this literature also suggest techniques that foreign actors may use to strengthen institutions given sufficient resources, including building capacity, persuading or coercing elites, influencing electoral outcomes, shaping public opinion, and imposing changes in laws or regulations. While works in this literature do recognize limits to the power of interveners, in general they observe that with more resources foreign actors can overcome domestic opposition and build better institutions.

A second theory is more skeptical of foreign intervention because state institutions are path dependent, meaning that preexisting structures and practices influence how institutions develop. These works analyze the history of political development in Western societies to identify the rare conditions that facilitate domestically driven political development, including military competition in western Europe, elite constraint of the monarchy during the Glorious Revolution in England, and social mobilization against clientelism in the United States in the nineteenth and early twentieth centuries.[27] These conditions are unlikely to emerge amid foreign intervention. Even if they were to emerge, the process of domestically driven political development could take decades because path dependence also means that state institutions are slow to change. By some accounts, foreign intervention has been more successful in societies with a history of strong political development, such as Germany and Japan.[28] From these observations, I derive the prediction that foreign-supported institution building is likely to fail except where there is a history of higher-quality state institutions. Indeed, the presence of an international mission may even hinder reform since the provision of services by foreign actors may diminish the incentive for domestic actors to seek reform on their own.[29]

International resources and path dependence do offer some insight for most of the reform efforts studied in this book, although the domestic opposition theory usually offered the most compelling explanation. Examining these two perspectives along with my own domestic opposition theory is nevertheless useful both to isolate which factors determine success and to enable the case studies to provide the most complete explanation for the process and outcome of reform.

My theory of domestic opposition builds on a growing number of works exploring how foreign interveners and domestic actors sometimes have divergent interests and a competitive or conflictual relationship. For example, Stephen Stedman notes that some domestic actors may act as spoilers, undermining peace processes.[30] Michael Barnett, Songying Fang, and Christoph Zürcher use game theory to explain how the "strategic interactions between international peacebuilders and domestic actors" often leads to "compromised peacebuilding."[31] Zürcher and several coauthors also argue that domestic elites respond to foreign efforts to build democracy based on the perceived "adoption costs." They note that elites may perceive a threat to their own security or to the achievement of their "primary political objectives," some of which—such as independence, ethnic autonomy, or retaining power—are associated with the interests I identify of nationalist goals and patron-client networks.[32] Séverine Autesserre explains how everyday practices of interveners can limit their ability to understand and address local conflict dynamics.[33] Recognizing the value of domestic buy-in for reform, some works cite the need for "local ownership" of foreign-led reform. Others claim that pursuing "local ownership" wrongly assumes that domestic actors typically want the same reform that foreign actors seek.[34] Other works have explored the specific dynamics between foreign interveners and domestic actors in particular societies or reform efforts.[35]

This book builds on these works in several ways. First, it offers insight into an understudied but critical policy question: What demands or recommendations should foreign reformers adopt to maximize success? As mentioned above, because most existing work studies success at the country level, few works suggest theories that can explain why some reform efforts within a society succeed while others fail or why a reform effort may vary in success over time.[36] This makes it hard for the existing literature to answer the policy question of how to select demands or recommendations to maximize the success of reform. Second, much of the existing work focuses on local elites without exploring how elite decision-making may be shaped by mass opinion. The focus on the problematic behavior of elites sometimes seems to imply that elite attitudes are not reflective of the society and that foreign actors may be able to coerce or replace elites to achieve reform. By contrast, I explain how elite advocacy for nationalist goals is expected to receive broad popular support while elite defense of patron-client networks is less popular, which impacts the potential for reform. I also show how mass mobilization can directly undermine the effectiveness of intervention.[37] Third, where there is work analyzing how domestic interests may motivate conflict or collaboration between domestic and foreign actors across different reform efforts, these works typically focus on a single society.[38] My analysis instead spans multiple regions of the world.

Finally, scholars who study how foreign goals can provoke elite opposition typically take this behavior as the almost inevitable product of the character of the international community or a given society.[39] Zürcher and colleagues, for example, emphasize that some elites are likely to be implacable opponents to intervention. As a result, they argue that interveners should lower expectations and "pursue a policy of selective intervention," pursuing intervention "only for cases likely to produce wins," where local elites may be more supportive.[40] Similarly, in their analysis of compromised peace building, Barnett, Fang, and Zürcher do not analyze in detail how foreign interveners might be able to adjust their stated preferred outcome to account for potential opposition.[41] My analysis differs by arguing that elite and mass opposition is often avoidable and that foreign reformers have the ability to limit opposition and achieve greater success by adjusting their stated demands and recommendations.

JUDGING THE SUCCESS OF INSTITUTION BUILDING

One challenge of studying foreign intervention is evaluating success. Works in the literature use such criteria as the maintenance of peace, the creation of basic democratic governance, the achievement of conditions believed to sustain peace after an intervener departs, and the development of a legitimate state.[42] Evaluating of these criteria is often difficult or controversial, which is one reason I analyze particular state institutions rather than studying intervention at the level of the society. In brief, this book assesses relative success by judging how an institution's effectiveness, accountability, and compliance with the law improved over time.

Western countries and international organizations who pursue reform seek to make state institutions in partner countries reflect the desirable qualities of state institutions in Western, developed countries.[43] Building from Fukuyama's work on political development, I identify three separable, desired qualities of state institutions: (1) effectiveness, meaning that state institutions can make and enforce rules as well as provide services;[44] (2) accountability, meaning that state institutions are overseen by an elected government and are responsive to the society as a whole, including minorities;[45] and (3) the rule of law, meaning that written laws exist and state institutions comply with them. These three dimensions do not always go together.[46] State institutions may be effective but not accountable, such as in the case of a repressive police force, or may be legally compliant without being effective, as in the case of a well-governed but ill-equipped military. Given the problems that unaccountable or ineffective state institutions may pose for a society's future development, progress on all three dimensions is desirable and indicative of success.

Various works use slightly different concepts or terms to describe the desired qualities of state institutions. For example, some highlight the creation of impersonal and rational-bureaucratic "Weberian" institutions, referring to the German sociologist Max Weber.[47] Others observe a "liberal" model for intervention, defined as making state institutions in other countries more similar to those in Western countries.[48] Nevertheless, across US and international intervention and institution building, as the case studies below indicate, there is general consensus and little disagreement about these overarching objectives.[49]

The United States and its partners have at times accepted or supported state institutions that do not reflect these desired qualities based on particular political or security objectives, as in the case of US cooperation with autocratic regimes during the Cold War.[50] Frustration can develop when Western organizations help to build institutions that are not accountable or compliant with the law. This frustration may develop both from a normative perspective and an instrumental one since many interveners believe that state institutions are more effective and sustainable if they are accountable and legally compliant. This book does argue against attempting to replicate Western institutional forms without taking local politics into account. It simultaneously affirms the overarching goal of making state institutions in partner countries achieve the desirable qualities of Western state institutions and rejects reform to build repressive or unaccountable institutions. Indeed, this book's metric for success implies that such reforms would be counterproductive. As detailed in the conclusion, the book claims that it is possible to select demands and recommendations that improve multiple facets of a state institution without provoking domestic opposition.

While the ultimate goal of foreign-supported reform may be to enable partner state institutions to achieve similar standards as institutions in highly developed Western countries, this is not a realistic goal for judging reform efforts. Instead, I use the state institutions in neighboring countries as a point of comparison. For example, it is more reasonable to compare state institutions in Kosovo with those in Serbia, Albania, or Macedonia rather than Germany or France.[51] Regional standards of governance offer a real and achievable goal for postwar societies and one that citizens in these societies recognize. The case studies include regional comparisons, especially at the beginning and end of the analysis to provide a benchmark for the quality of the state institution, and the appendix elaborates on the choices of regional comparisons.

There are several available statistics tracking the quality of governance in different countries, but they all have problems that make it infeasible to use them to evaluate success and failure based on my criteria. One fundamental problem is that existing statistics study overall changes in the quality of governance in a society rather than measuring changes in particular state institutions. Existing databases also do not provide consistent cross-national measures of the different effectiveness, accountability, and rule of law of the military and police. While existing measures might be useful as an indicator of the quality of central government, they are insufficiently sensitive to identify the changes that occur during a foreign reform effort. For example, the World Bank Governance Indicators for Iraq barely changed from 2003 to 2011, despite significant changes in the country's institutions: on a −2.5 to 2.5 scale, government effectiveness varied from −1.70 to −1.57; voice and accountability from −1.5 to −1.07; and the rule of law from −1.64 to −1.45.[52] One possible reason for the small variation in the World Bank statistics is that they are designed to be globally comparable. Making the index more sensitive to reforms in a particular country could make it harder to compare Iraq with other countries with more stable institutions, such as Saudi Arabia or Italy. Other databases that might speak to the quality of central government, such as Polity, do not include measurements of the relevant cases, because the international presence created an interruption in government.[53] Analysts have also questioned the conceptual consistency of these datasets.[54]

Because of these challenges, I propose a new scoring system for the quality of a state institution. The score system evaluates each of the three desired dimensions listed above—effectiveness, accountability, and compliance with the law—from 0 to 3, with 0 corresponding to the absence or complete dysfunction with respect to that dimension; 1 meaning that the institution has some basic framework or structure but little else with respect to that dimension; 2 meaning that the institution has some desired characteristics but does not meet regional standards for that dimension; and 3 corresponding to an institution that operates at or above the level of comparable institutions in neighboring countries with respect to that dimension. The appendix provides specific questions that the case studies use to make these assessments. By adding the results of the scores for the three dimensions, the scoring system yields an overall score for the quality of an institution ranging from 0 to 9.

The case studies repeatedly apply this scoring system over the course of the reform effort to evaluate the quality of an institution over time and thereby judge the success of reform following a rubric shown in table 1.1. The case studies seek to be as transparent as possible in making this assessment, although the result is inevitably subjective and some improvement or decline in quality may not alter the score. This scoring system offers a useful, if not always precise, metric for evaluating competing theories and for comparing the relative improvement of state institutions across different countries and regions.

TABLE 1.1. Change in Score and Associated Level of Success

Change in 0–9 score	Judgment of success	Description
0 or negative	Counterproductive	Violence or major nonviolent protest occurred, or the state institution was worse off than when the stage of reform began.
0	None/Minimal	There may be identifiable improvements in rules, practices, or organization, but an outside observer would likely not notice the difference between the quality of the state institution before and after.
0–1	Limited	There were some changes in the rules or functioning of the state institution, which might have lasting effect, but the general quality of the state institution remained similar.
2–3	Moderate	There were clear improvements to the state institution.
4–9	High	The state institution experienced rapid and dramatic improvement.

PLAN OF THE BOOK AND RESEARCH DESIGN

The book proceeds with six chapters and a methodological appendix. In chapter 2 I provide the background and hypotheses of my domestic opposition theory, the international resource theory, and the path dependence theory.

Seven case studies in chapters 3–6 evaluate these hypotheses. Chapters 3, 4, and 5 each considers two reform efforts from highly resourced post-conflict interventions, with chapter 3 examining reforms of central government institutions; chapter 4, reforms of defense institutions; and chapter 5, reforms of police institutions (see table 1.2). The reform efforts studied in these chapters occurred in Bosnia, Kosovo, East Timor, and Iraq, which, among interventions with a strong state-building mandate, had the highest level of international resources (see the appendix for details). Following the international resource theory, if reform success is likely to occur anywhere, it would occur in these societies.[55] Within these countries, I chose reforms that cover the full range of variation in threat to domestic interests and international resources and that provide useful comparisons for causal inference. The appendix also shows there is substantial variation in the preintervention level of development of these countries, which the path dependence theory expects would lead to different outcomes. Chapter 6 explores the wider applicability of my domestic opposition theory by considering defense reform in Ukraine, which had a very different context from the reform efforts examined in chapters 3–5. Ukraine was not a post-conflict society, the local government was the driver of reform rather than the international community, and Western organizations had far fewer resources to encourage the changes that they desired. The fact that similar dynamics of domestic opposition occurred in Ukraine suggests that my theory applies to a wide range of US and international institution-building efforts, as I discuss in the conclusion.

The case studies use three logics of causal inference to test the hypotheses. A first type of causal inference, congruence testing, simply compares the observed outcome to the outcomes predicted by the various theories. The case studies also use causal process tracing, which means to scrutinize the events of the reform to identify information indicating whether the logic of the process hypotheses is operating as expected.[56] Finally, I use the comparative method to isolate the impact of different variables and rule out competing explanations. The case studies compare reforms of the same institution in different countries, different state institutions within the same country, and variation over time within stages of the same reform.[57] The appendix offers additional detail on these methods.

The case studies draw on a wide range of official documents, news reports, think tank analysis, and academic work. The case studies on reform efforts in

TABLE 1.2. Case Studies

Reform	Stage	Threat of reform	Form of opposition	Resources	Relative success
Chapter 3					
Central government reform in Kosovo	Constitutional framework 1999–2001	None	Public	High, with gaps	High
	Standards before status 2001–4	NGs and PCNs	Private and public	High, with gaps	None, violence
	After riots 2004–8	None	Limited	High, with gaps	Moderate
Central government reform in Iraq	CPA-led process May–November 2003	None/ ambiguous	Public	Medium	Limited
	Accelerated transition November 2003–June 2004	None	Private and limited public	Medium	Moderate
Chapter 4					
Defense reform in Bosnia	State C2 May 2003–December 2004	None	None	High	Moderate
	Eliminate entity militaries January 2005–December 2006	None	None	High then medium	Limited
	Through 2016	None	None	Medium	Limited
Defense reform in Timor-Leste	UNTAET plans no military 1999–2000	NGs and PCNs	Public	Medium	None
	Establishment of F-FDTL June 2000–May 2002	None	None	Medium	Limited
	Successor missions 2002–6	None	None	Low	None, violence

Chapter 5					
Police reform in Bosnia	Ashdown December 2004–January 2006	NGs	Public	High	None
	Schwarz-Schilling and Lajcak May 2006–November 2007	NGs and PCNs	Public	Medium	None, delegitimation
Police reform in Iraq	CPA May 2003–June 2004	None	Public and private	Medium	Limited
	July 2004–May 2006	Limited, some threat to PCNs	Private	Medium	None
	Maliki government May 2006–10	Variable PCNs	Private	Medium–low	Limited
Chapter 6					
Defense reform in Ukraine	February 2014–February 2015	None	None	Very low	Limited
	February 2015–June 2018	Variable PCNs	Variable private	Low	Moderate

Note: CPA = Coalition Provisional Authority; NG = nationalist goal; PCN = patron-client network.

Bosnia, Kosovo, and East Timor make use of more than 160 interviews from over ten months of fieldwork in these countries. I also conducted additional in-person and phone interviews in the United States. The interviews offer a first-hand perspective and fill gaps in the written record.[58] Because nearly all interviews were conducted on a not-for-attribution basis, and because the discussion is not available to the reader, I provide a written source to support evidence from interviews wherever possible. For the Ukraine case study, I also draw on the results of RAND's publicly released report on security sector reform, which relied extensively on interviews. In the case of Iraq, I make use of the academic record of the US presence as well as unclassified materials from the CPA provided to the RAND Corporation.[59]

These sources offer a range of ways to gauge the motivation of domestic elites and foreign officials, which is an essential tool for evaluating the theories. Public statements or interview responses are a useful starting point and are most telling when actors have little reason to dissemble. Private discussions and correspondence can be the most compelling evidence but is rarely available. Comparing actors' responses to different or similar events can also be informative. Where possible, especially for key judgments, the case studies triangulate across multiple sources.

Following the theory chapter, chapter 3 considers the creation of central government institutions in Kosovo and Iraq. The UN Mission in Kosovo quickly established a constitution and parliament to govern Kosovo from 1999 to 2001 but faced riots in 2004 after it changed its policy to indefinitely delay negotiations about Kosovo's independence, the main Kosovo Albanian nationalist goals. After 2004 the UN began negotiations that would lead to independence, achieving a greater improvement in Kosovo's institutions. In Iraq in 2003 the CPA sought an extended occupation to build democratic institutions. However, the CPA had to compromise when it faced an elite boycott, spearheaded by Shia religious leader Grand Ayatollah Ali al-Sistani, who argued that the CPA's plan was insufficiently democratic. Both cases show how even high-resource missions with effective sovereign control cannot overcome public opposition and how the missions achieved greater success during the stages of reform when they did not propose changes that threatened nationalist goals.

Chapter 4 compares defense reforms in Bosnia and Timor-Leste. In Bosnia, the Office of the High Representative (OHR) was able to eliminate the ethnically based "entity" militaries and create a single, civilian-controlled BiH military. This success depended on extensive international resources and, more importantly, on specifying demands that would merge the entity militaries while not threatening Serb nationalist goals or the ruling elites' patron-client networks. In Timor-Leste the nationalist importance of a pre-independence guerrilla movement opposing Indonesia's occupation compelled a UN transitional administration to establish a military, contrary to the UN mission's original intentions. Successor UN missions paid little attention to the military and therefore failed to improve its accountability and compliance with law. The problems within the military later contributed to violent conflict between elements of the Timorese police and military.

Chapter 5 describes police reform in Bosnia and Iraq. In Bosnia the success of defense reform led OHR to pursue the reorganization of the police and create new police district boundaries that crossed the border between the two entities. This demand threatened Serb nationalist goals by undermining the autonomy of the Serb-dominated regional entity of BiH, the Republika Srpska. The threat of OHR's demands led to public opposition by Bosnian Serb elites, which blocked the reform effort and contributed to the subsequent delegitimization of OHR's authority in Bosnia. In Iraq, from 2003 to 2011, Coalition forces attempted to create a police force to take over security when they departed. Shia elites engaged in private opposition, co-opting and undermining Iraq's internal security forces. Shia private opposition stemmed more from a desire for control and the legacy of oppression under Saddam Hussein than the threat of the Coalition effort to Shia political parties' networks, although Shia opposition was more intense where there was a greater threat to these patron-client networks.

Chapter 6 examines the case of defense reform in Ukraine after 2014. It shows how the Ukrainian domestic imperative to meet NATO standards led the international community to make recommendations that threatened the ruling elites' patron-client networks to varying degrees. The recommendations that posed the least threat to these networks were ultimately the most implemented, showing how the domestic opposition theory offers insight outside of highly resourced post-conflict interventions.

Chapter 7 concludes by summarizing the results of the case studies, discussing policy implications, considering the wider applicability of the domestic opposition theory, and proposing directions for future research. By looking across the diverse reform efforts studied in the book, shown in table 1.2, it is possible to observe some general patterns, including that resources appeared to have little consistent impact on success and that the most successful reforms tended to be those that posed the least threat to nationalist goals and patron-client networks. Chapter 7 concludes that institution builders should formulate their demands and recommendations to avoid provoking opposition while still improving state institutions. The chapter also explores how foreign organizations can implement this advice, including developing foreign officials' local knowledge, ensuring greater autonomy for deployed missions, and increasing the priority of improving partner institutions over other objectives.

NOTES

1 This is according to a subsequent Ukrainian MoD report. See Anton Lavrov and Alexey Nikoslky, "Neglect and Rot: Degradation of Ukraine's Military in the Interim Period," in *Brothers Armed: Military Aspects of the Crisis in Ukraine*, edited by Colby Howard and Ruslan Pukhov, 65–72 (Minneapolis, MN: East View Press, 2015).

2 For details, see our final report: Olga Oliker, Lynn E. Davis, Keith Crane, Andrew Radin, Celeste Ward Gventer, Susanne Sondergaard, James T. Quinlivan, Stephan B. Seabrook, Jacopo Bellasio, Bryan Frederick, Andriy Bega, and Jakub P. Hlavka, *Security Sector Reform in Ukraine* (Santa Monica, CA: RAND, 2016), https://www.rand.org/pubs/research_reports/RR1475-1.html.

3 See Andrew Radin, "The Limits of State Building: The Politics of War and the Ideology of Peace" (PhD diss., Massachusetts Institute of Technology, 2012); and Andrew Radin, "Domestic Opposition and the Timing of Democratic Transitions after War," *Security Studies* 26, no. 1 (January 2, 2017): 93–123.

4 See Adriana Lins de Albuquerque and Jakob Hedenskog, "Ukraine: A Defence Sector Reform Assessment," Swedish Defense Research Agency (FOI), 2015, https://www.foi.se/rapportsammanfattning?reportNo=FOI-R--4157--SE; and Oksana Bedratenko, "More Proof Ukraine Is Changing: Opaque Defense Sector Embraces Reform," October 26, 2016, https://www.kyivpost.com/article/opinion/op-ed/oksana-bedratenko-proof-ukraine-changing-opaque-defense-sector-embraces-reform.html?cn-reloaded=1.

5 "Ukraine to Take into Account RAND Corporation's Recommendations during Defense Ministry Reform," Interfax-Ukraine October 24, 2015, http://en.interfax.com.ua/news/general/298483.html.

6 Isabelle Facon, "Reforming Ukrainian Defense: No Shortage of Challenges," Institut Français des Relations Internationales, May 2017, https://www.frstrategie.org/web/documents/publications/autres/2017/2017-facon-ifri-reforming-ukrainian-defense.pdf, 23–24.

7 See Bedratenko, "More Proof Ukraine Is Changing."

8 On the role of institutions in the maintenance of peace, see Charles Call and Vanessa Wyeth, *Building States to Build Peace* (Boulder, CO: Lynne Rienner, 2008). On the role of governing institutions, democracy, and peace, see Benjamin Reilly, "Political Engineering and Party Politics in Conflict-Prone Societies," *Democratization* 13, no. 5 (2006): 811–27; Philip G. Roeder and Donald S. Rothchild, *Sustainable Peace: Power and Democracy after Civil Wars* (Ithaca, NY: Cornell University Press, 2005); and Caroline A. Hartzell and Matthew Hoddie, *Crafting Peace: Power-Sharing Institutions and the Negotiated Settlement of Civil Wars* (University Park: Pennsylvania State University Press, 2007). Call and Stanley emphasize the importance of the police as the largest security force and the one with the greatest interaction with citizens. Charles T. Call and William Stanley, "Protecting the People: Public Security Choices after Civil Wars," *Global Governance* 7, no. 2 (April 1, 2001): 151–72. Skendaj makes a similar assessment of which state institutions are most valuable for study. He identifies four "core state functions" and corresponding state bureaucracies: extraction and boundary maintenance

(associated with the customs service), coercion (associated with the police), executive (associated with the central administration and corresponding to my analysis of central government institutions), and legal order (associated with the judicial system). Elton Skendaj, *Creating Kosovo: International Oversight and the Making of Ethical Institutions* (Ithaca, NY: Cornell University Press, 2014), 14.

9 See Daron Acemoglu and James Robinson, *Why Nations Fail: The Origins of Power, Prosperity, and Poverty* (New York: Crown, 2012), chap. 3. In other work, they define political institutions as "the social and political arrangements that allocate de jure political power" and offer the example of a political institution as "an electoral rule that gives the right to decide fiscal policies to the party that obtains 51 percent of the vote." Daron Acemoglu and James A. Robinson, *Economic Origins of Dictatorship and Democracy* (Cambridge: Cambridge University Press, 2006), 21–22.

10 Francis Fukuyama, *The Origins of Political Order: From Prehuman Times to the French Revolution* (New York: Farrar, Straus and Giroux, 2011), 450.

11 "Institutional Capacity Building," Defense Security Cooperation Agency website (n.d.), https://www.dsca.mil/programs/institutional-programs.

12 The 2017 National Security Strategy states, "We will help our partners develop and responsibly employ the capacity to degrade and maintain persistent pressure against terrorists and will encourage partners to work independently of U.S. assistance." Similarly, the 2018 National Defense Strategy proposes building "a capable alliance and partnership network." White House, "National Security Strategy of the United States of America," December 2017, https://www.whitehouse.gov/wp-content/uploads/2017/12/NSS-Final-12-18-2017-0905.pdf, 11; see also Department of Defense, "Summary of the 2018 National Defense Strategy: Sharpening the American Military's Competitive Edge," https://dod.defense.gov/Portals/1/Documents/pubs/2018-National-Defense-Strategy-Summary.pdf, 4.

13 Office of the Secretary of Defense, "Fiscal Year (FY) 2019 President's Budget," February 2018, https://comptroller.defense.gov/Portals/45/Documents/defbudget/fy2019/Security_Cooperation_Budget_Display_OUSDC.pdf, 3. US doctrine and policy analysis describe efforts to help partners using various overlapping terms, such as security assistance, security force assistance, foreign internal defense, and building partner capacity. Security cooperation is usually the most inclusive. See, inter alia, Derek S. Reveron, *Exporting Security: International Engagement, Security Cooperation, and the Changing Face of the US Military*, 2nd ed. (Washington, DC: Georgetown University Press, 2016); and Taylor P. White, "Security Cooperation: How It All Fits," *Joint Forces Quarterly* 72, no. 1 (2014): 106–8.

14 The World Bank's International Development Association, for example, "works with ministries, agencies, and departments of the executive branch on managing public institutions and finances. On broader governance issues, IDA works with the legislative and judicial branches and other institutions that promote public accountability and greater engagement with society." See World Bank, "The ABCs of IDA—Governance and Institution Building," http://ida.worldbank.org/results/abcs/abcs-ida-governance-and-institution-building.

15 On peace building, see Michael W. Doyle and Nicholas Sambanis, *Making War and Building Peace: United Nations Peace Operations* (Princeton, NJ: Princeton University Press, 2006). Nation building in this context refers not to efforts to create a national identity but to efforts to "use military force to underpin a process of democratization." James Dobbins, John G. McGinn, Keith Crane, Seth G. Jones, Rollie Lal, Andrew Rathmell, Rachel M. Swanger, and Anga R. Timilsina, *America's Role in Nation-Building: From Germany to Iraq* (Santa Monica, CA: RAND, 2003), 1; and Jeremi Suri, *Liberty's Surest Guardian: Rebuilding Nations after War from the Founders to Obama* (New York: Free Press, 2012). On state building, see Paul D. Miller, *Armed State Building: Confronting State Failure, 1898–2012* (Ithaca, NY: Cornell University Press, 2013).

16 See Doyle and Sambanis, *Making War and Building Peace*, 46; James D. Fearon and David D. Laitin, "Ethnicity, Insurgency, and Civil War," *American Political Science Review* 97, no. 1 (2003): 75–90; Paul Collier, *Breaking the Conflict Trap: Civil War and Development Policy* (Washington, DC: World Bank, 2003); Lars-Erik Cederman, Kristian Skrede Gleditsch, and Halvard Buhaug, *Inequality, Grievances, and Civil War* (New York: Cambridge University Press, 2013); Marina Ottaway, "Rebuilding State Institutions in Collapsed States," *Development and Change* 33, no. 5 (November 1, 2002): 1001–23; and Call and Wyeth, *Building States to Build Peace*.

17 UN Security Council, "No Exit without Strategy: Security Council Decision-Making and the Closure or Transition of United Nations Peacekeeping Operations," S/2001/394, New York, April 20, 2001, para 10.

18 Roland Paris, *At War's End: Building Peace after Civil Conflict* (Cambridge: Cambridge University Press, 2004).

19 James D. Fearon and David D. Laitin, "Neotrusteeship and the Problem of Weak States," *International Security* 28, no. 4 (2004): 5–43; Ashraf Ghani and Clare Lockhart, *Fixing Failed States* (Oxford: Oxford University Press, 2008); Stephen D. Krasner, "Sharing Sovereignty: New Institutions for Collapsed and Failing States," *International Security* 29, no. 2 (October 1, 2004): 85–120; and Chester A. Crocker, "Engaging Failing States," *Foreign Affairs* 82 (2003): 32.

20 See, for example, Kenneth Pollack, "We Need to Begin Nation-Building in Syria Right Now," *New Republic*, September 24, 2014, https://newrepublic.com/article/119556/obamas-syria-strategy-must-include-nation-building. Jeremy Suri writes that Americans are "a nation-building people" and observes that American's commitment to building a democratic nation-state at home has ineluctably led them toward nation-building abroad. Suri, *Liberty's Surest Guardian*, 1–9.

21 By examining reforms within Kosovo, Elton Skendaj also examines institution-level reforms rather than intervention-level outcomes. Skendaj, *Creating Kosovo*, 3.

22 See, inter alia, Samuel P. Huntington, *Political Order in Changing Societies* (New Haven, CT: Yale University Press, 1968); Fukuyama, *Origins of Political Order*; Douglass C. North, John Joseph Wallis, and Barry R. Weingast, *Violence and Social Orders: A Conceptual Framework for Interpreting Recorded Human History* (New York: Cambridge University Press, 2009); and Acemoglu and Robinson, *Economic Origins of Dictatorship and Democracy*.

23 Francis Fukuyama, *Political Order and Political Decay: From the Industrial Revolution to the Globalization of Democracy* (New York: Farrar, Straus and Giroux, 2015), 320. See also Jason Brownlee, "Can America Nation-Build?," *World Politics* 59, no. 2 (2007): 314–40; and Jeremy M. Weinstein, "Autonomous Recovery and International Intervention in Comparative Perspective," Center for Global Development, April 2005, https://dx.doi.org/10.2139/ssrn.997377.

24 Ernest Gellner, *Nations and Nationalism* (Oxford: Blackwell, 1983).

25 Another group of works offers normative suggestions for what types of institutions foreign actors should build to achieve positive outcomes, including recommending specific electoral systems or suggestions of best practices for what form institution should take. Reilly, "Political Engineering and Party Politics"; Roeder and Rothchild, *Sustainable Peace*; David A. Lake, *The Statebuilder's Dilemma: On the Limits of Foreign Intervention* (Ithaca, NY: Cornell University Press, 2016), 15–16; and Organisation for Economic Co-operation and Development, *The OECD DAC Handbook on Security System Reform: Supporting Security and Justice* (Paris: OECD, 2007).

26 For example, Doyle and Sambanis, *Making War and Building Peace*; and Dobbins et al., *America's Role in Nation-Building.*

27 Acemoglu and Robinson, *Why Nations Fail*, chaps. 3, 4, and 7; Fukuyama, *Political Order and Political Decay*, chaps. 4 and 11; and Charles Tilly, "War Making and State Making as Organized Crime," in *Bringing the State Back In*, ed. Peter B. Evans, Dietrich Rueschemeyer, and Theda Skocpol (Cambridge: Cambridge University Press, 1985), 169–91.

28 Brownlee, "Can America Nation-Build?"; Francis Fukuyama, *State-Building: Governance and World Order in the 21st Century* (Ithaca, NY: Cornell University Press, 2004), 38–39.

29 William Easterly, *The White Man's Burden: Why the West's Efforts to Aid the Rest Have Done So Much Ill and So Little Good* (New York: Penguin, 2007); and Fukuyama, *State-Building*, 139.

30 Stephen John Stedman, "Spoiler Problems in Peace Processes," *International Security* 22, no. 2 (1997): 5–53.

31 Michael Barnett, Songying Fang, and Christoph Zürcher, "Compromised Peacebuilding," *International Studies Quarterly* 58, no. 3 (September 1, 2014): 609.

32 Christoph Zürcher, Carrie Manning, Kristie Evenson, Rachel Hayman, Sarah Riese, and Nora Roehner, *Costly Democracy: Peacebuilding and Democratization after War* (Stanford, CA: Stanford University Press, 2013), 29. Stephen Biddle, Julia Macdonald, and Ryan Baker also describe how the divergent interests between the United States and elites in partner countries can undermine security force assistance, but they do not explore in detail how particular local interests lead to different forms of opposition. "Small Footprint, Small Payoff: The Military Effectiveness of Security Force Assistance," *Journal of Strategic Studies* 41, no. 1–2 (February 23, 2018): 89–142.

33 Séverine Autesserre, *The Trouble with the Congo: Local Violence and the Failure of International Peacebuilding* (Cambridge: Cambridge University Press, 2010).

34 Astri Suhrke writes, "[The concept of local ownership] in itself accentuates the external origin of the programmes; local ownership clearly means 'their' ownership of 'our' ideas,

rather than the other way around." Astri Suhrke, "Reconstruction as Modernisation: The 'Post-Conflict' Project in Afghanistan," *Third World Quarterly* 28, no. 7 (2007): 1292; see also Timothy Donais, "Empowerment or Imposition? Dilemmas of Local Ownership in Post-Conflict Peacebuilding Processes," *Peace & Change* 34, no. 1 (January 2009): 3–26.

35 For example, Philippe Leroux-Martin, *Diplomatic Counterinsurgency: Lesson from Bosnia and Herzegovina* (Cambridge: Cambridge University Press, 2013); Louis-Alexandre Berg, "From Weakness to Strength: The Political Roots of Security Sector Reform in Bosnia and Herzegovina," *International Peacekeeping* 21, no. 2 (2014): 149–64; Stefanie Wodrig and Julia Grauvogel, "Talking Past Each Other: Regional and Domestic Resistance in the Burundian Intervention Scene," *Cooperation and Conflict* 51, no. 3 (September 2016): 272–90; and James D. Savage, *Reconstructing Iraq's Budgetary Institutions: Coalition Statebuilding after Saddam* (Cambridge: Cambridge University Press, 2013).

36 See, for example, Berg, "From Weakness to Strength"; and Skendaj, *Creating Kosovo*. While Skendaj studies specific institution-building efforts, he predicts that building effective state institutions is more successful when international missions "insulate public administration from political and societal influences" and that "democracy is enhanced through international support of public participation and contestation." His argument about state institutions is contrary to my domestic opposition theory—by insulating state institutions from societal influences, institution builders ignore domestic political concerns and risk domestic opposition. I contrast our arguments in chapter 3 in analyzing the development of central government institutions in Kosovo.

37 See also Pellumb Kelmendi and Andrew Radin, "UNsatisfied? Public Support for Post-Conflict International Missions," *Journal of Conflict Resolution* 62, no. 5 (May 2018): 983–1011.

38 See Lisa Gross, *Peacebuilding and Post-War Transitions: Assessing the Impact of External-Domestic Interactions* (New York: Routledge, 2017); and Skendaj, *Creating Kosovo*.

39 For example, Christopher Paul and colleagues emphasize the importance of the alignment of aims of the US and partner nations for security cooperation but does not examine how shifting US objectives influence this alignment of interests. Christopher Paul, Colin P. Clarke, Beth Grill, Stephanie Young, Jennifer D. P. Moroney, and Christine Leah, *What Works Best When Building Partner Capacity and under What Circumstances?* (Santa Monica, CA: RAND, 2013), 38–39.

40 Zürcher et al., *Costly Democracy*, 148–50.

41 Barnett, Fang, and Zürcher, "Compromised Peacebuilding," 616–17.

42 Doyle and Sambanis, *Making War and Building Peace*; Paris, *At War's End*, 55; Lake, *Statebuilder's Dilemma*; and Dobbins et al., *America's Role in Nation-Building*.

43 For example, Fukuyama, drawing on the work of Lant Pritchett and Michael Woolcock, finds the goal of foreign state builders is "getting to Denmark," "a mythical place that is known to have good political and economic institutions." Fukuyama, *Origins of Political Order*, 14–16; and Lant Pritchett and Michael Woolcock, "Solutions When the Solution Is the Problem: Arraying the Disarray in Development," *World Development* 32, no. 2 (2004): 192–93. See also Colin Jackson, "Government in a Box:

Counter-Insurgency, State Building, and the Technocratic Conceit" in *The New Counterinsurgency Era in Critical Perspective*, ed. Celeste Ward Gventer, David Martin Jones, and Michael Lawrence Rowan Smith (Basingstoke, UK: Palgrave Macmillan, 2014), 82–110.

44 This definition of effectiveness draws on Fukuyama's definition of "governance as a government's ability to make and enforce rules, and to deliver services, regardless of whether that government is democratic or not." Francis Fukuyama, "What Is Governance?," *Governance* 26, no. 3 (July 1, 2013): 350.

45 Accountability is closely associated with the concept of "democratic" institutions but is intended to include a broader sense of whether institutions reflect the interest of the entirety of society rather than just the majority.

46 There is also debate about how the sequencing of these objectives—for example, some claim that effective institutions should be built before elections are held. See, e.g., Paris, *At War's End*; Miller, *Armed State Building*; and Thomas Carothers, "The 'Sequencing' Fallacy," *Journal of Democracy* 18, no. 1 (2007): 12–27.

47 For example, Marina Ottaway writes, "For the international community, rebuilding institutions in collapsed states means organizing government departments and public agencies to discharge their functions both efficiently and democratically, following models found in Weberian states." Ottaway, "Rebuilding State Institutions in Collapsed States," 1003–4. See also Max Weber, *From Max Weber: Essays in Sociology*, ed. H. H. Gerth and C. Wright Mills (Oxford: Oxford University Press, 1958).

48 Roland Paris, "International Peacebuilding and the 'Mission Civilisatrice,'" *Review of International Studies* 28, no. 4 (2002): 638.

49 Pritchett and Woolcock observe that there is "a broad consensus on objectives" and on the "adjectives" associated with good institutions: "'accountable,' 'sustainable,' 'responsive,' and 'transparent.'" Pritchett and Woolcock, "Solutions When the Solution Is the Problem," 203–4. Institution-building efforts by non-Western organizations may have fundamentally different goals and methods, such as Russia's institution-building efforts in the Donbass in Ukraine or Syria, or China's engagement in Africa. See, e.g., David Dollar, *China's Engagement with Africa: From National Resources to Human Resources*, Brookings Institution, 2016, https://www.brookings.edu/research/chinas-engagement-with-africa-from-natural-resources-to-human-resources/; and Lance Davies, "Russia's 'Governance' Approach: Intervention and the Conflict in the Donbas," *Europe-Asia Studies* 68, no. 4 (April 20, 2016): 726–49.

50 Reveron, *Exporting Security*, 131–32.

51 See also Paddy Ashdown, *Swords and Ploughshares: Bringing Peace to the 21st Century* (London: Weidenfeld & Nicolson, 2007), 27.

52 Variation in the World Governance Indicators in other study countries was similarly small. World Bank, "World Governance Indicators" (2018), http://info.worldbank.org/governance/wgi/#home. Other measures tend to be highly correlated, such as in the case of the rule of law. Mila Versteeg and Tom Ginsburg, "Measuring the Rule of Law: A Comparison of Indicators," *Law & Social Inquiry* 42, no. 1 (December 1, 2017): 100–137.

53 Polity IV, for example, lists interruptions in BiH for the period of study and in Iraq from 2003 to 2009, and only codes Kosovo after 2008. Center for Systemic Peace, "INSCR Data Page" (2018), http://www.systemicpeace.org/inscr/p4v2017.xls. Freedom House's "Freedom of the World" (2017) index does not specifically study effectiveness, accountability, and the rule of law; see https://freedomhouse.org/report/fiw-2017-table-country-scores.

54 Cullen Hendrix notes a range of different metrics of state capacity, some with significant flaws, and observes that the validity of these metrics may vary across countries with different export profiles and levels of development. Similarly, there is extensive criticism of the various available cross-national indicators of democracy. Cullen Hendrix, "Measuring State Capacity: Theoretical and Empirical Implications for the Study of Civil Conflict," *Journal of Peace Research* 47, no. 3 (2010): 273–85. See also Michael Coppedge, John Gerring, David Altman, Michael Bernhard, Steven Fish, Allen Hicken, Matthew Kroenig, Staffan I. Lindberg, Kelly McMann, Pamela Paxton, Holli A. Semetko, Svend-Erik Skanning, Jeffrey Staton, and Jan Teorell, "Conceptualizing and Measuring Democracy: A New Approach," *Perspectives on Politics* 9, no. 2 (2011): 247–67; and "Indicators of Governance and Institutional Quality" (n.d.), http://siteresources.worldbank.org/INTLAWJUSTINST/Resources/IndicatorsGovernanceandInstitutionalQuality.pdf.

55 This selection is similar to the "folk Bayesian" approach identified by Timothy McKeown. See Henry E. Brady and David Collier, eds., *Rethinking Social Inquiry: Diverse Tools, Shared Standards* (Lanham, MD: Rowman & Littlefield, 2004), chap. 9.

56 In the course of recounting the events of the reform effort, the case studies describe details or data points or "causal process observations" that offer evidence in support or opposition to the proposed process hypotheses of the different theories. See James Mahoney, "After KKV: The New Methodology of Qualitative Research," *World Politics* 62, no. 1 (2010): 125–29; Alexander L. George and Andrew Bennett, *Case Studies and Theory Development in the Social Sciences* (Cambridge, MA: MIT Press, 2005), chap. 10; and Brady and Collier, *Rethinking Social Inquiry*. For an application of process tracing in studying state building, see Oisín Tansey, "Evaluating the Legacies of State-Building: Success, Failure, and the Role of Responsibility," *International Studies Quarterly* 58, no. 1 (March 2014): 175–77.

57 See George and Bennett, *Case Studies and Theory Development in the Social Sciences*, chap. 8.

58 All interviews cited below were conducted by the author. Where I cite interviews conducted by others, I cite the work in which they are quoted or described.

59 See James Dobbins, Seth Jones, Benjamin Runkle, and Siddharth Mohandas, *Occupying Iraq: A History of the Coalition Provisional Authority* (Santa Monica, CA: RAND, 2009).

CHAPTER TWO

The DOMESTIC OPPOSITION THEORY *and* ALTERNATIVE THEORIES

In 2008 I made my first field research trip to Bosnia and Herzegovina (Bosnia, or BiH). The postwar mission in Bosnia had begun in 1995, and by the time I arrived the international community had pursued a wide range of efforts to help build peace, strengthen state institutions, and encourage the development of a multiethnic society. Some of the most well-resourced efforts to remake the country had achieved little, such as a police restructuring effort (see chapter 5). More practical, incremental efforts that avoided core political interests had the most success, such as the creation of a value added tax and a defense-reform effort (see chapter 4).

Bosnia was my first observation of the dynamic I would later observe firsthand in Ukraine. On one hand, foreign reformers must advocate for changes to correct the problems they observe, or else those problems will persist. On the other hand, any changes they seek have consequences for elites leading the government, the officials working within an institution, and the broader population of the society. Reforms of state institutions are inherently political, even if foreign actors may claim that they are pursuing only technical changes. Threatening core interests can provoke domestic opposition that makes a reform effort less successful than it might have been if the reformer had asked for less in the first place. International resources and preexisting institutions did set the context for reform, but the occurrence or absence of domestic opposition typically proved more important.

To understand the dynamics I observed in Bosnia, I developed a domestic opposition theory to understand when and how domestic actors can oppose reform. I also used the literature to derive competing predictions about how international resources and path dependence shape reform. This chapter presents the hypotheses of these theories, which I draw on in the case studies in chapters 3 through 6. I first present a framework for dividing reform efforts into multiple stages for analysis. Then I explore the origins of foreign demands and recommendations. The next three sections lay out the domestic opposition theory, considering in turn nationalist goals, patron-client networks, and reforms that threaten both interests or neither interest. The final sections of the chapter detail the alternative theories, on international resources and path dependence.

FRAMEWORK FOR ANALYZING THE STAGES OF A REFORM EFFORT

The domestic opposition theory and the case studies divide reform efforts into multiple stages. During a stage of reform, the foreign actor seeks to implement particular demands or recommendations. Each stage of reform is divided into the four steps shown in figure 2.1.

In the first step, foreign actors formulate and articulate the changes in the target state institution that they seek to accomplish. These changes may include adjustments in the formal rules, structures, or common practices of the institution. Desired changes may be framed as demands or recommendations depending on the international resources and the political and legal structure in place, including whether a foreign reformer has legal authority over a society or is acting more as an adviser to the sovereign government of the country. Where possible, I identify specific changes rather than general goals, for example, focusing on the requirement that a police institution is subordinate to the central government rather than a general goal that the accountability of the police force is improved. In identifying demands and recommendations, the case studies also focus on practical and realistic changes that foreign reformers sought to achieve rather than aspirational goals that they may have articulated. In the second step, domestic actors, including both elites and mass publics, decide whether to accept the reform or to oppose it either

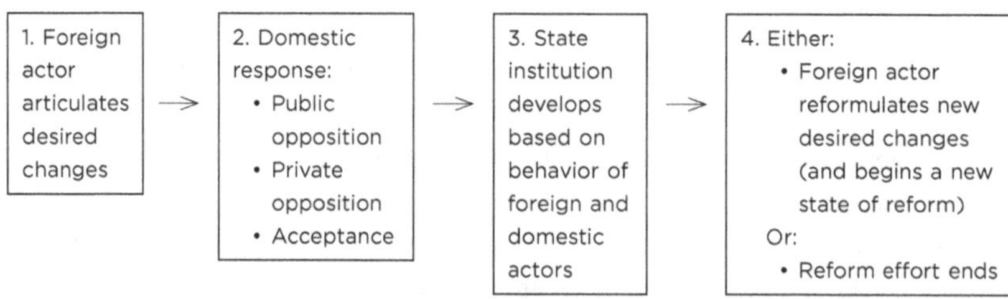

FIGURE 2.1. Steps in a Stage of Reform

publicly or privately. In the third step of a reform stage, a state institution is more or less improved due to the behavior of foreign and domestic actors. In the fourth step, the foreign actor may either end the reform effort or may reformulate a new set of demands or recommendations and begin a new stage of reform. The new set of desired changes may be developed because of a recognition of past failure or because of some external decision, such as pressure from the countries supporting the foreign mission.

This framework builds on the existing works analyzing peace or state building as a strategic interaction between foreign and domestic actors.[1] The framework presented here breaks new ground by focusing on specific state institutions rather than society-level dynamics. The proposed steps in a stage of a reform effort do not necessarily happen in sequence. For example, the ruling elites may oppose a reform over the course of several years at the same time as the state institution is being gradually improved. Through its simplification of more complex reform efforts, the framework offers a means to understand how different actors' decisions contribute to the ultimate outcome of reform.

ORIGINS OF FOREIGN DEMANDS AND RECOMMENDATIONS FOR REFORM

Why do foreign reformers pick particular demands or recommendations? Understanding the origin of reformers' proposed changes can help build confidence that these changes are indeed the cause of the success of reform efforts. There could potentially be some other factor determining both the success of reform efforts and foreign demands or recommendations. In practice, while factors such as international resources do shape the changes that foreign reformers propose, demands and recommendations are highly variable and generally unpredictable. Understanding the origin of demands and recommendations is also useful for gaining insight about how foreign actors can improve reform efforts in the future.

My experience in Ukraine, described in the previous chapter, demonstrates a common approach by which foreign reformers identify demands or recommendations, which is also reflected in other case studies. According to this approach, foreign reformers first analyze the problems with a state institution. Based on this analysis, they identify structures or practices from developed countries that, if put into practice, would correct these flaws. These structures or practices then become their demands or recommendations. Given that nationalist goals or the ruling elites' patron-client networks may be the cause of flaws of a particular state institution, it is not surprising that reforms often threaten these interests and, hence, provoke domestic opposition.

Several works explain how particular ideas within the organizations that pursue intervention may lead reformers to take this approach without paying sufficient attention to local practices. Lant Pritchett and Michael Woolcock explain that international development efforts tend to adopt a strategy of "skipping straight to Weber," meaning that they seek to "reach service delivery performance goals in developing countries by simply mimicking (or adopting through colonial inheritance) the organizational forms of a particular 'Denmark,'" meaning a model developed country.[2] Roland Paris similarly observes, "Without exception, peace-building missions in the post-Cold War period have attempted to 'transplant' the values and institutions of the liberal democratic core into the domestic affairs of peripheral host states."[3] Liberal ideas may shape demands in other ways.[4] One core liberal idea is respect for human rights. Pursuing human rights may lead foreign actors to demand free and fair elections, the protection and inclusion of minorities and women, and the universal application of judicial procedures.[5] Liberal values are also associated with integrative approaches to resolving ethnic conflict, including attempting to reduce the political importance of ethnicity, undermining segregation, and prioritizing individual over collective group rights.[6] In societies where nationalist goals include political rights and privileges for a particular ethnic group, liberal values may thus lead foreign actors' demands to threaten nationalist goals or perhaps patron-client networks.

Foreign missions with greater resources may be more likely to pursue ambitious demands or recommendations that threaten domestic interests. Officials within these missions may believe that their resources enable them to achieve greater change in state institutions. Higher resources, especially a stronger mandate, may lead foreign missions to formulate their desired changes as obligatory demands rather than as recommendations. There may also be pressure from the countries funding the mission for more rapid improvements in state institutions. However, foreign missions with higher resources do not consistently propose more threatening demands or recommendations, as indicated by the range of threats in the case studies (see table 1.2 in the previous chapter). Reforms that are framed as demands are also not necessarily more likely to be threatening or lead to opposition than those that framed as optional recommendations, as shown by opposition to defense reform in Ukraine, described in chapter 6.

Part of the reason for variation in the threat of reform is that different individuals leading or supervising foreign missions may adopt different strategies or priorities based on their own experience and perspective. There are also other political, bureaucratic, or cultural pressures within peace-building organizations that influence the choice of demands or recommendations. Lise Morjé Howard notes that UN organizations may have vested political interests in carrying out peacekeeping operations in certain ways or with particular goals in mind, which may not always maximize the potential success of state building.[7] Astri Suhrke, for example, shows how the mandate for the peacekeeping mission in East Timor in 1999 developed from preexisting ideas about impartiality and the United Nations' recent experience in developing the peacekeeping mission in Kosovo.[8] Séverine Autesserre highlights how everyday practices and beliefs can undermine the effectiveness of interveners, especially by reducing their ability to understand and adapt to local circumstances. She notes that interveners tend to emphasize "thematic" or generally accepted technical knowledge over "local" knowledge about the society where they are active. This tendency can lead to a range of dysfunctional practices, such as a preference for "short deployments and rapid turnover" of personnel, which leads to a lack of institutional memory and knowledge of events in the society; the selective recruitment of local partners who may provide a biased perspective of events on the ground; and a tendency to adopt one-size-fits-all approaches across different societies.[9] Assessments of US counterinsurgency and state-building efforts in Iraq and Afghanistan are also critical of the problems of rapid rotation, lack of training in local languages, and a focus on general technical principles without attention to their applicability to local circumstances.[10]

In a given intervention, there are often three levels of authority: a foreign mission, a headquarters overseeing the mission, and the country or countries that provide funds and staff the mission. The varying objectives of these separate organizations can also lead to the selection of counterproductive demands or recommendations.[11] The headquarters may, for example, have an incentive to demonstrate to the mission's backers that the mission is abiding by liberal principles or other ideals, which may lead the headquarters to ask the mission to seek particular demands even if they are not achievable. For example, Reo Matsuzaki shows in the case of US colonial policy in the Philippines that policymakers in Washington preferred a concept of bottom-up democratization based on the American historical experience of small New England towns. This policy was inappropriate in the Philippines since the municipalities in the Philippines did not have the capacity or will to run effective local administrations.[12] Alternatively, the headquarters may have an incentive to declare success even if the mission is not making progress and thus encourage skewed reporting.

Another possibility is that particular domestic actors are able to influence foreign actors' demands or recommendations to suit their interests. Foreign actors must to some degree take into account the interests of domestic-interest groups and draw their insight about what is good for the society through discussions with domestic actors. Few foreign actors seek direct involvement in local political competition, even though they recognize that their intervention will have an impact on it. The influence of particular domestic actors may mean that reform poses less of a threat to domestic interests in general, or it may lead foreign actors to adopt demands or recommendations that threaten the interests of competing domestic parties or groups.

Some foreign actors are able to modulate their demands or recommendations to the particularities of domestic politics, without being captured by particular domestic-interest groups, and thereby maximize the success of reform. Indeed, foreign actors sometimes learn from their failure and achieve greater success in later stages of reform. Drawing from the observed cases of success below, the concluding chapter also observes that foreign officials who have greater knowledge of domestic politics and the autonomy to select demands tend to be better able to avoid domestic opposition.

NATIONALIST GOALS

Political mobilization in defense of nationalist goals is an underappreciated factor influencing the outcome of foreign-supported institution building. Public opposition based on the threat of reform to nationalist goals is a bottom-up process that may involve both elites and the mass population but that is fundamentally driven by the popularity of nationalism among the population of a society. Because of the power of popular mobilization, my theory sees nationalist goals as an upper limit for what reform efforts can achieve.

Nationalism refers to the idea that a specific group should govern a territory.[13] In societies where nationalism is politically important, individuals within the society tend to associate themselves with one or more identifiable "groups" distinguished by a "salient political cleavage" within their society.[14] Elites and political parties in these societies often compete for support within their particular group.[15] For example, postwar Bosnia was, and perhaps remains, an "ethnocracy": there were three main groups—Bosnian Muslim, Croat, and Serb—each with their associated political parties, and political competition focused on the identity and relative political position of these three groups.[16] In some cases, such as the Shia or Sunnis of Iraq, groups may not seek independence within a territory but may have beliefs for how a shared state is governed, such as seeking a dominant position or minimum representation for their group.[17] I include these sentiments as part of nationalism since they amount to a group-based vision for the governance of a society. Nationalism can also be politically important in societies without strongly defined ethnic groups. In Timor-Leste, there was only one main group after 1999, as supporters of Indonesia had largely fled. Nevertheless, the nationalist discourse of the achievement of independence remained politically important.[18]

The importance of nationalist goals in explaining institution building depends on a scope condition: whether or not nationalism is politically important in the relevant society. This condition is met in some but by no means all societies where foreign actors pursue institution building. In societies where there is little history or likelihood of popular mobilization around group identities, this element of the theory is unlikely to explain the process or outcome of reform. In neopatrimonial societies where patronage relationships dominate politics, for example, group identity may be more important for structuring patron-client networks than as a means of mass mobilization, and mass mobilization in response to a threat to nationalist goals may be unlikely.[19]

Scholars have noted several reasons for the political importance of nationalism, including the specific history of political and economic modernization, the mobilizing role of elites, and a history of violent conflict. While nationalist leaders may claim that ethnic identities go far back in history, scholars have traced the origins of nationalism in many countries to processes associated with economic and political modernization that occurred in the eighteenth to early twentieth centuries, including mass literacy, industrialization, and the rise of widely distributed media.[20] Many works also highlight how elite rhetoric and competition reinforce nationalist ideas and show that elite participation is an essential part of nationalist mobilization.[21]

A recent experience of war often leads to an increase in the political importance of nationalism. Carrie Manning, for example, observes that many political parties emerging from wartime into the postwar period continue to use "war-time packages of collective incentives," meaning appeals that include reference to general wartime objectives, depending on whether the "major war-time cleavage remains relevant in the post-war political arena."[22] Elizabeth Wood explains how individuals' experience of war or violence can influence the lasting development of particular political beliefs through mechanisms such as the military recruitment of individuals into rebel groups.[23] Laia Balcells documents in the case of Spain that experiences of victimization are often socialized into subsequent generations, which can lead wartime identities to have a long-standing political impact.[24] Roger Petersen argues that the experience of violence may create emotional residues that create a resource for subsequent political mobilization.[25] When many individuals identify with nationalist beliefs and elites begin to depend on nationalist identities for political power, it becomes very difficult for foreign actors to diminish the importance of nationalism.

To understand whether a reform threatens nationalist goals, it is first necessary to identify the dominant nationalist goals for the relevant groups. Nationalist goals refer to the minimum political objectives associated with a group's nationalist aspirations. Identifying these goals is not always straightforward since individuals within groups have varying political objectives. Some individuals may espouse more radical preferences for secession or takeover of the central government, while more moderate individuals may seek improved political representation or greater autonomy. The balance of radical and moderate preferences may shift over time. Each of the case studies in chapters 3 through 6 analyzes the history of the society, elite discourse, and surveys (where possible) to map the nationalist beliefs of the key groups within the society. From this analysis, the case studies identify the dominant nationalist goals, meaning the minimum goals that were most consistently articulated by the group's leaders and backed by the members of the group (summarized in table 2.1). These assessments are meant to distinguish widely shared nationalist goals that, if challenged, would generate widespread popular unrest from the more fringe goals, which are likely to inspire a smaller reaction.

The case studies then evaluate the threat to nationalist goals by considering whether foreign demands or recommendations, if implemented, would undermine the relevant groups' nationalist goals or make them unachievable. For example,

TABLE 2.1. Dominant Nationalist Goals of the Major Groups in the Case Studies

Society	Group	Desired territory	Dominant nationalist goals
Bosnia	Bosniaks	Entire country	Political participation in unified Bosnia
	Serbs	Republika Srpska (RS)	Autonomy within RS
	Croats	Croat cantons of the Federation	Autonomy within Croat cantons
Kosovo	Albanians	Kosovo	Independence
Timor-Leste	n/a[a]	Timor-Leste	Independence
Iraq	Shia	Iraq	Dominance over the Iraqi government in a unified Iraq
	Sunnis	Iraq	Political participation in unified Iraq
	Kurds	Kurdistan	Autonomy within Kurdistan
Ukraine	Ukrainians[b]	Ukraine	Integrity and defense of Ukraine

[a] Because East Timor was a case of successful secession, there were no group divides in the post-conflict political arrangement.

[b] As discussed in chapter 6, while there were linguistic and social divisions in Ukraine, including around the usage of the Russian language, there were not clearly delineated or stable groups, and pro-Ukrainian nationalism strengthened throughout the country after 2014. See Fedorenko, Rybiy, and Umland, "The Ukrainian Party System before and after the 2013–2014 Euromaidan," 624.

a reform effort may threaten nationalist goals by eliminating local control over a police force, which would undermine an institution critical to regional autonomy. Demands may also threaten nationalist goals by requiring changes to the constitution that would reduce ethnic dominance or autonomy. Finally, as in Kosovo, foreign actors who exercise temporary sovereignty over a territory may threaten nationalist goals by indefinitely delaying the territory's self-governance. Some members of a group may claim for political reasons that foreign demands or recommendations threaten nationalist goals even if there is little threat. Determining which foreign demands or recommendations actually threaten a group's dominant nationalist goals inevitably involves some subjective judgment, so the case studies seek to be as transparent as possible in their assessments. Where there is uncertainty, the analysis errs on the side of not identifying a threat.

Many works observe that nationalist goals are an obstacle to peace because they offer a motivation or means for elites to obstruct international efforts. For example, Stephen Stedman describes how elites may "spoil" peace processes depending on their interests and capabilities.[26] Similarly, Zürcher and his coauthors observe that elites may have the primary objective of ethnic dominance or independence, objectives that I refer to as nationalist goals, and they claim these may be threatened by the development of democracy.[27] As mentioned in chapter 1, few works recognize that elite pursuit of nationalist goals reflects the widespread popularity of nationalist goals and that popular support for nationalist goals plays a bottom-up role in blocking reform, as I discuss next.

Hypotheses for Reform Threatening Nationalist Goals

The domestic opposition theory expects that a reform that threatens a major group's nationalist goals will have an outcome of little or no improvement in the quality of the state institution (Hypothesis 1).[28] Below I specify several process hypotheses for how the theory expects that this outcome could occur (see table 2.2). The more that the process of given reform effort follows these predictions, the more that the domestic opposition theory offers insight for that particular reform. The outcome hypotheses are numbered 1–6, while the process predictions are numbered based on the associated outcome prediction (e.g., H1A, H1B, . . . , H2A, H2B).

When a reform effort threatens nationalist goals, the theory expects elites and the mass population to engage in public opposition, meaning open and unconcealed efforts to stop or undermine reform (Hypothesis 1A). Public opposition can undermine reform by convincing the foreign actor that the population opposes reform, that the demands or recommendations associated with a reform are illegitimate, and that the reform should therefore be abandoned or altered. While there

TABLE 2.2. Hypotheses Given a Threat to Nationalist Goals

Outcome	Process
H1: Little or no improvement in the quality of state institutions.	H1A: There is widespread and recurring public opposition in the form of elite objections or mass demonstrations. H1B: Within the group whose nationalist goals are threatened, public satisfaction toward the mission or reform will decline. H1C: Widespread and recurring elite objections convince foreign actors that if they persist with their demands or recommendations, the state institution they seek to build will not be effective or legitimate. H1D: Widespread and recurring public demonstrations create cognitive dissonance with foreign reformers' belief in popular sovereignty. H1E: The desire to avoid threatening nationalist goals can make foreign reformers preemptively adjust their demands or recommendations.

is an extensive literature on the role of public demonstrations in political change, there is relatively limited focus on the role of public demonstrations against the international community.[29]

Public opposition depends on the attitudes and behavior of both the mass population and the elites but may be executed by either actor. Elites execute public opposition primarily through elite objections, in which they voice their opposition to reform in public speeches or written statements, media appearances, discussions with foreign officials, or votes against legislation. Public opinion often motivates elites to object to a reform and makes elite objections more credible. The mass population can also execute public opposition through mass demonstrations, including protests, rallies, or riots where the intent of the demonstration is to oppose the foreign actor or a specific reform effort. Elites often have a role in setting the stage for or responding to mass demonstrations, but actions by non-elites are what characterizes mass demonstrations.

The relative threat of nationalist goals influences the size and scale of public opposition, which in turn determines whether this opposition will be effective. In cases where reform threatens nationalist goals, public opposition becomes widespread and recurring, and therefore compelling to foreign reformers. Large-scale public opposition depends on the interaction between mass attitudes and elite behavior. Elites compete with one another, so they have a strong incentive to gain support by opposing unpopular reform threatening nationalist goals. Elites may engage in "outbidding," meaning the adoption of increasingly extreme positions to compete for leadership within their group, resulting in an overall cascade of elites voicing more radical, pronationalist views. The literature on nationalist mobilization and ethnic violence explains that elite outbidding, in combination with popular sentiment opposing reform, enables and encourages large-scale mass demonstrations.[30] As the literature on civil resistance explains, larger public protests are usually more effective in creating political change.[31] Elite outbidding also can create an elite consensus that makes it difficult for foreign actors to find popular elites who support the reform. For example, in the case of the Shia in Iraq (discussed in chapter 3), an elite boycott emerged in which the leading Shia officials refused to accept the CPA's demands, and the CPA was forced to compromise. Absent a threat to nationalist goals, elites can still make statements or use their networks to organize small demonstrations, as discussed in the next section on patron-client networks. Small-scale demonstrations or elite objections that are not supported by public opinion are unlikely to be compelling to foreign reformers.

Public opinion can therefore be an important indicator of whether elite objections or mass demonstrations are indeed motivated by popular opposition to the reform effort. Hence, when reform threatens a group's nationalist goals, public opinion within the group toward the mission or reform is expected to decline (Hypothesis 1B).

The occurrence or even potential for widespread and recurring public opposition can persuade foreign reformers to weaken or abandon reform through at least two different mechanisms. First, elite objections can convince foreign actors that if they persist with their demands or recommendations, the state institution they seek to reform will not be effective or legitimate (Hypothesis 1C). In the face of widespread elite objections, especially an elite boycott, foreign reformers may come to believe that few if any credible elites participate in the state institutions that the foreign actor seeks to create. Mass opinion plays a role in determining which elites are credible and in convincing interveners that an elite opposition is indeed representative of their views. To ensure the effectiveness and accountability of the state institutions they seek to build, foreign actors may decide to reconsider their demands or recommendations to encourage popular elites to participate in government, as occurred in Iraq following the Shia elite boycott in 2003.

Second, widespread and recurring mass demonstrations show foreign actors that continuing with the reform effort is incompatible with norms underpinning the intervention (Hypothesis 1D). As discussed earlier, Western interveners subscribe to liberal norms, including popular sovereignty, which is the idea that the citizens of a country should select and hold accountable those who rule the country.[32] In the face of widespread and recurring mass demonstrations, foreign actors who believe in liberal norms therefore face facts that are incompatible with their beliefs—in other words, cognitive dissonance.[33] The theory expects that foreign officials can resolve their cognitive dissonance only by abandoning or reformulating the demands or recommendations that are provoking public opposition. In Kosovo, for example, as discussed in chapter 3, riots in 2004 convinced UN officials that their demands were not achievable, and the UN was forced to alter its demands to accommodate Kosovar Albanian concerns.

Nationalist goals can shape reform even when foreign actors do not actually make demands threatening these goals. As they develop and articulate their demands or recommendations, foreign actors may sense that their desired changes will trigger public opposition and adjust them accordingly (Hypothesis 1E). The absence of foreign demands or recommendations threatening nationalist goals therefore does not necessarily imply that nationalist goals are not important in shaping the outcome for foreign-supported reform.

The failure of reform due to public opposition is damaging in several ways. First, failed reform wastes the limited time and resources available to foreign interveners. Second, failure in the face of public opposition makes future reform more difficult. When foreign actors yield to public opposition and reduce their demands or recommendations, domestic elites may come to believe that interveners are not as committed to reform as they originally perceived. Everything else being equal, elites may therefore become more inclined to oppose foreign-supported reform. Indeed, the 2004 riots in Kosovo and public opposition to police reform in Bosnia from 2004 to 2007 reduced local perceptions of the credibility of the international community and thereby hurt the prospects for future reform, as detailed in chapters 3 and 5. Third, when public opposition makes foreign actors reformulate their desired changes, they may select new demands or recommendations that cause long-term problems for the society. For example, in Iraq, after the CPA was forced to accelerate its time line for elections in the face of public opposition, it selected a simple single-district electoral system rather than an electoral system designed to account for Iraq's complex ethnic balance. This decision undermined Sunni support for future elections.[34]

Nationalist goals play a powerful role in the politics of many societies where foreign actors pursue reform. This makes reforms threatening nationalist goals particularly unproductive because they provoke damaging domestic opposition. It is relatively rare for foreign actors to seek changes that threaten nationalist goals and thereby provoke public opposition, in part because foreign actors recognize the likely consequences. It may also be more common for foreign reformers with significant resources and influence to make demands that threaten nationalist goals than lower-resourced missions. Still, the potential for damaging public opposition makes it important to understand what happens when reform threatens nationalist goals.

PATRON-CLIENT NETWORKS

Patron-client networks refer to personal links between the ruling political elite and their lower-status clients, who may include officials in the government or other citizens in the society who support elites. In these networks elites provide resources or protection for clients, and clients reciprocate with support and assistance.[35] Patrimonialism, the logic of governance associated with patron-client networks, operates under a fundamentally different, personalist logic from the rational-bureaucratic, Western-style state institutions that foreign actors typically seek to build.[36] Foreign actors thus often select demands or recommendations that threaten the ruling elites' patron-client networks. Ruling elites have both a strong incentive to obstruct reforms that threaten these networks and the ability to use these same networks to privately oppose reform.

Patron-client networks can play a dominant role in societies where foreign actors pursue reforms for at least two reasons. First, patrimonialism represents a baseline form of government. Scholars of political development trace patrimonialism far back in human history. They differentiate between the historically dominant patronage-based political orders, referred to as "limited-access orders" or "extractive political institutions," and the modern, democratic political institutions that foreign actors seek to replicate in many societies.[37] However, since patron-client networks appear to remain present in all societies to some degree, it may make sense to distinguish a continuum of the political influence of patronage, ranging from "neopatrimonial societies," where patrimonialism "is the core feature of politics"; to societies with some degree of democratic practice but where patronage remains important (e.g., Russia); to liberal democracies such as the Nordic states where personal patronage plays a much smaller role.[38]

Second, war and violence often facilitate the development of persistent patron-client networks, often associated with criminality or corruption, which transition into the postwar period. Paul Staniland notes that only insurgent groups with strong networks—including links between urban and rural areas, and connections between political leaders and military cadres—are likely to be successful in fighting and winning civil wars.[39] One reason such networks are important is that the groups that fight civil wars need revenue, and their networks are often developed in part to conduct illicit economic activities—such as smuggling drugs, cigarettes, or oil—to fund their operations.[40] When the war ends, the groups or organizations who fought the war often are encouraged to cease their illegal activities and transition to political parties with broad bases of support. Nevertheless, the networks and patron-client systems that developed during war typically carry over to the postwar period.[41] Political leaders often emerge from leaders of the warring groups and draw on political and economic networks from the war and prewar period.[42] The bonds between the leaders of the movement and the fighters are not easily broken or substituted, and leaders may retain an obligation to provide patronage to veterans.[43]

There are at least four common ways in which ruling elites use their patron-client networks to maintain power. First, elites use their patron-client networks to distribute resources to supporters, especially to secure votes. Elites typically work through "brokers," who ensure the support of larger numbers of individuals. Although direct "vote buying" may occur, providing resources to party members or to groups who might be more likely to support the party ("pork-barrel politics") appears more common.[44] Ethnicity often offers a means for elites to identify supporters and target patronage more narrowly.[45]

Second, elites can use their networks to restrict or unfairly skew electoral competition. Elites or their proxies may use blackmail, intimidation, or murder to prevent, dissuade, or harm opponents pursuing political office. Elite proxies may include private security organizations or criminal groups, or elites may be able to use their networks to manipulate state organizations, such as the police, to pursue individual, party, or group agendas.[46] Elites may also use their networks to control organizations that regulate or mediate electoral competition, such as the media or election boards.[47]

Third, elites may use their networks to gather resources to enrich themselves or fund their political activities. Some parties may be able to draw on legal, locally generated financial support or may receive donations from foreign sources, such as a diaspora. Other parties may use their patron-client networks to expropriate state resources, draw proceeds from private or state-owned enterprises, or rely on connections with criminal organizations.[48]

Fourth, patron-client networks help elites govern and exercise control over state institutions. Elites' personal networks extend throughout the government and into state institutions and therefore offer elites informal channels to gather and exchange information. Even in developed societies, personal connections between senior officials and subordinates establish trust beyond formal hierarchies.

A foreign-supported reform effort can often threaten the ruling elites' use of their patron-client networks to maintain power. Measuring or anticipating the potential threat can be challenging since patron-client networks are often secret, diffuse, and constantly evolving. Each case study assesses the threat to patron-client networks using a three-step process. The case studies first identify the ruling elites by pinpointing the main political parties within governing coalitions during the reform effort. Some case studies focus only on elites within a particular ethnic group who had the greatest potential to oppose reform.

The case studies then describe the patron-client networks that are believed to be essential to elites' power and relevant to the particular state institution. I use interviews, investigative journalism, criminal investigations, think tank reporting, and academic writing to identify these networks. In some cases it is possible to uncover the networks of specific political parties. The case studies considering BiH, for example, draw on an account from Louis-Alexandre Berg that the leadership of the Srpska demokratska stranka, or Serb Democratic Party (SDS), in BiH in 2002 to 2006 was not as dependent on connections with wartime leaders as the prior SDS leadership.[49] Other cases draw on accounts of the general types of patron-client networks that are politically important in a given society. For example, interviewees in Kosovo asserted that each of the major parties depended on revenue from oil smuggling.[50]

Finally, the case studies evaluate to what extent foreign demands or recommendations, if implemented, would indeed threaten elites' ability to use their networks to maintain power. Reforms could threaten elite networks by restructuring an institution to reduce the influence of politically linked officials; changing recruitment or vetting to limit the ability of the ruling elite to control an institution; or strengthening a state institution in a way that would weaken elites, such as by bolstering anticorruption mechanisms. Not all reform efforts that touch on elite networks are necessarily threatening, however. To be assessed as a threat to patron-client networks, the reform must realistically impact elite networks in a way that would reduce elites' power or influence.

Hypotheses for Reform Threatening Patron-Client Networks

The domestic opposition theory expects that when there is a threat to the patron-client networks of the ruling elite, reforms will fail to make improvements unless moderate or high levels of international resources are present. If such resources are present, the ultimate improvement in state institutions is expected to be modest at best (Hypothesis 2). As for nationalist goals, I specify process hypotheses for how the theory expects this outcome to occur (see table 2.3).

When reform threatens the patron-client networks of the ruling elite, the theory expects these elites to engage in private opposition, meaning concealed, denied, or other nonpublic efforts to undermine reform (Hypothesis 2A). Public opposition is expected to be more effective, but elites may not be able to rally public opposition because their patron-client networks tend to be unpopular, so reforms that threaten elites' networks often have public support (Hypothesis 2B). Elites find it more difficult to sway public opinion by using patron-client networks than by using nationalist appeals because patron-client networks typically benefit a relatively small portion of the population, often at the expense of the larger society. Surveys indicate frustration with corruption in post-conflict societies or other societies where foreign actors pursue reform.[51] Analysts in Bosnia and Kosovo, for

TABLE 2.3. Hypotheses Given a Threat to the Ruling Elites' Patron-Client Networks

Outcome	Process
H2: No significant improvements unless moderate or high international resources are present. If such resources are present, modest improvements are likely.	H2A: Elites may attempt public opposition, but it is unlikely to be effective. Elites will mainly use private opposition. H2B: Public opinion is expected to support or not strongly oppose reform. H2C: Private opposition involves delay, theft, and informal co-optation of state institutions. H2D: Techniques specified by international resource theory can mitigate the impact of private opposition to some degree.

example, also observe that many people in these societies support outside intervention in part because they hope foreign actors will strengthen anticorruption initiatives, prosecute senior officials for criminal activities, or strengthen the police to enable them to address high-level criminality.[52] Even if they lack broad public support, in some cases elites may still attempt to publicly oppose reform by voicing their objections or by rallying small-scale protests. These activities are unlikely to be effective since foreign actors will not perceive broad support for elite opposition and may in some cases view such opposition as an attempt to defend networks associated with illicit or criminal activities.

Some elites may have larger networks that can reach more people within a society. However, as elite networks grow, the average benefits provided to individuals within the networks become smaller and less likely to motivate individual participation in public protests. In smaller societies where patron-client networks dominate the state and the economy, such as neopatrimonial regimes, patronage networks may be relatively more influential.[53] In such societies it may be easier for elites to rally broad public protests, as observed in the case of patronage-linked protests in Timor-Leste (see chapter 4). Nevertheless, the theory expects nationalist appeals to be generally more effective at swaying public opinion than elites' use of their networks.

Elite private opposition can occur through at least three mechanisms: delay, theft, or co-optation (Hypothesis 2C). For each of these mechanisms elites make use of their networks within the target state institution. The intensity and tactics that elites use to oppose reform may vary across the different foreign demands or recommendations, depending on the threat posed to their networks and their ability to block reform. Similarly, if there is variation in the intensity of foreign efforts to undermine elite networks in different regions, issue areas, or echelons of an institution, elites are expected to engage in greater private opposition in areas where there is the greatest threat.

Delay tactics are one easy way for domestic elites to limit the impact of foreign reform. Officials may ignore foreign requests, seek more time to comply, or be purposefully absent. The presence of foreign trainers or advisers is expensive and therefore time limited, while domestic officials will remain in control for the indefinite future. For example, one foreign account explained that Iraqi officials used the expression "they have the watches, we have the time. Translation: the Americans (like the British and others) will be here for a while and then be gone; be patient, we will frustrate and exhaust them, and we will have our country to ourselves."[54] Delay tactics are especially effective when foreign officials rapidly rotate since newly deployed foreign officials often have little information about what has been achieved or agreed on in the past. Over multiple years, delay tactics may convince foreign actors to curtail or abandon their reform goals and spend their limited resources elsewhere.

Elites may also oppose reform by extracting resources from state institutions. This may include siphoning off payrolls, engaging in contract fraud, or even stealing equipment or arms. For example, "ghost payrolls," in which more individuals are paid than those who actually work, is a persistent problem in Afghanistan and other societies.[55] Theft degrades the capabilities of the state institution that foreign actors seek to support, and it reallocates international resources to local actors.

Elites can also co-opt or politicize a state institution. Elites may influence recruitment or promotion decisions, ensure the selection of loyal officials to senior positions, or build informal organizations under their personal control within state institutions. In Iraq, for example, as discussed in chapter 5, Badr militia groups seized control of the Ministry of Interior and developed militias outside of official control within the Iraqi police. In Kosovo, international officials observed that elites had personal relationships with judges and prosecutors and could prevent prosecution of their supporters.[56] As in the case of theft, co-optation and politicization can redirect state institutions to fulfill the private interests of elites, undermining accountability and the rule of law.

The theory expects that, where moderate or high levels of international resources are present, the impact of private opposition can be mitigated and at least some meaningful improvement can be achieved (Hypothesis 2D). Reform threatening the ruling elites' patron-client networks creates a competition between foreign actors who use the techniques specified by the international resource theory (described below) to pursue reform and elites who use various means of private opposition. Resources to address elite obstruction may include a powerful mandate that enables the removal or sanction of elites, a high-functioning bureaucracy that can coordinate across foreign organizations and make swift decisions, and sufficient money and personnel to observe the functioning of state institutions. Gerard Toal and Carl Dahlman, for example, show how domestic officials in Bosnia were able to delay and disrupt minority return, in part by ignoring internationally backed decrees and laws. They write that the international community in Bosnia was eventually able to achieve greater minority return thanks to increased authority to remove politicians and pass laws, improved coordination between international organizations, and more personnel in areas where return was happening.[57]

There are two factors that limit foreign-supported reform in the face of private opposition, even when high international resources are present. First, foreign actors ultimately rely on domestic officials to run state institutions. So long as domestic officials are involved, there is likely some means for ruling elites to use their networks to block reform. All contemporary foreign interventions involve some form of "indirect rule," meaning that foreign reformers exercise influence through local officials and that domestic officials are ultimately responsible for providing most state services.[58] Even in well-resourced missions in Germany, Japan, and Kosovo, domestically recruited police were quickly substituted for foreign-provided officers.[59] And liberal, Western-led interventions generally assume that authority and governance will eventually be transferred to domestic actors.[60]

Second, foreign actors have limited local knowledge, meaning that they lack a detailed understanding of how a state institution or society operates.[61] To counter private opposition, foreign actors must be able to distinguish it from normal bureaucratic friction. This requires identifying some details of elites' networks; recognizing when and how elites attempt to co-opt or undermine state institutions; and attributing delays, missing equipment, or ineffectiveness to intentional obstruction. Few foreign officials have such local knowledge.[62] In Kosovo, for example, observers noted that UN Mission in Kosovo officials were "remarkably incurious about the Kosovo Albanians."[63] Another common challenge is that few foreign officials speak the local language and must instead communicate through a translator or depend on local officials' foreign-language skills. Given inevitable gaps in local knowledge, the theory expects that the effectiveness of foreign reform facing private opposition will be modest.

PREDICTIONS FOR REFORMS THREATENING NEITHER OR BOTH NATIONALIST GOALS OR PATRON-CLIENT NETWORKS

Some reform efforts may pose a threat to neither nationalist goals nor patron-client networks. In such cases, the theory predicts that foreign actors will be able to improve state institutions depending on the resources they possess, following the international resource theory described below (Hypothesis 3). Table 2.4 outlines the process hypotheses for reforms threatening neither and both nationalist goals and patron-client networks.

Without a threat to nationalist goals or patron-client networks, the theory expects that elites and the mass population will generally support reform and will

TABLE 2.4. Hypotheses for Reforms Threatening Neither and Both Key Interests

Threat of demands or recommendations to domestic interests	Outcome	Process
No threat to nationalist goals or ruling elites' patron-client networks	H3: The international resource theory applies—greater resources will lead to more improvement.	H3A: There will be limited systematic public or private opposition. H3B: Public opinion is expected to support or not strongly oppose reform. H3C: Higher international resources will enable greater improvement, according to the techniques suggested by the international resource theory. H3D: Elites may engage in low-level private obstruction to protect interests absent a threat to their networks, but it will be of lower intensity. H3E: If significant private or public opposition does emerge, it will limit reform as predicted by H1 and H2. H3F: Reforms that do not identify changes that improve the effectiveness, accountability, or rule of law of a state institution will achieve little improvement.
Threat to both nationalist goals and ruling elites' patron-client networks	H4: No improvement in state institutions.	H4A: Public opposition is most likely because it is most effective, but private opposition is also possible.

not engage in significant public or private opposition (Hypothesis 3A). As in the case of reform threating patron-client networks, the theory expects general public support for reform (Hypothesis 3B). Greater international resources are expected to enable greater improvement in the state institution, according to the techniques suggested by the international resource theory (Hypothesis 3C). Still, the absence of a good reason to oppose reform does not necessarily mean that elites and bureaucracies will take positive action to implement it. Ruling elites may still engage in limited private opposition even in the absence of a significant threat to their networks, but their opposition is likely to be less intense than if these networks were under major threat (Hypothesis 3D).

The specific politics of particular countries vary, and there may be significant private or public opposition even in the absence of threatening demands or recommendations. If such unpredicted public or private opposition occurs, the theory expects opposition to limit reform as these hypotheses predict: widespread and recurring public opposition should block reform, and private opposition should limit reform depending on the available international resources (Hypothesis 3E).

One possibility is that avoiding targeting nationalist goals and patron-client networks will water down reform efforts and prevent meaningful changes in the relevant state institutions. When foreign demands or recommendations do not specify changes that will make a meaningful impact on the effectiveness, accountability, or rule of law of a state institution, the theory expects that the institution will not improve (Hypothesis 3F).

Alternately, a reform effort could pose a threat both to nationalist goals and to the ruling elites' patron-client networks. If this occurs, the theory expects that reform will fail (Hypothesis 4). The theory expects that failure resulting from public opposition is most likely since elites will prefer to use the most effective means to block reform—namely, rallying public demonstrations through elites' objections. Still, elites may also attempt to prevent reform through private opposition (Hypothesis 4A).

ALTERNATIVE THEORY 1: INTERNATIONAL RESOURCES

The previous sections specify the predictions of my domestic opposition theory, but domestic opposition is not the only factor that determines the process and outcome of reform. Specifying hypotheses for the two alternative theories is essential to understand how international resources and preexisting conditions shape and set the context for reform.

The international resources theory reflects the common belief that the stronger that foreign actors are, the more they are likely to achieve success. International resources may include anything that is provided by foreign actors, including troops, equipment, or money; more abstract resources such as the authority provided by the mission's mandate; or bureaucratic resources such as planning, organizational learning, and interorganizational coordination. This section adapts arguments from the literature on intervention to the specific problem of institution building and identifies testable hypotheses for the case studies.

A core line of reasoning in the literature is that foreign missions can succeed when they have sufficient resources to overcome the problems present in a given society. The RAND series on nation building, for example, emphasizes that "among the controllable factors the most important determinant [of success] seems to be the level of effort—measured in time, manpower, and money."[64] The authors of the series recognize the constraints posed by domestic conditions, such as the destructiveness of the war and the preexisting level of development, but believe that "resistance can be overcome, but only through a well-considered application of personnel and money over extended periods of time."[65] Michael Doyle and Nicholas Sambanis use a statistical model to demonstrate that the greater international authority (measured as strength of mandate) and the more money transferred to the target society, the better the expected outcome of peace-building missions.[66] Paul Miller similarly claims that sufficient and appropriate application of resources can correct problems with state institutions: "State builders should apply attention, resources, and effort to the parts of the state that are broken, and should apply more efforts the more broken the state is."[67] The clear implication is that greater resources are expected to overcome preexisting problems and local resistance and thereby increase the effectiveness of intervention.[68]

These and related works highlight how four key international resources can enable intervention success. I also draw from existing measures to categorize low, medium, and high levels of resources in each category.

The first and perhaps most important resource is the mandate of a foreign mission. The mandate not only specifies the goals and authority of a mission but, as Doyle and Sambanis write, is also a "proxy for the mission's strength, its technical and military capabilities, and the level of international commitment."[69] Drawing from Miller, I identify three categories of mandates as low, medium, and high, respectively: monitor, which includes observing and reporting on events; train and equip, which includes a range of activities to strengthen state institutions; and administer, which involves a foreign actor directly exercising executive authority over the target society.[70] The mandate for an intervention or institution-building effort is typically decided prior to its deployment and may be formalized in a UN Security Council resolution, legislation, or an executive decision. One reason that mandates are significant is because Western institution builders are typically constrained by law. Although Western institution builders or military forces may at times exceed their legal authority, such violations are the exception rather than the rule.[71]

A second critical resource is personnel. Missions need skilled leadership and qualified staff. Civilian personnel with experience working in a foreign cultural environment may have greater success as advisers, trainers, or mentors. The literature emphasizes the need for troops and police proportionate to the size of the relevant society. Drawing from the average number of personnel deployed during the first year of eight past peace missions, Dobbins and his coauthors estimate future requirements based on a ratio of thirteen foreign soldiers per one thousand inhabitants.[72] I use this ratio as a proxy for overall personnel resources and use Dobbins and colleagues' proposed requirements as an indicator of medium personnel resources. I assess personnel resources as high when the ratio of troops to inhabitants is greater and low when the ratio is smaller. Ultimately, the absence of international troops can weaken the international community's hand in enforcing its will on domestic officials. Philippe Leroux-Martin notes, for example, how a small international troop presence limited the international community's options in imposing laws against the opposition of BiH Serb leader Milorad Dodik (see chapter 5).[73]

The third resource is money. Interventions are expensive. Dobbins and colleagues estimate that in a hypothetical country of 5 million people, total costs for a "heavy" peace enforcement mission will be approximately $15.6 billion per year, compared with only $1.5 billion for a "light" peace enforcement mission.[74] More money permits paying additional foreign personnel, reconstructing basic infrastructure, encouraging economic development, and funding nascent state institutions. Annual per capita development assistance averaged $231 in the first two years in ten major post-conflict missions (in 2000 dollars).[75] Although the needs of societies vary, this figure is useful as a rough proxy of a medium level of financial resources, with low and high financial resources assessed accordingly. This estimate does not, however, include spending for foreign troops and police—each American or other Western soldier costs approximately $200,000 per year, and each police officer $155,000 per year.[76]

The fourth resource is bureaucratic capacity, which includes the interactions within and between the foreign organizations that collaborate in reform efforts. The literature considers at least three elements of bureaucratic capacity—planning, coordination, and organizational learning. The case studies assess bureaucratic resources as high if there were no significant reports of problems with bureaucratic capacity in these areas, medium if some problems were visible, and low if participants highlighted bureaucratic problems as a perceived cause of failure.

Planning failures are often identified as a cause of failed intervention. In preparing for its mission in Timor-Leste, for example, UN planners were reportedly told to "take the Kosovo plan and reconfigure it for East Timor," despite the clear differences between these countries.[77] The problems in the planning for the Timor-Leste mission led to the slow deployment of UN officials and hurt the mission's ability to incorporate Timorese views into the mission's activities. In Iraq, flaws in the planning process for the postwar stabilization phase are also believed to have undermined the development of governance.[78] Planning failures appear to stem most often from flawed assumptions, dysfunctional organizations, or political circumstances, although a shortage of available personnel may also play a role.

Unity of effort is another component of bureaucratic capacity. There are either multiple organizations with different mandates that comprise an intervention or there may be a single organization composed of suborganizations.[79] When these organizations do not coordinate—or, worse, actively disagree—intervention outcomes are expected to suffer. Domestic actors may be able to play different organizations against one another, and disagreeing organizations may inefficiently allocate resources to tasks or adopt tasks that are poorly suited to their own capabilities.[80] Deployed international organizations must also coordinate with states and international organizations outside of the mission. One way to address coordination problems is to alter the formal structure of the organizations deployed on the ground, such as by centralizing control over different international organizations, as was attempted in the case of Kosovo.[81] Even when there is a single hierarchy of civilian organizations, in many interventions, including Kosovo, there is also a separate military command structure, which tends to produce coordination problems between the civilian and military efforts. Changes in leadership may also improve coordination. Arguably, Paddy Ashdown, the High Representative of the international community in Bosnia from 2002 to 2006, was more able to coordinate international organizations than his predecessors and successors (see chapters 4 and 5).

A final component of bureaucratic capacity is organizational learning. Lise Morjé Howard writes that peacekeeping success depends on organization learning, as indicated by an organization's ability to gather information, coordinate internally, engage with the environment, and exercise leadership.[82] Similarly, Thorsten Benner and his coauthors observe that, to succeed, "the UN Peace operations apparatus had to transform itself into a 'learning organization,' "—in other words, adapt its structure to respond to changing circumstances.[83]

Hypotheses for the International Resources Theory

Much of the literature on international resources evaluates the success of intervention at the level of the society rather than at the level of the state institution. Using the arguments above, I draw out specific hypotheses for how resources are likely to impact the outcome and process of reform, summarized in table 2.5.

The literature points to a clear outcome prediction: greater resources lead to more successful institution building (Hypothesis 5). The case studies assess this

TABLE 2.5. Hypotheses for the International Resources Theory

Predicted Outcome	Process Hypotheses
H5: Greater resources tend to lead to more successful institution building.	H5A: Capacity building can improve the quality of state institutions. H5B: Foreign actors can use their resources to persuade or coerce domestic elites. H5C: Interveners may seek to influence who wins elections. H5D: Foreign organizations can temporarily substitute for local state institutions and thereby enable the longer-term development of state institutions. H5E: Foreign organizations can encourage reform by engaging the mass public through publicity campaigns and developing civil society. H5F: Foreign organizations can impose changes in laws or regulations.

hypothesis by aggregating the measures of the four categories of resources described above to develop an overall assessment of the level of resources in a given stage of a reform effort. The case studies then consider whether the level of improvement in the state institution accords with this level of resources.

The literature also identifies six techniques that foreign actors can use to improve state institutions, which I specify as process hypotheses. First, foreign actors can engage in capacity building to improve the quality of state institutions (Hypothesis 5A). Capacity building refers to the range of activities intended to strengthen the target state institution to perform its specified functions, including mentoring, advising, training, providing equipment, or building infrastructure.[84] Although capacity building may primarily improve the effectiveness of a given state institution, it may also support compliance with the law (such as by providing human rights training to police) or accountability (by enhancing minority participation or transparency). Capacity-building activities benefit from a stronger mandate, money, and the presence of skilled international personnel.

Second, depending on their resources, foreign actors can persuade or coerce domestic elites to improve state institutions (Hypothesis 5B). Foreign reformers can offer advice, make a locally desired political outcome conditional on the fulfillment of reform, and, given executive authority, threaten to replace or actually fire officials who do not comply with foreign requests.[85] Attempts to advise or persuade elites or local officials is common, but the skill of foreign personnel determines whether it will be effective. Conditionality can be especially effective when reforms are required for EU or NATO accession or the transfer of power from foreign actors to domestic officials.[86] However, the effectiveness of conditionality depends on the political context and the presence of sufficient bureaucratic resources to ensure that promised rewards are provided only in return for compliance.

Third, interveners may seek to influence who wins elections (Hypothesis 5C). The literature notes the potential for "electoral engineering" in postwar societies, in part with the goal of encouraging the selection of "moderate" elites who are likely to support reform. Techniques to achieve this goal include formulating electoral systems to reward moderate candidates, providing training or advice to specific parties, or sanctioning or excluding parties that might undermine international objectives.[87]

Fourth, foreign actors can temporarily substitute for a given state institution and thereby enable longer-term development (Hypothesis 5D). Substitution for local capacity is common early in interventions, such as in the case of foreign police helping to provide basic law and order in the absence of a functioning local police force.[88] In some cases substitution may continue after domestic institutions have begun to operate, especially when the functioning of these organizations falls far below the standards set by foreign actors. While the same foreign personnel may be responsible for both capacity building and substitution, the two activities are different: the former seeks to train local officials, while the latter seeks to perform services on their behalf. The path dependence theory, below, argues that the provision of government functions by foreign actors in fact discourages domestic actors from developing their own capacities. Nevertheless, many foreign actors believe that the temporary fulfillment of basic functions is essential to avoid collapse and enable subsequent reform.

Fifth, foreign institution builders can make reform more popular through publicity campaigns and developing civil society (Hypothesis 5E). Public opinion in any society is important for the success of reform. Ashdown notes that "the struggle to reconstruct a state and society cannot be won without first gaining the support of the local population," and he emphasizes that public consent is ultimately required for foreign actors to use their executive powers.[89] Former US ambassador to Afghanistan Zalmay Khalilzad similarly observes that "effective communication is vital to the success of any reconstruction program."[90] Developing civil society organizations is also believed to strengthen the ability of the mass public to exercise their opinion and potentially encourage elites to improve state institutions.[91]

Sixth, foreign organizations with executive legal authority can improve the quality of state institutions by imposing changes in laws or regulations without the approval of domestic officials (Hypothesis 5F).[92] For example, in Kosovo, Timor-Leste, and Iraq, international administrations used their authority to create the basis for a legal code in the absence of an elected legislature. Imposition is feasible only if there is an administer mandate, and it likely also depends on bureaucratic capacity, as effective planning and unity of effort are critical to ensure that the imposed law has a meaningful impact and that domestic actors accept imposition.[93] Changing the law or formal rules does not necessarily make it more likely that domestic officials will comply with the law, however.

To be sure, adherents of the international resources theory recognize that resources are not always available and that any progress depends to some degree on the domestic conditions in which institution building occurs. Nevertheless, the core claim of the international resource theory is that higher resources can compensate for poor conditions and enable foreign actors to improve state institutions.

ALTERNATIVE THEORY 2: PATH DEPENDENCE

The second alternative theory draws on the literature studying political development absent foreign intervention. Based on the history of Western Europe and more recent modernization and democratization in countries such as South Korea, scholars have observed the specific and rare conditions that give elites incentives to create the inclusive institutions associated with political development. Absent periods of significant change or critical junctures, institutions are durable and likely to persist into the future.[94] Although it is hypothetically possible for foreign actors to provide the kind of critical juncture that will enable self-sustaining improvements, the works analyzing the history of political development are generally skeptical of this occurring. Entrenched prior institutions and the difficulty of changing societies from the outside, from this perspective, make it unlikely for foreign actors to achieve a meaningful improvement in state institutions.

The literature identifies several different gradual processes of how political institutions are developed and consolidated. Modernization theory argues that political, economic, and social development (including, e.g., urbanization, education, and civil society) are mutually reinforcing, and finds that economic growth enables the development of democracy and desirable state institutions.[95] Charles Tilly, by contrast, claims that strong states in Western Europe emerged due to the imperatives of external military competition. He explains how the leaders of polities needed to gather resources to fight wars and, by gathering revenue through taxation or other means, sometimes inadvertently ended up creating strong state institutions.[96] Fukuyama identifies two potential paths for political development: one mirroring the path described by Tilly, which he observes in Prussia, France, and China, and another a process of "peaceful political reform" and social mobilization, which he finds occurred in the United States and Britain in the late nineteenth and early twentieth centuries.[97]

Other scholars describe political development as the movement from an undesirable "extractive" or "limited-access" political order dominated by elites to a more desirable inclusive or "open access" political order. Under an extractive political order, elites use the threat of violence and distribution of patronage to limit potential opposition by the rest of the population.[98] Shifting to inclusive political institutions requires that elites recognize that they have an interest in agreeing to new institutions that would limit their power, as occurred during the Glorious Revolution in England, for example.[99] After such critical junctures, a self-reinforcing path dependence can occur, leading the development of increasingly effective and accountable political institutions. However, the specific conditions associated with the transitions from extractive to inclusive institutions are disputed, complex, and difficult to identify even in retrospect. Douglas North, John Wallis, and Barry Weingast highlight the importance of the "rule of law for elites, perpetually lived organizations in the public and private sphere, and consolidated control of the military," while Acemoglu and Robinson note the role of civil society, "shocks," economic inequality, and globalization.[100] From this perspective, foreign actors are unlikely to be able to intentionally bring about a major transition in political order during a foreign intervention. Even if the right conditions were to emerge, the process of moving toward a more inclusive political order could take decades, far longer than the interventions studied here.

Further, scholars studying the history of political development are in broad terms skeptical of the ability of foreigners to encourage domestic reform. Acemoglu and Robinson doubt that foreign intervention can "'engineer' prosperity."[101] Fukuyama writes that "each society must adapt [Western models of development] to its own conditions and build on indigenous traditions."[102] These authors doubt that political development is feasible unless domestic actors would seek it on their own, absent foreign encouragement.[103] These authors also recognize that foreign actors often attempt to persuade domestic actors to support reform, such as through the use of conditionality or public campaigns. However, they argue such efforts often fail because Western organizations are often obliged to continue to provide assistance even if countries do not meet foreign demands.[104]

Foreign intervention can also occur in societies where there is a history of strong political development. In a review of works on US-led nation building, Jason Brownlee argues that preexisting institutions, rather than resources, determine the relative success of US intervention.[105] In Japan, for example, Brownlee claims that successful state building "was based from start to finish upon institutions the Japanese had already developed . . . including the country's bureaucracy, its parliament, and, symbolically, its monarch."[106] In societies such as the Philippines, Haiti, and Iraq, where US efforts had less to build on, Brownlee argues that US-led nation-building efforts were therefore less successful. Statistical studies of peace building similarly observe that societies with lower levels of prewar economic development or democracy are less likely to achieve desirable outcomes and, hence, pose a higher level of "difficulty" for foreign actors.[107] Economist Moses Abramovitz also observes that after violent conflict, societies with strong levels of development (in his terms, "social capability") experience a "catch up" phase of rapid economic growth.[108]

Hence, the literature on path dependence expects it to be difficult, if not impossible, for foreign interveners to build high-quality state institutions in societies without a history of democracy and economic development. However, rapid improvement from postwar destruction may be feasible in societies with a strong history of political development, although the extent to which foreign assistance is necessary or beneficial to facilitate this rebuilding is uncertain.

Hypotheses for the Path Dependence Theory

The works described above mainly focus on explaining continuity and change in the overall level of political development of a society. In the following, I draw from these arguments to make specific hypotheses that are applicable to foreign-supported institution building (see table 2.6).

Regarding the outcome of reform, the path dependence theory expects that a reform effort will improve a state institution to match the highest historic quality of the relevant state institution in that society and no higher (Hypothesis 6). This hypothesis focuses on the historical development of the target state institution rather than the broader level of political development in the society. The past quality of the target state institution is likely to be more relevant for a foreign reform effort and can be measured in a way that is consistent with the quality of the institution during and after reform. Still, the overall level of past political development and

TABLE 2.6. Hypotheses for the Path Dependence Theory

Predicted Outcome	Process Hypotheses
H6: Foreign-led institution building is likely to be successful only when there is a history of higher-quality state institutions.	H6A: New and reformed state institutions will likely follow the forms and models of previously existing state institutions within the target society. H6B: State institutions that exceed the quality of other institutions within the society will rapidly decline in quality once international resources are reduced. H6C: Foreign support reduces the desire of domestic actors to seek reform.

past quality of a key state institution are expected to be closely connected. Absent a history of higher-quality preexisting state institutions, the path dependence theory does not expect foreign-supported reform to succeed.

The process of how reform progresses offers another opportunity to evaluate the claims articulated by the path dependence theory. If past institutions inform and constrain what institutions may be developed, new and reformed state institutions should follow the forms and models of previously existing state institutions within the target society rather than foreign models (Hypothesis 6A). Preexisting forms and models of state institutions may include formal rules, structures, or informal practices. Evidence against this hypothesis could include observations that officials in societies where there is low prewar political or economic development can rapidly adopt rational-bureaucratic state institutions.

If, contrary to Hypothesis 6A, a well-resourced foreign intervention does manage to rapidly improve a state institution, the path dependence theory expects the quality of this state institution to decline to the historical level of development once international resources are reduced (Hypothesis 6B). This hypothesis is based on the recognition that foreign officials often execute governance on behalf of local officials during reform efforts.[109] It also is based on the premise that reform may not be sustainable since the quality of state institutions depends on the broader socioeconomic development of a society. The potential unsustainability of reform questions the premise that improvements in some state institutions can facilitate the broader political development of a society in the long term.

Some scholars analyzing the potential for domestically driven reform claim not only that foreign-supported institution building is unlikely to succeed but also that it is likely to reduce domestic demand for reform (Hypothesis 6C).[110] Robert Bates, for example, emphasizes that external financial assistance diminishes the incentive for domestic elites to build state revenue institutions on their own, undermining a critical path toward political development.[111] In Kosovo interviewees also claimed that so long as international officials were investigating corruption and organized crime, domestic actors had little incentive to put themselves at risk by investigating such crimes. Recognizing that strong foreign action may dissuade domestic officials from pursuing reform, some foreign missions have explicitly adopted more restrained approaches to institution building. In BiH from 2006 to 2007, High Representative Christian Schwarz-Schilling argues, the only way to make Bosnian officials strengthen state institutions was for the international community to "step back."[112] Nevertheless, even if foreign actors take a more restrained approach, they do not necessarily create the conditions that would lead domestic actors to seek reform in the absence of foreign intervention. Domestic officials also recognize that foreign actors who do "step back" still have the authority and resources to pursue reform, even if they do not use it.

Some of the predictions of the path dependence theory overlap with my domestic opposition theory. Indeed, one reason why a state institution may be path dependent is that elites could see a threat to their interests and block reform. My domestic opposition theory differs from the path dependence theory by arguing that changes that threaten nationalist goals or the ruling elites' patron-client networks are particularly unlikely to be achieved, while other reforms are more feasible. The path dependence theory is generally skeptical of any rapid changes to an institution.

CONCLUSION

This chapter describes three alternative theories explaining the process and outcome of reform. My domestic opposition theory emphasizes the political importance of nationalist goals and patron-client networks. It expects the greatest success when foreign reformers avoid demands or recommendations that threaten these core interests while still finding ways to improve state institutions. The international resources theory, by contrast, argues that foreign reformers can overcome opposition given sufficient resources. The path dependence theory claims that the quality of past institutions determines the potential for future improvements. The case studies in the following four chapters systematically evaluate these theories' hypotheses.

NOTES

1 Barnett, Fang, and Zürcher's game theoretic model observes that Western interveners often make demands for a more liberal government than domestic elites will accept. Barnett, Fang, and Zürcher, "Compromised Peacebuilding," 611–12. See also Lake, *Statebuilder's Dilemma*; Michael Barnett and Christoph Zürcher, "The Peacebuilders' Contract: How External Statebuilding Reinforces Weak Statehood," in *The Dilemmas of Statebuilding: Confronting the Contradictions of Postwar Peace Operations*, ed. Roland Paris and Timothy D. Sisk (New York: Routledge, 2009), 23–52; and Zürcher et al., *Costly Democracy*.

2 Pritchett and Woolcock, "Solutions When the Solution Is the Problem," 193, 201.

3 Paris, "International Peacebuilding and the 'Mission Civilisatrice,'" 638. See also Paris, *At War's End*; and Roland Paris, "Saving Liberal Peacebuilding," *Review of International Studies* 36, no. 2 (2010): 337–65.

4 On the role of liberal ideas, see also Patrice C. McMahon and Jon W. Western, *The International Community and Statebuilding: Getting Its Act Together?* (London: Routledge, 2012), chap. 2; and Autesserre, *Trouble with the Congo*, 103–14.

5 Michael Freeman argues that "liberalism has, however, generally had an uneasy relationship with nationalism, because liberalism is strongly individualistic and rationalistic, and

often perceives nationalism to be, by contrast, collectivist and irrational." "The Perils of Democratization: Nationalism, Markets, and Human Rights," *Human Rights Review* 2, no. 1 (October 2000): 40. See also Ghia Nodia, "Nationalism and Democracy," *Journal of Democracy* 3, no. 4 (October 1992): 9–11.

6 On integrative approaches to addressing ethnic conflict, see Benjamin Reilly, *Democracy in Divided Societies: Electoral Engineering for Conflict Management* (Cambridge: Cambridge University Press, 2001), 20–21. See also Roberto Belloni, "Peacebuilding and Consociational Electoral Engineering in Bosnia and Herzegovina," *International Peacekeeping* 11, no. 2 (2004): 334–53; Arend Lijphart, *Democracy in Plural Societies: A Comparative Exploration* (New Haven, CT: Yale University Press, 1977); and Donald L. Horowitz, *A Democratic South Africa? Constitutional Engineering in a Divided Society* (Berkeley: University of California Press, 1991).

7 Lise Morjé Howard, *UN Peacekeeping in Civil Wars* (Cambridge: Cambridge University Press, 2008), 12–13.

8 Astri Suhrke, "Peacekeepers as Nation-Builders: Dilemmas of the UN in East Timor," *International Peacekeeping* 8, no. 4 (Winter 2001): 1–20.

9 Séverine Autesserre, *Peaceland: Conflict Resolution and the Everyday Politics of International Intervention* (New York: Cambridge University Press, 2014), 70–93.

10 On rapid rotation of Coalition personnel, see, for example, Bruce Pirnie and Edward O'Connell, *Counterinsurgency in Iraq (2003–2006)* (Santa Monica, CA: RAND, 2008), 81–82. Rory Stewart writes about the importance of personnel who are "much more focused on the history and culture of Afghanistan, more attentive to the realities of rural life. The massive influx of international money and staff has made this group of specialists a tiny minority. They are drowned out by the vast, rapidly expanding organizations with eye-watering budgets." Rory Stewart and Gerald Knaus, *Can Intervention Work?* (New York: Norton, 2011), 84–85.

11 See also the literature on the principal-agent dilemmas, including Gary J. Miller, "The Political Evolution of Principal-Agent Models," *Annual Review of Political Science* 8, no. 1 (2005): 203.

12 Reo Matsuzaki, *Statebuilding by Imposition: Resistance and Control in Colonial Taiwan and the Philippines* (Ithaca, NY: Cornell University Press, 2019), chap. 5 and 6.

13 Nationalism is typically defined as the belief that the state and the national unit should be congruent. Gellner, *Nations and Nationalism*, 1.

14 Daniel N. Posner, "The Political Salience of Cultural Difference: Why Chewas and Tumbukas Are Allies in Zambia and Adversaries in Malawi," *American Political Science Review* 98, no. 4 (2004): 529–45; and Laia Balcells, "Continuation of Politics by Two Means: Direct and Indirect Violence in Civil War," *Journal of Conflict Resolution* 55, no. 3 (2011): 397–422.

15 See, e.g., Kanchan Chandra, "What Is an Ethnic Party?," *Party Politics* 17, no. 2 (March 1, 2011): 151–69; and Kanchan Chandra, *Why Ethnic Parties Succeed: Patronage and Ethnic Headcounts in India* (Cambridge: Cambridge University Press, 2004).

16 ICG, "Elections in Bosnia & Herzegovina," Bosnia Report No. 16, September 22, 1996; Gerard Toal and Carl T. Dahlman, *Bosnia Remade: Ethnic Cleansing and Its*

Reversal (Oxford: Oxford University Press, 2011), chap. 6; and Elizabeth M. Cousens and Charles K. Cater, *Toward Peace in Bosnia: Implementing the Dayton Accords* (Boulder, CO: Lynne Rienner, 2001), chap. 4, 6, 7.

17 See discussion of the nationalist goals of Iraqi groups in chapter 3.

18 Tanja Hohe describes the 2001 election as a "totem poll . . . rooted in the manipulation of indigenous values, symbols and the history of the resistance fight." "'Totem Polls': Indigenous Concepts and 'Free and Fair' Elections in East Timor," *International Peacekeeping* 9, no. 4 (2002): 70.

19 See Michael Bratton and Nicolas Van de Walle, "Neopatrimonial Regimes and Political Transitions in Africa," *World Politics* 46, no. 4 (July 1, 1994): 453–89. On the challenges of peacekeeping and institution building in these contexts, see Alex De Waal, "Mission without End? Peacekeeping in the African Political Marketplace," *International Affairs* 85, no. 1 (January 1, 2009): 99–113.

20 See, e.g., Gellner, *Nations and Nationalism*; Benedict R. Anderson, *Imagined Communities: Reflections on the Origin and Spread of Nationalism* (London: Verso, 1983); Eugen Weber, *Peasants into Frenchmen: The Modernization of Rural France, 1870–1914* (Stanford, CA: Stanford University Press, 1976); and Keith Darden and Harris Mylonas, "Threats to Territorial Integrity, National Mass Schooling, and Linguistic Commonality," *Comparative Political Studies* 49, no. 11 (September 1, 2016): 1446–79.

21 In a 2000 review, for example, Fearon and Laitin note that "if there is a dominant or most common narrative in the texts under review, it is that large-scale ethnic violence is provoked by elites seeking to gain, maintain, or increase their hold on political power." James D. Fearon and David D. Laitin, "Violence and the Social Construction of Ethnic Identity," *International Organization* 54, no. 4 (2003): 846; see also Stuart J. Kaufman, "Spiraling to Ethnic War: Elites, Masses, and Moscow in Moldova's Civil War," *International Security* 21, no. 2 (Fall 1996): 108–38.

22 Carrie Manning, "Party-Building on the Heels of War: El Salvador, Bosnia, Kosovo and Mozambique," *Democratization* 14, no. 2 (2007): 255.

23 Elizabeth Wood, "The Social Processes of Civil War: The Wartime Transformation of Social Networks," *Annual Review of Political Science* 11, no. 1 (2008): 539–61.

24 Laia Balcells, "The Consequences of Victimization on Political Identities: Evidence from Spain," *Politics & Society* 40, no. 3 (2012): 311–47.

25 Roger D. Petersen, *Western Intervention in the Balkans: The Strategic Use of Emotion in Conflict* (Cambridge: Cambridge University Press, 2011).

26 Stedman, "Spoiler Problems in Peace Processes."

27 Zürcher et al., *Costly Democracy*, 29.

28 This section draws in part on Radin, "Domestic Opposition."

29 On the role of public demonstrations in political change, see Erica Chenoweth and Maria J. Stephan, *Why Civil Resistance Works: The Strategic Logic of Nonviolent Conflict* (New York: Columbia University Press, 2011); Doug McAdam, John D. McCarthy, and Mayer N. Zald, *Comparative Perspectives on Social Movements: Political Opportunities, Mobilizing Structures, and Cultural Framings* (Cambridge: Cambridge University Press, 1996); and Adria Lawrence, "Triggering Nationalist Violence: Competition

and Conflict in Uprisings against Colonial Rule," *International Security* 35, no. 2 (Fall 2010): 88–122. On public demonstrations against the international community, see the literature on international administrations, which notes that these missions generally have weak formal channels of accountability. Simon Chesterman, *You, the People: The United Nations, Transitional Administration, and State-Building* (Oxford: Oxford University Press, 2004), 152; Dominic Zaum, *The Sovereignty Paradox: The Norms and Politics of International Statebuilding* (Oxford: Oxford University Press, 2007), 67–69; and Richard Caplan, *International Governance of War-Torn Territories: Rule and Reconstruction* (Oxford: Oxford University Press, 2005), chap. 9.

30 Kaufman writes that elite outbidding "requires either the presence of mass hostility, or the preconditions for mass hostility, so the masses will have reason to respond to extremist appeals." "Spiraling to Ethnic War," 109. See also Mia M. Bloom, "Palestinian Suicide Bombing: Public Support, Market Share, and Outbidding," *Political Science Quarterly* 119, no. 1 (April 1, 2004): 61–88; and Lawrence, "Triggering Nationalist Violence."

31 Chenoweth and Stephan, *Why Civil Resistance Works.*

32 Paddy Ashdown, for example, emphasizes limits of executive authority in international missions, including in Bosnia, where the Bonn Powers gave the internationally appointed High Representative for BiH the authority to veto laws or move politicians. Ashdown writes, "Like any law, [the Bonn Powers] rested on public consent. Any decision using the Bonn powers depended, just as any law does, on the ultimate acceptance of the people to whom it was being applied." Ashdown, *Swords and Ploughshares*, 219. See also Paddy Ashdown, *A Fortunate Life* (London: Aurum, 2009), 352–53.

33 A belief in liberal norms and popular sovereignty are a scope condition for cognitive dissonance to emerge in foreign actors pursuing institution building. Autocratic organizations pursing state building will likely be less susceptible to popular protest or elite objections. See Miller, *Armed State Building*, 5.

34 L. Paul Bremer, *My Year in Iraq: The Struggle to Build a Future of Hope* (New York: Simon & Schuster, 2006), 367; and Larry Diamond, *Squandered Victory: The American Occupation and the Bungled Effort to Bring Democracy to Iraq* (New York: Holt, 2006), 268–69.

35 More formally, following James Scott's definition, these relationships can be understood "as a special case of dyadic (two-person) ties involving a largely instrumental friendship in which an individual of higher socioeconomic status (patron) uses his own influence and resources to provide protection or benefits, or both, for a person of lower status (client) who, for his part, reciprocates by offering general support and assistance, including personal services, to the patron." I focus on the specific case of ruling political elites, but there may be other types of elites (e.g., economic) with their own patron-client networks. James C. Scott, "Patron-Client Politics and Political Change in Southeast Asia," *American Political Science Review* 66, no. 1 (March 1, 1972): 92.

36 See Max Weber, *From Max Weber: Essays in Sociology*, ed. H. H. Gerth and C. Wright Mills (Oxford: Oxford University Press, 1958).

37 North, Wallis, and Weingast, *Violence and Social Orders*; Acemoglu and Robinson, *Why Nations Fail*; and Fukuyama, *Political Order and Political Decay.*

38 Michael Bratton and Nicolas Van de Walle characterize neopatrimonal practices as "the chief executive maintains authority through personal patronage, rather than through ideology or law," and further observe, "The interaction between the 'big man' and his extended retinue *defines* African politics, from the highest reaches of the presidential palace to the humblest village assembly." Bratton and Van de Walle, "Neopatrimonial Regimes and Political Transitions in Africa," 458–59. On societies with some degree of democratic practice but where patronage remains important, see Steven Levitsky and Lucan Way, *Competitive Authoritarianism: Hybrid Regimes after the Cold War* (New York: Cambridge University Press, 2010), 28; Keith Darden, "The Integrity of Corrupt States: Graft as an Informal State Institution," *Politics & Society* 36, no. 1 (March 1, 2008): 35–59; and Herbert Kitschelt and Steven Wilkinson, *Patrons, Clients, and Policies: Patterns of Democratic Accountability and Political Competition* (Cambridge: Cambridge University Press, 2007).

39 Paul Staniland, *Networks of Rebellion: Explaining Insurgent Cohesion and Collapse* (Ithaca, NY: Cornell University Press, 2014).

40 See, for example, Vanda Felbab-Brown, *Shooting Up* (Washington, DC: Brookings Institution Press, 2009), http://www.brookings.edu/research/books/2010/shootingup.

41 Manning, "Party-Building on the Heels of War."

42 Michael Pugh, "Postwar Political Economy in Bosnia and Herzegovina: The Spoils of Peace," *Global Governance* 8, no. 4 (October 2002): 470–71. See also Peter Andreas, *Blue Helmets and Black Markets: The Business of Survival in the Siege of Sarajevo* (Ithaca, NY: Cornell University Press, 2008); and Michael Pugh, "Rubbing Salt into War Wounds: Shadow Economies and Peacebuilding in Bosnia and Kosovo," *Problems of Post-Communism* 51, no. 3 (June 2004).

43 Sarah Zukerman Daly, "Organizational Legacies of Violence: Conditions Favoring Insurgency Onset in Colombia, 1964–1984," *Journal of Peace Research* 49, no. 3 (May 1, 2012): 473–91.

44 See, inter alia, Susan C. Stokes, Thad Dunning, Marcelo Nazareno, and Valeria Brusco, *Brokers, Voters, and Clientelism: The Puzzle of Distributive Politics* (New York: Cambridge University Press, 2013), 7; and Kitschelt and Wilkinson, *Patrons, Clients, and Policies*, 2–19.

45 See, for example, Chandra, *Why Ethnic Parties Succeed*.

46 In Iraq, for example, the major Shia political parties were affiliated with militias that appeared in part comprised of police or other members of the security forces. ICG, "The Next Iraqi War? Sectarianism and Civil Conflict," Middle East Report No. 52, February 27, 2006.

47 Levitsky and Way write, "Bribery, blackmail, proxy ownership and other illicit exchanges are often critical to sustaining authoritarian governing coalitions." *Competitive Authoritarianism*, 28.

48 See, for example, James Cockayne, "Chasing Shadows," *RUSI Journal* 158, no. 2 (April 1, 2013): 16.

49 Berg, "From Weakness to Strength," 156.

50 Interviews with local analysts and former UN Mission in Kosovo (UNMIK) customs officials, Pristina, January 2010.

51 See, for example, Philippe Le Billon, "Corrupting Peace? Peacebuilding and Post-Conflict Corruption," *International Peacekeeping* 15, no. 3 (June 1, 2008): 344–61.

52 On Bosnia, see UN Development Programme, "The Silent Majority Speaks" (2007), 46–48, http://www.ba.undp.org/content/bosnia_and_herzegovina/en/home/library/democratic_governance/the-silent-majority-speaks.html. On Kosovo, see Gallup, "Balkan Monitor Insights and Perceptions: Voices from the Balkans" (2009), http://www.balkan-monitor.eu/files/BalkanMonitor-2009_Summary_of_Findings.pdf, 14. Interviews with local analysts, Bosnia and Kosovo, 2008–10.

53 Bratton and Van de Walle, "Neopatrimonial Regimes."

54 Don E. Eberly, *Liberate and Leave: Fatal Flaws in the Early Strategy for Postwar Iraq* (Grand Rapids, MI: Zenith, 2009), 40.

55 "Pentagon Asked to Explain Reports of Afghan 'Ghost Soldiers' on Payrolls," *RFE/RL*, October 7, 2016, http://www.rferl.org/a/afghanistan-pentagon-ghost-soldiers/28038302.html.

56 For example, the International Crisis Group report notes, "On two occasions in 2007, Crisis Group witnessed department chiefs receive phone calls apparently from advisers to two separate ministers seeking information about specific investigations in which their family members or party associates were allegedly involved." ICG, "The Rule of Law in Independent Kosovo," Europe Report No. 204, May 19, 2010, 6.

57 Toal and Dahlman, *Bosnia Remade*, chap. 7.

58 Fukuyama, *Political Order and Political Decay*, chap. 20.

59 Dobbins et al., *America's Role in Nation-Building*.

60 Paris, "Saving Liberal Peacebuilding," 357–58.

61 Fukuyama, *Political Order and Political Decay*, 320.

62 Autesserre, *Peaceland*, chap. 2. See also Michael N. Barnett and Martha Finnemore, "The Politics, Power, and Pathologies of International Organizations," *International Organization* 53, no. 4 (1999): 723.

63 Henry H. Perritt, *The Road to Independence for Kosovo: A Chronicle of the Ahtisaari Plan* (Cambridge: Cambridge University Press, 2009), 66; and Iain King and Whit Mason, *Peace at Any Price: How the World Failed Kosovo* (Ithaca, NY: Cornell University Press, 2006), 78. See also Stewart and Knaus, *Can Intervention Work?*, 34–50, 77–87; and Rajiv Chandrasekaran, *Little America: The War within the War for Afghanistan* (New York: Knopf, 2012), 170–89.

64 Dobbins, *America's Role in Nation-Building*, xix, xxv. Pierre Englebert and Denis Tull note that "Western policymakers assume that the chances of successful state building increase with the intensity of outsiders' inputs such as per capita assistance or the strength and mandate of UN peacekeeping missions." "Postconflict Reconstruction in Africa: Flawed Ideas about Failed States," *International Security* 32, no. 4 (April 1, 2008): 135.

65 James Dobbins, Seth G. Jones, Keith Crane, and Beth Cole DeGrasse, *The Beginner's Guide to Nation-Building* (Santa Monica, CA: RAND, 2007), xx–xxi. See also Seth Jones, Jeremy Wilson, Andrew Rathmell, and Jack Riley, *Establishing Law and Order after Conflict* (Santa Monica, CA: RAND, 2005).

66 Doyle and Sambanis, *Making War and Building Peace*, 94.

67 Miller, *Armed State Building*, 80.

68 Roger Petersen also describes a dominant Western approach of attempting to wield sticks and carrots that depends on international resources to shape local behavior. Petersen, *Western Intervention in the Balkans*, 5. See also James C. O'Brien, "Lawyers, Guns, and Money: Warlords and Reconstruction after Iraq," *U.C. Davis Journal of International Law & Policy* 11, no. 1 (December 2004): 99–100; and Jackson, "Government in a Box."

69 Doyle and Sambanis, *Making War and Building Peace*, 84.

70 Miller, *Armed State Building*, 77–78.

71 International organizations seek to build the rule of law and base their legitimacy in part on claiming to represent legal authority—violating their mandate would undermine such claims. Michael N. Barnett and Martha Finnemore, *Rules for the World: International Organizations in Global Politics* (Ithaca, NY: Cornell University Press, 2004).

72 Dobbins, *Beginner's Guide to Nation-Building*, 41, 72. Dobbins and colleagues also estimate approximately 161 international police may be required per 100,000 inhabitants if no domestic police force is present.

73 Leroux-Martin, *Diplomatic Counterinsurgency*.

74 Dobbins, *Beginner's Guide to Nation-Building*, 256.

75 This estimate is calculated by averaging the assistance in missions listed in table A.1 in the appendix. The data is from James Dobbins, Seth G. Jones, Keith Crane, Andrew Rathmell, Brett Steele, Richard Teltschik, and Anga R. Timilsina, *The UN's Role in Nation-Building: From the Congo to Iraq* (Santa Monica, CA: RAND, 2005), 239; and James Dobbins, Seth G. Jones, Keith Crane, Christopher S. Chivvis, Andrew Radin, F. Stephen Larrabee, Nora Bensahel, Brooke Stearns Lawson, and Benjamin W. Goldsmith, *Europe's Role in Nation-Building: From the Balkans to the Congo* (Santa Monica, CA: RAND, 2008), 259.

76 Dobbins, *Beginner's Guide to Nation-Building*, 42–43, 70.

77 Suhrke, "Peacekeepers as Nation-Builders," 7. Samantha Power writes that "UN Staff joked that Security Council Resolution 1272 was a 'delete Kosovo, insert East Timor' resolution." *Chasing the Flame: Sergio Vieira de Mello and the Fight to Save the World* (New York: Penguin Press, 2008), 300.

78 Nora Bensahel and colleagues write, "The evidence suggests that the United States had neither the people nor the plans in place to handle the situation that arose after the fall of Saddam Hussein." Nora Bensahel, Olga Oliker, Keith Crane, Rick Brennan Jr., Heather S. Gregg, Thomas Sullivan, and Andrew Rathmell, *After Saddam: Prewar Planning and the Occupation of Iraq* (Santa Monica, CA: RAND, 2008), xx.

79 See Barnett and Finnemore, "Politics, Power, and Pathologies," 724; and Julian Junk, "Designing Mulitdimentional Peace Operations: The Cases of International Interim-Administrations in Bosnia, Kosovo, and East-Timor" (Thesis, Universitat Konstanz, 2006), 1–2.

80 See Stephen Knack and Aminur Rahman, "Donor Fragmentation and Bureaucratic Quality in Aid Recipients," *Journal of Development Economics* 83, no. 1 (May 2007):

176–97; and Roland Paris, "Understanding the 'Coordination Problem' in Postwar Statebuilding," in *The Dilemmas of Statebuilding: Confronting the Contradictions of Postwar Peace Operations*, ed. Roland Paris and Timothy D. Sisk (New York: Routledge, 2009), 53–78. See also, for example, the challenges with coordination among international organizations in Bosnia: Toal and Dahlman, *Bosnia Remade*, chap. 6; and Cousens and Cater, *Toward Peace in Bosnia*, chap. 4, 6, 7.

81 See William G. O'Neill, *Kosovo: An Unfinished Peace* (Boulder, CO: Lynne Rienner, 2001), 37. On formal organizational structures for intervention, see also Alexander Cooley, *Logics of Hierarchy: The Organization of Empires, States, and Military Occupations* (Ithaca, NY: Cornell University Press, 2005).

82 Howard, *UN Peacekeeping in Civil Wars*, 15–16.

83 Thorsten Benner, Stephan Mergenthaler, and Philipp Rotmann, *The New World of UN Peace Operations: Learning to Build Peace?* (Oxford: Oxford University Press, 2011), 4, 10.

84 For example, the UN Development Programme defines capacity development as "the process through which individuals, organizations and societies obtain, strengthen and maintain the capabilities to set and achieve their own development objectives over time." UNDP, "Supporting Capacity Development, The UNDP Approach" (2008), 4, http://www.undp.org/content/undp/en/home/librarypage/capacity-building/support-capacity-development-the-undp-approach/. See also Deborah Eade, *Capacity-Building: An Approach to People-Centered Development* (Oxford: Oxfam, 1997); and Deborah Eade, "Capacity Building: Who Builds Whose Capacity?," *Development in Practice* 17, no. 4–5 (2007): 630–39.

85 Oisín Tansey, *Regime-Building: Democratization and International Administration* (Oxford: Oxford University Press, 2009), 55.

86 See Judith Green Kelley, *Ethnic Politics in Europe: The Power of Norms and Incentives* (Princeton, NJ: Princeton University Press, 2004); and Wade Jacoby, *The Enlargement of the European Union and NATO: Ordering from the Menu in Central Europe* (Cambridge: Cambridge University Press, 2004).

87 On electoral systems, see Reilly, *Democracy in Divided Societies*, 7; and Horowitz, *Democratic South Africa?* On electoral training or advice, see Thomas Carothers, "Democracy Assistance: The Question of Strategy," *Democratization* 4, no. 3 (1997): 113; and Paris, *At War's End*, 191–99. On sanctioning or excluding parties, see, e.g., Stedman, "Spoiler Problems in Peace Processes," 9–12.

88 Jones et al., *Establishing Law and Order after Conflict*; and David Bayley, *Changing the Guard: Developing Democratic Police Abroad* (New York: Oxford University Press, 2006).

89 Ashdown, *Swords and Ploughshares*, 128, 147–48, 219.

90 Zalmay Khalilzad, "How to Nation-Build: Ten Lessons from Afghanistan," *National Interest* 80 (Summer 2005): 23–24.

91 Paris, *At War's End*, 194–99. See also Katia Papagianni, "Participation and State Legitimacy," in *Building States to Build Peace*, ed. Charles Call and Vanessa Wyeth (Boulder, CO: Lynne Rienner, 2008), 63; and Dobbins et al., *Beginner's Guide to Nation-Building*, 200–207.

92 Tansey, *Regime-Building*, 42.

93 See, for example, Leroux-Martin, *Diplomatic Counterinsurgency*.

94 Acemoglu and Robinson, *Economic Origins of Dictatorship and Democracy*, 24. On critical junctures, see James Mahoney, "Path Dependence in Historical Sociology," *Theory and Society* 29, no. 4 (2000): 507–48.

95 See, inter alia, Seymour Martin Lipset, "Some Social Requisites of Democracy: Economic Development and Political Legitimacy," *American Political Science Review* 53, no. 1 (1959): 69–105; Huntington, *Political Order in Changing Societies*, 5–8; and Acemoglu and Robinson, *Why Nations Fail*, 443–45.

96 Charles Tilly, "War Making and State Making as Organized Crime," in *Bringing the State Back In*, ed. Peter B. Evans, Dietrich Rüschemeyer, and Theda Skocpol (Cambridge: Cambridge University Press, 1985), 169–91.

97 Fukuyama, *Political Order and Political Decay*, chap. 13.

98 See, e.g., North, Wallis, and Weingast, *Violence and Social Orders*, chap. 2 and 3.

99 Acemoglu and Robinson, *Why Nations Fail*, chap. 4.

100 North, Wallis, and Weingast, *Violence and Social Orders*, 26; and Acemoglu and Robinson, *Economic Origins of Dictatorship and Democracy*, 31–42.

101 Acemoglu and Robinson, *Why Nations Fail*, 446–55. Michael Mazarr similarly observes, "Forcible state building simply cannot be accomplished by outsiders in any sustainable or authentic way." "The Rise and Fall of the Failed-State Paradigm: Requiem for a Decade of Distraction," *Foreign Affairs* 93 (2014): 117–18.

102 Fukuyama, *Political Order and Political Decay*, 320.

103 Fukuyama explains, "The majority of cases of successful state building and institutional reform have occurred when a society has generated strong domestic demand for institutions. . . . Insufficient domestic demand for institutions or institutional reform is the single most important obstacle to institutional development in poor countries. . . . What we know about the techniques and prospects for generating demand for institutions from the outside is both extensive and discouraging." Fukuyama, *State-Building*, 47–48. See also Timothy Donais, *Peacebuilding and Local Ownership: Post-Conflict Consensus-Building* (London: Routledge, 2012), 3–4.

104 Fukuyama, *State-Building*, 48; and Acemoglu and Robinson, *Why Nations Fail*, 453–55.

105 Brownlee adds, "Where present, this political infrastructure has enabled the U.S. to rejuvenate and modify antecedent institutions, often quite rapidly. In less propitious settings, nation-building has foundered—sometimes despite prolonged attempts at institutional development. . . . The United States has succeeded at nation-building most demonstrably (and most quickly) when its interventions have built upon local institutions and traditions." "Can America Nation-Build?," 315, 339. For a similar argument, see Fukuyama, *State-Building*, 51–52.

106 Brownlee, "Can America Nation-Build?," 325.

107 These statistical studies use prewar economic and political development as a control variable and measure state building success or failure based on whether a society reaches a particular threshold of political development. Doyle and Sambanis, *Making War and Building Peace*; James Dobbins, Laurel E. Miller, Stephanie Pezard, Christopher S.

Chivvis, Julie E. Taylor, Keith Crane, Calin Trenkov-Wermuth, and Tewodaj Mengistu, *Overcoming Obstacles to Peace: Local Factors in Nation-Building* (Santa Monica, CA: RAND, 2013), 205–8.

108 Moses Abramovitz, "Catching Up, Forging Ahead, and Falling Behind," *Journal of Economic History* 46, no. 2 (June 1, 1986): 385–406.

109 See Fukuyama, *State-Building*, 139.

110 Fukuyama writes that because the international community "comes so richly endowed and full of capabilities that it tends to crowd out rather than complement the extremely weak state capacities of the targeted countries." Another reason foreign-supported institution building can undermine local capacity is internal "brain-drain" in which highly skilled individuals may seek relatively higher-paying jobs within international or nongovernmental organizations. Fukuyama, *Political Order and Political Decay*, 139; see also Easterly, *White Man's Burden*.

111 Robert H. Bates, *Prosperity and Violence: The Political Economy of Development* (New York: Norton, 2010), chap. 4.

112 High Representative's TV Address to the Citizens of BiH, January 31, 2006, http://www.ohr.int/?p=38178; see also Valery Perry and Soeren Keil, "The OSCE Mission in Bosnia and Herzegovina: Testing the Limits of Ownership," *Nationalities Papers* 41, no. 3 (2013): 371–94; and Edward Joseph, "Ownership Is Over-Rated," *SAIS Review of International Affairs* 27, no. 2 (Summer–Fall 2007): 109–23.

CHAPTER THREE

CREATING CENTRAL GOVERNMENTS *in* KOSOVO *and* IRAQ

Following the 1999 war, Kosovo was in chaos. The UN Mission in Kosovo (UNMIK) was mandated to administer Kosovo until the territory's final status was determined, meaning Kosovo would gain independence, remain part of Serbia, or some other alternative. From 1999 to 2001 UNMIK made rapid progress in creating a temporary, UN-run administration and subsequently establishing a "provisional" elected government, whose powers were specified by a constitutional framework. The mission achieved this early success in large part because it seemed to be making progress toward Kosovo's independence, the key Albanian nationalist goal. In 2002 UNMIK shifted to a policy of delaying final status negotiations (and, hence, independence) until Kosovo's institutions met high standards of governance. This threatened Albanian nationalist goals, which in turn led to growing popular and elite discontent, culminating in deadly riots in March 2004. Despite extensive resources, UNMIK was compelled to reduce its demands and begin final status negotiations. UNMIK's record of building central government in Kosovo, the first case study in this chapter, thereby offers a clear example of how the threat of foreign demands to domestic interests can create opposition that damages or delays reform.

UNMIK and the Coalition Provisional Authority (CPA) in Iraq—the subject of the second case study in this chapter—are among only a few examples in which a highly resourced mission sought to build a central government from scratch.[1] Kosovo and Iraq are also striking since they have little in common aside from international intervention. Kosovo was a small, relatively poor European country (population of 2 million) where the dominant majority group welcomed foreign intervention, while

Iraq had a population of 28 million, oil wealth, a different ethnosectarian structure, and little local support for the Coalition presence.

Despite these differences, both missions were compelled to compromise in the face of public opposition. In Iraq the CPA developed a plan for an extended occupation to build democratic institutions. However, Shia religious leader Grand Ayatollah Ali al-Sistani argued that the CPA's plan was insufficiently democratic because the proposed constitution-writing body would not be elected. Sistani spearheaded an elite boycott, which forced the CPA to shorten its occupation of Iraq and compromise its vision for Iraq's institutions. The CPA-proposed institutions did recognize the Shia majority in Iraq and were therefore not clearly threatening to Shia nationalist goals as coded below. Still, Sistani was able to organize effective public opposition because of his unique stature. Both case studies show how foreign reformers can achieve the most success when they select their demands to avoid domestic opposition, although the origins of domestic opposition may sometimes diverge from the two interests proposed in my theory depending on the unique characteristics of some societies.[2]

DEVELOPMENT OF CENTRAL GOVERNMENT IN KOSOVO, 1999–2008

From 1999 to 2008 UNMIK undertook a number of ambitious efforts to build Kosovo's provisional institutions, including creating a central government that met Western standards of effectiveness, accountability, and the rule of law. These institutions would eventually transform into the governing institutions of an independent Kosovo after 2008. When UNMIK's proposed institutions interfered with independence and elite networks, it would face strong opposition. When they did not, UNMIK was more able to improve governance in Kosovo.

Context

In the course of the 1990s, following the breakup of Yugoslavia, the Serbian government exerted increased control over Kosovo, which had previously been an autonomous region within the Socialist Republic of Serbia. Kosovo played an important role in Serbian nationalist discourse, in part because Serbs had at one time made up a majority of the population. However, the Serb population diminished, and by 1990 more than 80 percent of the population consisted of Kosovo Albanians. Despite the minority position of Serbs, the Belgrade government repressed the Albanian majority and excluded it from state-run institutions.[3]

Kosovo Albanians resisted Serbian oppression in several ways. They established a system of "parallel institutions" and, later, formed an armed guerrilla group called the Kosovo Liberation Army (KLA). In 1999, after attacks by the KLA on Serbian authorities, Serbia moved security forces into Kosovo, and the conflict escalated. After failed peace talks at the Rambouillet conference in France in February 1999, NATO intervened militarily and bombed Serbian targets in Kosovo and Serbia.[4]

The war ended with an agreement, codified in UN Security Council Resolution 1244, that required Serbian forces to withdraw from Kosovo and specified that the territory would gain provisional political autonomy from Serbia under a UN administration, namely UNMIK. Kosovo's final political status, however, remained undetermined.[5] In addition to Serbia's staunch opposition to Kosovo's independence, many other countries opposed granting independence following the KLA's violent separatist campaign. Rather than face a controversial debate on Kosovo's independence in 1999, the United States, its allies, and other members of the international community decided to indefinitely delay the question of Kosovo's future status.[6]

UNMIK set out to provide "an interim administration for Kosovo under which the people of Kosovo can enjoy substantial autonomy" and to develop "provisional institutions for democratic and autonomous self-government."[7] To accomplish these goals, UNMIK had overall high resources, albeit with some gaps. From its mandate, UNMIK had "full legislative and executive powers, including the administration of the judiciary."[8] UNMIK also benefited from large numbers of foreign personnel, although it did face some early difficulties in recruiting and deploying foreign personnel, and there were accusations of foreign corruption and malfeasance.[9] Kosovo Force (KFOR), the international military mission mandated by Resolution 1244 to enforce the peace agreement, had a peak size of 45,000 in 2000 (19.3 per 1,000 inhabitants). There were also 4,731 civilian police in 2002, which amounted to 2.38 per 1,000 inhabitants, a much higher level than the desired standard specified in chapter 2. Kosovo also benefited from $526 per capita economic assistance in the first two years after the war, the second highest (after Bosnia) listed in the RAND nation-building study.[10]

UNMIK, however, had only moderate bureaucratic resources. UNMIK officials explicitly learned from the coordination problems in Bosnia, where multiple organizations were present without clear leadership.[11] In Kosovo the special representative of the secretary-general (SRSG) had final authority over the four "pillars" of the mission, although there are reports of problematic day-to-day coordination between the pillars.[12] The mission demonstrated some degree of organizational learning, in particular revising its demands following the 2004 riots. Nevertheless, KFOR was under NATO—not UN—control, and there were still identifiable gaps in planning and coordination. For example, prior to 2004 there was no clear plan for pursuing final status negotiations.

When UNMIK first arrived in June and July 1999, Kosovo's physical infrastructure was largely destroyed, and its central government institutions were effectively nonexistent. Tim Judah writes that "it is impossible to underestimate the chaos of Kosovo in the wake of the war," and a UN official at the time explained that Kosovo was "like the Wild West now, except they didn't have grenades and AK-47s in the Wild West."[13] There was also violence between Kosovo political factions—in 2009 Nazim Blaca confessed to having killed seventeen people on behalf of the Democratic Party of Kosovo (or Partia Demokratike e Kosovës, PDK), mainly during the initial postwar period.[14] Albanian-led institutions, including the previously developed "parallel" institutions and the more recently KLA-established "provisional government," also claimed authority.[15] Nevertheless, the central government after the war was effectively nonexistent. For effectiveness, accountability, and adherence to law, I score the central government 0 out of 3 in each category, for a total score of 0 out of 9.

Kosovo did have a history of some degree of self-government. During the 1970s "golden age," Kosovo gained status as an autonomous republic of Serbia and had its own parliament, government, and police, although the territory was less prosperous than the rest of Yugoslavia (I score effectiveness as 2 out of 3).[16] By 1970 two-thirds of the Communist Party and local administration were Albanians, and by 1981 three-quarters of the security forces were Albanian, implying that Albanians had a degree of participation in state institutions, although Serbs were still somewhat overrepresented (I score accountability as 1 out of 3).[17] There was a well-developed judiciary and rule of law in Kosovo during the Yugoslav period—Albanian lawyers who had been trained and practiced in the former Yugoslavia were eventually merged into the UNMIK-governed judiciary[18]—but the history of discrimination against Albanians, a record of lower economic development, and instability indicated lower rule of law in comparison to other Yugoslav republics (I score rule of law as 2 out of 3).[19] Based on these scores, the overall historical quality score of central governance was 5 out of 9. Skendaj also observes that the population "developed shared and high expectations" about the need for the state to provide protection and services, which would shape Albanian views of governance under UNMIK.[20]

Serbia's repression of the Kosovo Albanians in the 1990s not only destroyed Kosovo's governing institutions but set the stage for interethnic conflict to continue as a major issue in Kosovo in the postwar period. While many Serbs left after the war, preferring not to live in an Albanian-controlled territory, some stayed. There were reports of violence by Albanians against Serbs.[21] Rather than protect Albanians from Serbs as originally anticipated, UNMIK would instead focus more on securing the rights of Kosovo Serbs in an Albanian-dominated polity. Nevertheless, Serbs largely boycotted the institutions UNMIK established. Hence, even though debates about the development of Kosovo's institutions focused on the rights of Kosovo Serbs, the outcome of UNMIK's reform efforts hinged on the interaction between Kosovo Albanian factions and UNMIK, which is the focus of the case study below.[22]

Two main Kosovo Albanian factions opposed Serbian authority during the 1990s, and some of these factions, or elements of these factions, in turn developed into major political parties after 1999. These parties drew on wartime rhetoric and patron-client networks to campaign and bolster their position. The most established faction was the Democratic League of Kosovo (or Lidhja Demokratike e Kosovës, LDK), led by Ibrahim Rugova. The LDK adopted a policy of nonviolence and created an elected government of "parallel institutions" that provided services of education and health care outside of the Serbian-dominated government.[23] Its funding came in part from informal taxes, from funds collected from the Albanian diaspora abroad, and, according to interviews, through smuggling networks and criminal activities. The patron-client networks associated with the parallel institutions and fundraising appear to linger into the postwar period.[24]

The other main faction emerged from the KLA, which was organized into several largely autonomous regional organizations, each loyal to the local regional commander. Hashim Thaçi, from the Drenica region, was a political leader of the KLA. Thaçi later became the leader of the PDK, which developed into one of Kosovo's main political parties. Ramush Haradinaj led a second political party that emerged from the KLA, the Alliance for the Future of Kosovo (or Aleanca për Ardhmërinë e Kosovës, AAK), which drew much of its support from the Dukagjini region.[25] The KLA had its own fundraising efforts abroad.[26] Analysts and officials also observe that the KLA was in significant part funded by illegal activities, such as drug trafficking.[27] Fifteen years after the end of the war, experts alleged that the PDK and AAK continued to raise money through protection rackets, corruption, election fraud, and the smuggling of drugs, cigarettes, and oil.[28] The parties that emerged from the KLA also had loyalty and responsibility to individuals who had joined the KLA during the war, and they sought to ensure employment for them in the postwar period.[29]

Kosovo Albanians sought a range of nationalist objectives, which can be understood as different solutions for how the final status of Kosovo could be resolved: Kosovo could remain part of Serbia, achieve independence, be unified with Albania and other majority Albanian areas in surrounding countries, or continue under international administration. Pellumb Kelmendi and I demonstrate that the proportion of Albanians voicing a preference for independence increased over the course of UNMIK's administration. In particular, the number of Albanian respondents supporting the more radical option of unification with Albania decreased from a high of 18 percent in July 2002 to a low of 2.5 percent in 2006.[30] Even with some support for the more radical nationalist goal of unification with Albania, elite political discourse focused on independence throughout UNMIK's tenure. As one of Thaçi's advisers observed in 1999, "It is almost impossible to differentiate' among the [various parties'] platforms. They all have three key issues: number one, independence; number two, independence; number three, independence."[31] The major political parties continued to campaign on nationalist rhetoric focused on independence throughout UNMIK's tenure.[32] As detailed below, Albanian leaders were not enthusiastic to grant special political rights to the Serbs, but as long as such rights were linked to the achievement of an independent, Albanian-dominated Kosovo, Albanian leaders were willing to compromise. The priority of achieving independence shaped Kosovo Albanian reactions to UNMIK's effort to build representative institutions, and these reactions in turn influenced UNMIK's success.

Below, I analyze three separate stages of reform shown in table 3.1—UNMIK's initial effort to develop interim institutions from 1999 to 2001, the standards before status policy from 2002 to 2004, and the final status negotiations from 2005 to 2008.

Stage 1: Development of Provisional Central Governing Institutions, June 1999–December 2001

During stage 1, UNMIK pursued three main demands: establishing a temporary government, developing a framework for an elected government, and ensuring the election of this government. These demands did not threaten the Kosovo Albanian nationalist goal of achieving independence, because these institutions were necessary for progress toward that goal. An independent Kosovo would need some sort of central governing institutions. UNMIK's proposed institutions could transition into central governing institutions for an independent Kosovo even if UNMIK did not yet articulate a plan for ceding authority. UNMIK's demands also did not threaten the ruling elites' patron-client networks, because UNMIK's institutions incorporated the major political parties. Given the absence of threats to nationalist goals or patron-client networks, the domestic opposition theory expects that elites and the population would not engage in major opposition. Indeed, there was little organized opposition to UNMIK up until 2001, although Kosovo Albanian elites did seek to parlay their role in the wartime and prewar parallel structures into political authority within these new institutions.

In July 1999 the first permanent SRSG of UNMIK, Bernard Kouchner, arrived in Kosovo to take over for interim SRSG Sérgio Vieira de Mello. To develop Kosovo's governing institutions, Kouchner first worked to create an interim

TABLE 3.1. Development of Central Governing Institutions in Kosovo

Stage	Threat of UNMIK's demands	Form of opposition	Relative success	International resources	Quality of institution at the end of the stage (out of 9)
Highest level of development before the intervention (1970s "Golden Age")	—	—	—	—	5
Quality of institutions at beginning of intervention (June 1999)	—	—	—	—	0
1. Constitutional framework (1999–2001)	None	Limited public	High	High, with some gaps	3
2. Standards before status (2002–4)	NGs and PCNs	Private and public	Limited but with violence	High, with some gaps	4
3. Beginning final status negotiations (2005–8)	None	Limited public	Limited	High, with some gaps	5

Note: NG = nationalist goal; PCN = patron-client network; UNMIK = UN Mission in Kosovo.

structure by which UNMIK could temporarily govern Kosovo and secure full control over the territory from competing, locally led parallel structures. A day after Kouchner arrived, the first meeting of the Kosovo Transitional Council was held, which was intended to offer a formal structure for Kosovar elites, both Albanian and Serb, to advise UNMIK.[33] On July 25, 1999, Kouchner issued UNMIK's first regulation, asserting UNMIK's authority: "All legislative and executive authority with respect to Kosovo, including the administration of the judiciary, is vested in UNMIK and is exercised by the [SRSG]."[34] In effect, Kouchner used the authority granted to UNMIK by Resolution 1244, backed by his military and bureaucratic resources, to negotiate with Kosovar elites and provide substitute governance.

Kosovo Albanian officials were not especially supportive of UNMIK's initial efforts. Kosovo elites used the Kosovo Transitional Council "as a platform for politicking for the various participants, [rather] than for any serious participation in UNMIK's policy-making process," according to one report.[35] Thaçi complained that Kosovo remained under Serbia despite UNMIK's presence and that Albanians were "not allowed to give our contribution."[36] UNMIK received similar complaints that it was not sufficiently taking into account local opinion from LDK and the Kosovo Serbs. This concern soon led Kouchner to create the UNMIK-led Kosovo-UNMIK Joint Interim Administrative Structure (JIAS) to temporarily govern Kosovo until elections were held.[37] The agreement creating the JIAS stipulated that the Kosovar-controlled parallel institutions "shall be transformed and progressively integrated" into the JIAS, assuaging concerns that Kosovo leaders would not be able to maintain their patron-client networks in the new government.[38] Pressure on Thaçi by the United States and Britain also apparently helped to convince him to follow UN demands.[39]

Under the JIAS, UNMIK was able to establish the beginnings of central governing institutions in Kosovo. UNMIK directed ministry-like "administrative departments," each of which had an international and local co-leader. These departments also established a legal code and collected and allocated tax revenue.[40] The JIAS, however, was unelected. It also at times faced local obstruction. Thaçi, for example, complained of "harassment" by UNMIK police, while LDK officials dragged their feet in eliminating the parallel structures.[41] Nevertheless, domestic opposition to the JIAS was not particularly widespread or systematic.

One reason for the lack of opposition is that there was general public support for UNMIK. An early poll showed UNMIK was perceived as more legitimate than the Albanian parallel structures.[42] Similarly, a focus group in April 2000 indicated that "Kosovo Albanians strongly support independence, but seem patient. Albanians believe Kosovo's future should be decided by the people who live there, but many accept that their future will be determined by the international community, and even consider this desirable."[43] An International Crisis Group (ICG) report observed that "although the number of Albanians who do not believe that their homeland should eventually be independent could comfortably fit inside a phone booth, most understand that independence now is not possible and many would also argue that it is not desirable at the present moment."[44]

After the JIAS, the next step was to develop a document specifying the powers of an elected government, including a parliament and executive, that would not prejudice Kosovo's final status. Initial discussions within the international community led to the drafting of a "legal framework," which was approved by the NATO Quint (United States, Germany, France, Italy, and the United Kingdom) and the UN Secretariat in early 2001. In March 2001 Kouchner's successor, Hans

Haekkerup, initiated a joint working group of UN and Kosovar representatives to finalize the framework.[45]

Local participants objected to elements of the framework. Albanian officials pushed for a time limit on UNMIK's governance over Kosovo, the creation of a constitutional court, the ability to call referenda, and a reduction in the seats reserved for minorities within the parliament. Legal scholars noted precedent from Kosovo's experience in Yugoslavia to argue for greater autonomy, showing how past governance experience can lead to path dependence.[46] Oisín Tansey notes that Kosovar members were able to shape the development of the document, including winning the addition of several chapters and convincing UNMIK to call the document a "constitutional" rather than "legal" framework.[47] Nevertheless, some Albanians dropped out of the process in the face of UNMIK's unwillingness to compromise, and Thaçi opposed the document on the grounds that it would "hold hostage the aim of the people of Kosovo, which is independence."[48]

Despite the limited Kosovar opposition, UNMIK issued the constitutional framework as UNMIK Regulation 2001/9 on May 15, 2001.[49] The framework called for elections to determine the new leadership of the Provisional Institutions of Self-Government (PISG). The framework also put in place protections for minority rights and created a judicial system with the authority to limit the activities of the new government. Still, UNMIK reserved control of many authorities normally held by sovereign central governments—including finance and budgets, the appointment and assignment of judges, and control of law enforcement and security institutions. Further, the constitutional framework explicitly did not limit the SRSG's authority under UN Resolution 1244, meaning that the SRSG could overrule the newly elected government.[50]

Even Kosovar officials who had voiced opposition to the framework participated in the November 2001 elections. LDK won 46 percent of the vote, PDK 26 percent, AAK won 8 percent, and a coalition of Serbian parties won 11 percent. A broad coalition government, which included the Serbian parties, was established seven months after the election after UNMIK-mediated negotiations. Rugova, the head of the LDK, would become the president, while Bajram Rexhepi from PDK would become prime minister—in part, by some accounts, because of opposition from the United States to Thaçi, who was perceived as more radical.[51]

After the election, Albanian parties continued to voice their desire for greater authority and a path toward independence. The assembly supported resolutions opposing UNMIK negotiation of the border with Macedonia and approving of the KLA's wartime values. UNMIK subsequently overruled both resolutions.[52] Nevertheless, widespread Albanian opposition of the new Kosovo institutions was not particularly noticeable, in part because of a division between the more radical Thaçi and the more moderate LDK leaders. The newly elected government, overseen by

UNMIK, attempted to lead the territory and ensure that the government provided services, albeit not to a level that was satisfying to foreign observers.[53]

UNMIK had moderate success in establishing institutions of self-government in Kosovo. Kosovo's central governing institutions went from being effectively nonexistent to achieving a total score of 3 out of 9:

- Effectiveness (1 out of 3): The JIAS and PISG were able to make laws and deliver some services, although the Albanian representatives prioritized pursuing independence over executing effective governance.[54]
- Accountability (1 out of 3): There was an election, and some minority representatives were selected, but challenges to minority rights remained. Further, UNMIK retained final authority over legislation and governance.
- Rule of Law (1 out of 3): With the constitutional framework, a basic law for central government was established, but UNMIK could override it.

Absent more intense opposition, UNMIK was able to use its resources to improve Kosovo's central government institutions, as the international resource and domestic opposition theories predict.

Stage 2: Standards before Status and the Riots

After the election of the PISG, UNMIK developed a second set of demands, which was articulated in a policy eventually called "standards before status." According to this policy, UNMIK would allow final status negotiations to begin only after Kosovo had fulfilled certain standards for governance. Michael Steiner, who succeeded Haekkerup as SRSG in December 2001, explained, "Kosovo's final status cannot be considered in a meaningful way until its institutions, economy and political culture have evolved so that it can administer itself without extensive outside support or interference. Our philosophy, standards before status, express[es] a logical necessity."[55] Based on accounts of Steiner's private discussions, it appears that he believed that the institutionalization was necessary before beginning discussion about Kosovo's independence and that Kosovo could achieve the standards he specified.[56]

Over the next two years UNMIK requirements for what institutions Kosovo needed to fulfill became increasingly arduous and unachievable, thereby threatening the Albanian nationalist goal of independence. In April 2002 Steiner introduced eight main benchmarks.[57] UNMIK further specified these into 109 sub-benchmarks in November 2003 and later issued a 117-page document with more than 400 actions in March 2004. Many requirements were vague or beyond reasonable expectations for Kosovo. For example, the Kosovo Standards Implementation Plan included the requirement that "public figures (both centrally and in municipalities) unequivocally condemn statements condoning or likely to incite violence, inter-ethnic hatred or any other form of extremism."[58] One international official apparently joked that "if Kosovo met Steiner's standards, it should be immediately granted the chairmanship of the Council in Europe, because its human rights record would surpass that of any Western European country."[59] UNMIK also failed to develop clear criteria for evaluating progress, required improvements in government functions that had yet to be transferred to Kosovar responsibility, and delayed a formal evaluation of Kosovo's progress with respect to the standards.[60] While perhaps the most challenging standards concerned the creation of a government that would respect the rights of the Serbs, UNMIK's standards also included elements focusing on anticorruption and minority recruitment, threatening the ruling elites' patron-client networks.[61] Given a threat to both core domestic interests, the domestic opposition theory predicts widespread and recurring bottom-up public opposition as well as possibly elite-driven private opposition.

Both forms of opposition occurred. Although UNMIK's major challenge would become the public opposition culminating in the 2004 riots, its capacity-building efforts were also hindered by private opposition. Elton Skendaj explains that "party elites brought their village or town networks and employed family and friends in the new administration. In two to three months after the turnover in 2002, the central government was filled immediately with new people who did not have experience in administration."[62] Skendaj also claims Kosovo Albanians used their pursuit of independence as a means of silencing attacks on corruption and other malfeasance by branding critics as opponents of the Albanian cause.[63]

The political selection of unqualified officials, combined with the provision of extensive international advice, undermined the development of the central government. Kosovo's laws were often not based on research or forethought and instead were copied from other countries, some of which had incompatible legal frameworks.[64] Ministers and senior officials were widely perceived to receive kickbacks—Skendaj cites a public statement by a former minister: "I have abused my father's money. Why shouldn't I abuse the state budget?"[65] Nevertheless, there was no significant prosecution of corruption, in large part because of the politicization of the judiciary.

At the same time, through 2003 and early 2004 Kosovo Albanian leaders began to voice increasing objections to UNMIK, especially about the pace of transition and the flaws of the standards policy. By late 2003 Prime Minister Rexhepi, who was viewed as a moderate, stated that if UNMIK "refuses to transfer more power to us, then internationals here will face big demonstrations and everyone will be crying 'UNMIK go home.'"[66] At the same time as elites voiced their opposition, UNMIK's popularity among the Albanian population was also in decline, as the domestic opposition theory expects. Survey respondents who were satisfied with UNMIK dropped from 60 percent in November 2002 to 42 percent in July 2003, 28 percent in November 2003, and 23 percent in March 2004.[67]

The international community hoped to encourage practical cooperation between Albanian and Serbian representatives within the Kosovo Assembly. However, Albanian politicians instead attempted to extend the authorities of the Kosovo Assembly, pursued resolutions focused on nationalist objectives, and ignored practical minority concerns on language and education policy. Most Kosovo Serbs were reluctant to participate in the PISG and other UNMIK-backed institutions for fear that they might lead to Kosovo's independence, and the failure to gain broader support for their agenda may have contributed to the subsequent Serb decisions to boycott elections.[68]

Popular dissatisfaction with UNMIK, combined with elite opposition, eventually led to riots in March 2004. The riots included an estimated fifty thousand individuals and led to nineteen people killed, nine hundred injured, and seven hundred homes destroyed.[69] The reported trigger for the riots was a news story that several Albanian boys had drowned in the Ibar River after being chased by a group of Serbs. One report observed "a whirlwind mix on the one hand of incoherent anger searching for direction and outlets, and on the other of determined groups displaying cohesion and calculations."[70] Subsequent analysis drew a direct link between the riots and the delay of final status negotiations. A UK diplomat working within UNMIK described the protests as "an insurrection against the UN."[71] Similarly, a leading analyst of Kosovo, Henry Perritt, writes, "It is undeniable that the paroxysm of Kosovar Albanian rage directed against UNMIK and Kosovo Serbs on those two days reflected a deep-seated Albanian frustration with political affairs and with the pace of transition from UN administration of Kosovo to final status."[72] In a UN report Norwegian diplomat Kai Eide found that the lack of progress toward final status negotiations was a major cause of the violence. Eide wrote that "the international community failed to read the mood of the majority population, its frustrations and impatience." He found the continued pursuit of the standards before status policy to be "untenable."[73]

As the domestic opposition theory predicts, widespread Albanian public opposition hindered reform and, based on a recognition that the mission's demands were contrary to the popular will, compelled UNMIK to compromise its demands. Some international officials argued that the United Nations should not move forward with final status negotiations because the riots indicated that Kosovo was not ready for independence, and such action would reward violence. However, Søren Jessen-Petersen, the new SRSG appointed in June 2004, rejected further delays of the status negotiations. He explained, "The only terms on which I will agree to [become SRSG] is if I can be forthright about the need to move quickly to final status negotiations, and . . . decisive in devolving further power to the elected governmental institutions of Kosovo."[74] With this change in leadership, UNMIK would begin a new stage of the reform process.

From 2002 to mid-2004, the quality of Kosovo's central government institutions did appear to improve. They become more effective, achieving a score of 2 out of 3 as the government raised revenue and provided services. However, both the accountability and compliance with law of the central government remained poor, with a score of 1 out of 3 each, due to challenges with corruption, limited minority representation, and continued foreign administration. UNMIK had helped to encourage progress from a total score of 3 to 4 out of 9 from 2001 to 2004, but the occurrence of violent opposition undercut this success. If UNMIK had preemptively started final status negotiations rather than indefinitely delaying them, more progress would likely have been made, as shown by the events of the next period.

Stage 3: UNMIK's Push to Final Status, 2005–8

After the riots, the United Nations adopted new demands that included beginning the final status negotiations, transferring additional authority to the Kosovo government, and specifying a new set of reduced "priority" standards related to the protection of minority rights, the rule of law, and security. The priority standards focused on more achievable objectives such as greater minority participation in local government, the return of IDPs and refugees, improved tracking of cases in the judiciary, and minority Serb employment in the Ministry of Culture.[75] Some of the remaining standards from the Kosovo Standards Implementation Plan were also reformulated into the August 2006 European Partnership Action Plan, which specified the longer-term requirements for Kosovo's eventual EU accession process.[76] Although the outcome of the status negotiations depended more on international politics outside of Kosovo, the international community hoped that improving Kosovo's government would make independence more credible and that independence could serve as an incentive for reform.[77]

By initiating status negotiations and indicating that independence would likely be the result of the negotiations, UNMIK's policies no longer stood in the way of Albanian nationalist goals. Although UNMIK continued to officially seek to address corruption and related rule of law issues, the associated standards were not identified as a "priority." The specification of these priority standards reduced the potential threat of UNMIK's reform to existing patron-client networks. Given the absence of a threat to nationalist goals or patron-client networks, the domestic opposition theory predicts that organized opposition would diminish. The theory also expects some improvement in institutional quality given the international resources in Kosovo.

Indeed, Albanian popular support for UNMIK's demands appeared to increase in late 2004 and early 2005 due to UNMIK moving toward initiating final status negotiations. Following elections in October 2004, Haradinaj, the leader of the AAK, became prime minister in December 2004. Due to his background in the KLA, some international observers tended to perceive Haradinaj as a more radical leader, but he worked harder than his predecessor to build a more effective executive and fulfill the requirements set by UNMIK.[78] The United Nations noted "growing political maturity" in Kosovo, thanks to Haradinaj's efforts.[79] However, Haradinaj was indicted for war crimes by the International Criminal Tribunal for the former Yugoslavia in March 2005. He was acquitted in April 2008.[80]

Kosovar efforts to fulfill international standards continued after Haradinaj's indictment. For example, in June 2006 the Kosovo Assembly adopted an assembly standards plan that included requirements for the committees to meet more regularly and developed a more formalized structure for the drafting and development of laws.[81] Local participants cited the existence of greater capacity to react to complex and bureaucratic international demands. Reports by the SRSG to the Security Council also indicated greater adherence to the standards, in part, according to one UN report, "to enhance Pristina's credibility in the future status talks."[82] Still, as Skendaj notes, Kosovo leaders continued to undermine international efforts to establish a meritocratic central government in favor of securing their own political control.[83] According to former German diplomat Wolfgang Ischinger, UNMIK's provision of services also undermined Kosovar officials' incentives to develop state institutions: "The problem was a very large UN organization, with personnel of uneven quality. They did not give the Kosovo institutions enough to do. Even the license plates were printed locally by German diplomats. That meant that the Kosovo Albanians had little to focus on except final status."[84] Some of the failure to meet UNMIK's demands also stemmed from Serb opposition. The standards required minority recruitment into government, but Serbs had boycotted the 2004 election and generally declined to participate in government.[85]

The final status negotiations finally came to fruition in 2007 and 2008. After representatives from Kosovo and Serbia failed to come to an agreement on their own, in March 2007 Martti Ahtisaari, the Finnish diplomat leading the negotiations, issued a plan for Kosovo's "supervised" independence. Among other elements, the Ahtisaari plan created new rights for minorities, which according to the ICG, "go far beyond European standards."[86] These included the creation of Serb-controlled municipalities, which had the right to join with one another and receive benefits from Serbia, and a requirement that certain laws (for example, on municipal boundaries, elections, language, education, and religious freedom) require a dual majority of the overall and non-Albanian vote in assembly to pass. The Ahtisaari plan also proposed new international organizations that would have executive authority after independence, including the International Civilian Office and the EU Rule of Law Mission (EULEX).[87] Kosovo Albanians "grudgingly accepted" the Ahtisaari plan since, as one report explained, "they believed that was the price they would have to pay for independence."[88] Still, due to Serbian and Russian opposition, the Ahtisaari plan stalled throughout 2007. Ultimately, the UN Security Council did not approve the Ahtisaari plan, especially because of Russian opposition. With US support, Kosovo unilaterally declared independence in February 2008 under the terms of the Ahtisaari plan.[89] However, prior to the announcement of independence, little progress had been made in drafting the necessary legislation.[90] The new constitution and forty-one required laws were quickly passed by the assembly. Still, foreign actors played a major role in supporting this process, indicating the continuing limited capacity of the Kosovo governing institutions.[91]

When Kosovo declared independence on February 17, 2008, its central government institutions had been significantly improved, although some gaps remained. In aggregate, at independence, I score Kosovo's central government as 5 out of 9:

- Effectiveness (2 out of 3): While Kosovo's central government had improved, some issues remained. The 2009 European Commission assessments indicated gaps between the Kosovo central administration and, for example, that of Serbia.[92] These included reports of poorly qualified officials, challenges in creating a meritocratic civil service, incoherent laws, overdependence on foreign assistance, and limited substantive discussions about key policy issues.[93]
- Accountability (2 out of 3): Kosovo's government was democratically elected, and there were extensive guarantees for minorities specified under the Ahtisaari plan. There were also subsequent challenges with electoral fraud.[94] Because the United Nations did not approve the Ahtisaari plan, UNMIK officially retained final authority over Kosovo, although in practice the mission was "reconfigured" so that it did not govern Kosovo except in the Serb-dominated northern Kosovo.[95] These problems mainly stemmed from the international environment, rather than flaws in Kosovo's central government, but still undermined accountability.
- Rule of Law (1 out of 3): While Kosovo was ruled by a constitution, compliance with law in the central government remained a challenge due in part to corruption and clientelism. The judiciary did not appear to be independent and did not prosecute senior officials for corruption. There were also continuing reports of senior officials demonstrating limited respect for law. While EULEX attempted to remedy these problems, it would have little apparent impact.[96]

Overall, by accepting Kosovo's path to independence and leveraging its resources, UNMIK was able to achieve noticeable, albeit limited, progress moving the territory's central governing institutions from a score of 4 to 5 out of 9.

Conclusions: Central Governing Institutions in Kosovo

Overall from 1999 to 2008, I observe a change in the score of central governing institutions in Kosovo from 0 to 5 out of 9, a high success. The change in the numerical score, however, obscures the detail and variation over time in the trajectory of Kosovo's central governing institutions. My domestic opposition theory offers the best explanation for when and how UNMIK was able to improve these institutions. It explains that UNMIK achieved the most progress from 1999 to 2002 and from 2004 to 2008 because during these periods its demands did not threaten the Albanian nationalist goal of achieving independence. It also explains how public opposition and violence emerged from UNMIK's policy delaying Kosovo's independence. If UNMIK had begun the process of final status negotiations prior to 2005, rather than adopting the standards before status policy, Kosovo would likely have achieved greater progress. Finally, the case study explains how elites' patron-client networks motivated and enabled them to undermine the development of Kosovo's institutions. Even though UNMIK possessed great resources, its ability to counter and unravel patron-client networks was limited by a lack of local knowledge.

There was also some support for the alternative theories. The international resources theory explains how UNMIK leveraged its strong mandate and personnel. It also shows how resource limitations, such as a lack of coordination, effective planning, or language expertise, likely limited UNMIK's success.[97] The international resource theory cannot, however, explain the occurrence or effectiveness of Albanian domestic opposition. The path dependence theory accurately predicts that the quality of Kosovo's central government would achieve the highest historical level, that state institutions would follow historical models, and that foreign provision of services may have hindered local demand for improving institutions. Path dependence has a harder time explaining why UNMIK was so successful in developing a fairly functional central government that would appear to remain intact after UNMIK's authority diminished in 2008 and after the International Civilian Office closed in 2012.[98]

Skendaj offers an additional alternative argument that international efforts achieved less success because they permitted local ownership by elites, which facilitated the maintenance of patronage networks. He implies that the international community would have had more success if it had built impersonal, Western-style bureaucracy for the central government, as it did by starting from "scratch" in the customs authority and police in Kosovo.[99] There are several issues with this claim. UNMIK would have had difficulty building impersonal central governing institutions given the need to develop a locally legitimate government. UNMIK needed the support of the key Kosovar parties for its initial appointed government, which could not have been achieved if UNMIK started from scratch. Furthermore, entrenched patron-client networks would still likely have co-opted the new government institutions. Kosovo is a small country, and potential recruits could have been influenced by or brought into elite patronage networks. Finally, it is likely that greater elite opposition would have occurred if UNMIK had followed Skendaj's recommendation, and there is some indication that this opposition would have slowed the development of Kosovo's central government. Accepting elites' use of their networks instead increased elite buy-in and thus may have achieved greater progress than attempting to undermine their networks and provoking elite opposition.

BUILDING A NEW CENTRAL GOVERNMENT IN IRAQ, 2003–4

Unlike UNMIK, where the majority Albanian community welcomed UN intervention, there was little support in Iraq for the US-led invasion. Despite this difference in origin, the missions otherwise shared several common characteristics, including a mandate to exercise full executive, legislative, and judicial power.[100] Foreign reformers in both countries also pursued a similar general agenda, first establishing an interim appointed executive body supervised by the foreign administration and later developing a plan for a constitution and locally elected government. Like UNMIK, the CPA had some success but faced widespread public opposition that undermined the development of central governing institutions.

Context

In April 2003 a US-led Coalition invaded Iraq and brought down Saddam Hussein's regime. Prior to the invasion, the apparent US plan was for a short occupation and an "early transfer" of authority to an Iraqi government. This plan was premised on the rapid emergence of a legitimate and democratic Iraqi government following the war. Jay Garner, a retired US general, was the first civilian leader of the transition effort as the head of the Office of Reconstruction and Humanitarian Assistance (ORHA). ORHA primarily intended to respond to an anticipated humanitarian crisis and rapidly transfer of authority to Iraqis. However, following major hostilities, a vacuum in governance emerged, and President George W. Bush appointed L. Paul Bremer III to lead the civilian effort in Iraq. Bremer arrived in Baghdad on May 12, 2003, about a month after US forces had first occupied the city.[101]

Bremer initiated a major change in policy. Instead of rapidly transferring authority to Iraqis, Bremer intended to conduct a longer-term occupation to create peace and democracy in Iraq. He believed that the CPA would need to "not just install democratic institutions, but also create what [Bremer] called social 'shock absorbers,' institutions which form civil society—a press, trade unions, political parties, professional organizations."[102] Bremer sought to delay elections in Iraq until after these basic institutions were in place, both because of the practical challenges of holding elections and because of concerns voiced by post-conflict experts that early elections would undermine Iraq's democratic development.[103] By Bremer's account, President Bush supported his plan for a longer-term occupation, stating "I'm fully committed to bringing representative government to the Iraqi people. We're not going to abandon Iraq."[104]

Overall, the CPA had moderate resources, with high resources in some areas but gaps in others. The CPA had a strong mandate—as the administrator of the Coalition Provision Authority, Bremer had authority over "all executive, legislative, and judicial functions" in Iraq.[105] The US-led Coalition, however, faced shortfalls in troops relative to other societies, with only 6.5 foreign troops per 1,000 inhabitants, compared with the average of 13 per 1,000 for other interventions.[106] Assistance amounted to approximately $206 per capita in the first two years, which is moderate compared with other interventions.[107] In addition to the flawed prewar planning process, the CPA also faced a number of other bureaucratic challenges. Early on, the mission's internal organization was not well developed. For example, there were no established policy planning and coordination processes. Throughout its tenure, the mission also had difficulty coordinating its activity with the rest of the US government. The CPA further faced challenges spending authorized funds and experienced rapid staff turnover.[108] Still, the CPA showed a capacity for rapid adaption and learning over the course of the mission.

Iraq had at one time possessed fairly effective central state institutions, albeit with a poor record of accountability and weak rule of law. After the Ba'athist regime came to power in 1968, it developed an increasingly strong central state over the 1970s, drawing on Iraq's substantial oil wealth to rapidly increase service delivery to the population. Arguably, the high point of the Iraqi state came in 1979, when Saddam Hussein became president, followed by the Iran-Iraq War.[109] Authority was highly centralized and personalized within the Ba'ath Party, which exercised control through both an elaborate and complex bureaucracy and informal channels associated with the Ba'ath Party.[110] Although the Ba'ath Party's activities conflicted to a degree with the efficiency of the civil service, the government was nevertheless fairly effective by regional standards (I score effectiveness as 2 out of 3). In the 1970s, the regime also had some success in building an Iraqi "national" identity on top of existing ethnic and sectarian identities—that is, Shia, Sunni, or Kurdish—while at the same time actively repressing Shia Islamists groups.[111] I score the level of accountability and the rule of law in the late 1970s as 1 out of 3 each (for a total score of 5 out of 9) given the arbitrary arrest, repression, and the lack of free and fair elections. After the 1991 Gulf War, the Iraqi state conducted widespread human rights abuses and was significantly weakened due to sanctions, although the intelligence and security apparatus remained relatively effective up to 2003.[112]

After the Coalition invasion in 2003, Iraqi's central governing institutions largely collapsed. With the defeat and disappearance of the Iraqi security forces, widespread looting and violence broke out.[113] Remnants of the former regime reportedly took part in the looting and destruction to make it more difficult for the occupiers; indeed, the CPA faced significant challenges in reestablishing governance due to the destruction of government buildings, an inability to locate staff, and the disappearance of prewar official documentation.[114] Bremer recounts the observation at one of his first meetings in Iraq that "nobody had given me a sense of how utterly *broken* this country was."[115] Given the postwar destruction of Iraq, I score the quality of Iraq's central government as 0 in each category, for a total score of 0 out of 9, when the CPA began its effort.

Ethnosectarian identities arguably became increasingly politically important after 2003.[116] The Iraqi Shia constituted a slight majority of the population but had been marginalized and suffered atrocities under Saddam Hussein's regime. Different elements of the Shia political establishment articulated and pursued different goals for the future of Iraq, but some elements were widely shared and can be understood as dominant nationalist goals for the group. A first such goal was to gain control over the Iraqi government in proportion to their status as the majority of the population—by one account, as the "big brother or the senior partner in Iraq's multicommunal framework."[117] Ali Allawi identifies a significant shift in the political perspective of the Shia "from the politics of 'victimisation' to an insistence on their rights as a majority. This went beyond the simple assertion of majority rights and extended to the heart of the Iraqi state itself. . . . The Shia would now insist on moulding the state to their own perceptions and requirements."[118] A second goal, as indicated below, was the integrity of the Iraqi state, including preventing regions of the country from gaining extensive autonomy or seceding. The dominant Shia nationalist goals were not, however, explicitly anti-Sunni, and mainstream politicians did not specifically seek to exclude a Sunni role in the new state.[119] A final goal was to prevent the return of Ba'athism.[120] As I discuss in chapter 5, concern about Ba'athism would drive the violence perpetrated by more extreme Shia individuals or groups against Sunnis. From the perspective of the wider Shia community, this goal instead required the elimination of the Ba'athist party and leadership from power.

Shia politics was moderated and heavily influenced by Sistani, the most senior of the four grand ayatollahs of Najaf. While resisting a direct role in government bodies and refusing to meet with the CPA, Sistani played an influential role throughout the CPA's tenure, repeatedly expressing opinions that shaped the behavior of the full range of Shia elites, even the more secular ones, and the Shia population. According to Abbas Kadhim, Sistani was "very essential in keeping the majority of Shia from an open revolt" and, by August 2004, had "established himself as the most important man in Iraq, an indispensable force with a positive role."[121] I divide the leading Shia parties and leaders during the CPA period into three categories: the Supreme Council for the Islamic Revolution in Iraq and Dawa parties, who were Islamists and had opposed Saddam Hussein's regime from exile from Iran; exiled politicians close to the Western policymakers, such as Ahmed Chalabi; and the more radical anti-occupation movement led by Muqtada al-Sadr, which drew support mainly from poorer urban areas.[122] While violent opposition by Sadr's supporters was influential, there was not broader popular support for the movement. This meant that public opposition by al-Sadr and his supporters, even though it was justified based on a nationalist, anti-occupation sentiment, would not prove compelling to the CPA, as detailed below. The Shia parties also depended on a range of patron-client structures, especially the militias that would come to dominate the security forces, as discussed in the case study on the Iraqi police in chapter 5.

The Kurds, who made up approximately 20 percent of the population of Iraq, sought to secure autonomy in the north of Iraq. They also wanted some degree of participation in the central state and, as one participant explained, sought to "avoid alienating the Shia."[123] The Iraqi Sunnis, who made up approximately 19 percent of the population, had more complicated objectives. There was extensive division among the Sunni—David Patel notes that after 2003 there was "a lack of unifying nation-level Sunni Arab leaders" and difficulty articulating the preferences of the unified Sunni bloc.[124] Part of the reason for the absence of a cohesive Sunni political position during and after the occupation was the lack of a strong, preexisting, explicitly Sunni political identity under the previous regime, despite disproportionate Sunni dominance of the Iraqi state.[125] Many Sunnis went on to reject the Coalition and sectarian dynamics of Iraq, including contesting their status as a minority.[126] Many Sunnis also took up arms against the Coalition and after the CPA period participated in the sectarian civil war.[127] In chapter 5, I describe how Sunni leaders would later turn against al-Qaeda at the same time as the Coalition surge in 2006–7. While characterizing a coherent goal for the Sunnis is difficult given their political diffusion, politicians representing Sunnis consistently advocated for Sunni participation in the government and state institutions. I take this to be the dominant Sunni nationalist goal.[128] Sunnis and Kurds did play a role in shaping the development of central government institutions under the CPA. However, public opposition by the Shia would prove to be the main determinant of the CPA effort to develop Iraq's governing institutions.

The case study below describes the two stages of the CPA's reform effort (see table 3.2). The first stage was from May to November 2003, during which the CPA established the Governing Council and attempted to implement a "seven-step plan" for an extended occupation. The second stage was from November

TABLE 3.2. Development of Central Governing Institutions in Iraq

Stage	Threat of CPA demands	Form of opposition	Relative success	Resources	Quality of institution coding at end of stage (out of 9)
Highest level of development before the intervention (before Iran-Iraq War 1979)	—	—	—	—	5
Quality of institutions at beginning of intervention (after fall of regime, April 2003)	—	—	—	—	0
1. Bremer's arrival in May 2003 until November 2003	None/ ambiguous	Public—elite boycott	Limited	Medium	1
2. November 2003 to end of CPA in June 2004	None	Private and limited public	Moderate	Medium	3

2003 to June 2004, during which the CPA implemented a revised plan accommodating Sistani's objections.

Stage 1: The CPA Plans for an Extended Occupation, May 2003 to November 2003

To build central governing institutions, the CPA pursued two main demands. First, the CPA sought to create an appointed, interim governing body and functioning ministries. Second, the CPA sought Iraqi agreement for a proposed plan for the development of a constitution and eventual transfer of authority to Iraqis.

I assess that neither demand posed a significant threat to the nationalist goals or patron-client networks of the major local parties or groups who participated in the government. First, in establishing the interim governing body—what would become the Governing Council—the CPA incorporated the key political parties and preserved a balance that protected the major ethnosectarian groups' interests, including a Shia majority. While the CPA did articulate a desire to limit corruption, its initial concerns were rapidly establishing functioning ministries, which meant there was little practical challenge to existing patronage networks.[129] Members of the Governing Council could also maintain their patron-client networks by influencing recruitment decisions. Second, Bremer's transition plan—the "seven-step plan" detailed below—also did not pose a threat to core political interests because the future government's structure would be determined either by the ethnically proportionate Governing Council or by a popular vote.

Based on this assessment, my domestic opposition theory expects no major public or private opposition. However, intense public opposition did occur through a Shia elite boycott, which emerged due to Sistani's fatwa, discussed below. While my theory does not predict the origins of Shia public opposition, it does explain how Shia opposition compelled the CPA to revise its plans—namely, because the Shia elite boycott undermined the legitimacy of the institutions that the CPA sought to build.[130] Other individuals and parties, including Sadrists and Sunni insurgents, also engaged in public and violent opposition to the CPA. However, this opposition was not as widespread and, as noted in the following narrative, the CPA did not perceive it to be representative of broader public sentiment.[131]

In May 2003, after his arrival, Bremer immediately pursued his first demand: developing an interim governing body. Initially, he attempted to convince the G-7—a group of exiled Iraqi politicians who had been told by American officials prior to Bremer's arrival that they would receive power—to develop themselves into a more representative group. By mid-June, the CPA determined that the G-7 was not willing to enlarge itself to meet Bremer's expectations. Instead, the CPA decided to identify candidates on its own and on July 13 appointed the Iraqi Governing Council.[132] The twenty-five-member body included the leaders of several major political movements, and the membership was carefully selected to ensure a slim majority for Shia, equal representation for Sunnis and Kurds, and representation for other minorities and women.[133]

In line with my predictions, Iraqi elites did not appear to engage in significant private or public obstruction to the Governing Council. They did use their membership on the body to protect their personal interests and networks. Bremer's account of the recruitment of Iraqi senior leaders to the Governing Council notes that they were ultimately willing to serve but played "hard to get" by seeking to appoint subordinates or relatives to the Council in their stead or to gain advantage for themselves or their group as a condition of joining the Council.[134] Once on the Council, members sought to increase their own salaries, and they appointed their close associates or party members to ministries and other government bodies. Bremer, for example, quotes a Governing Council member explaining their choices for Iraqi ministers as "jobs for the boys."[135]

To build capacity, the CPA appointed advisers to Iraqi ministers, who, as Allawi writes, "acted not so much as liaisons but as actual administrators, even though some insisted on maintaining the fiction of Iraqi involvement in key decisions."[136] The US Agency for International Development also implemented a "Ministry in a Box" program to provide basic equipment. The CPA's de-Baathification order also removed the senior party members, including much of the middle management.[137] Nevertheless, the ability of foreign advisers to exercise control was limited. Ali Allawi writes that in addition to the officially established ministries and governing structures, there were "parallel, often dangerous, networks inside the government that continued to function, that owed their loyalties to the former Ba'ath regime, to political parties, to criminal gangs or to themselves alone."[138] Despite these problems, which reflected the challenges of path dependence and patron-client networks, the development of the Governing Council and ministries represented an initial success for the CPA and demonstrated how the CPA could use its authority and ability to persuade Iraqi elites to build representative institutions.

After the creation of the Governing Council, the CPA pursued its second demand—gaining Iraqi agreement for its "seven-step" plan for the transfer of sovereignty to Iraq. The plan, publicized in September 2003, was modeled off the 1925 constitutional process in Iraq.[139] It involved the creation of an appointed constitution-writing body, popular ratification of that constitution, and only then the election of a government to which the CPA would transfer sovereignty. The selection process for the constitution-writing body would be determined by the Governing Council–appointed Preparatory Committee. Because of the ethnically proportionate representation of the Governing Council, the major groups could in theory ensure that their nationalist goals were met, including achieving a Shia majority, participation for Sunnis, and autonomy for the Kurds.

The problem, however, was that in June 2003, before the CPA had even finalized the Governing Council, Sistani had issued a fatwa specifying his opposition to an appointed constitution-writing body. Instead, he insisted on an elected constitution-writing body and a referendum to approve the constitution.[140] Based on the same logic, Sistani opposed the CPA's seven-step plan. Sistani may have been motivated by concerns about the Shia nationalist goals—namely, their position as a majority group in Iraq. But his logic and justification were framed more broadly in terms of democratic values and a reference to Iraqis as a whole, not just the Shia.[141] Because of Sistani's stature, the fatwa meant that Shia officials, as Bremer writes, "could not risk openly defying him."[142] The Preparatory Committee, which was composed of a majority of Shia officials, thus also recommended general elections. Former CPA lawyer Noah Feldman explains that the Preparatory Committee "found itself completely constrained by the legal logic of the fatwa" and, after an audience with Sistani, "left unanimous that [Sistani's] argument could not be refuted" and dissolved itself.[143]

After the failure of the Preparatory Committee to adopt a proposal in line with the seven-step plan, Bremer still sought to convince the Governing Council to accept an alternative to direct elections. However, the Shia representatives of the Governing Council refused to accept any alternative that violated Sistani's demand for an elected constitution-writing body. Former CPA officials Feldman and Roman Martinez write that "the debate came to a head in November 2003, when the CPA and Iraqi leaders finally concluded that Sistani's demands would simply be impossible to circumvent."[144] In a memo on November 4, Megan O'Sullivan and Martinez warned of the "high political costs" of vetoing any Governing Council decision for direct elections of the constitution-writing body. They feared that a veto might provoke resignations by leading Shia of the Governing Council or "endanger our relationship with Iraq's Shi'a community writ large," and they noted that "if the religious Shi'a were to call for non-participation in the constitutional process, that process would be impossible to complete in a legitimate manner."[145] Bremer recognized that, due to the opposition of the Shia, "Our path to a constitution and sovereignty was now in jeopardy."[146] Reflecting on Sistani's opposition in his memoir, Bremer observed that Sistani's "inflexible position" on the need for an elected constitutional convention "would be the undoing of our first plan for Iraq's political process."[147]

Given that domestic opposition had undermined its initial approach to building Iraq's governing institutions, the CPA developed a new plan, which would become the "November 15 Agreement." Under this plan, the CPA would transfer authority to an elected transitional government of Iraqis by midsummer 2004. This body would follow a "Fundamental Law"—essentially an interim constitution—that would be written by a joint body of Iraqis and foreign officials. After the Transitional Government was in power, an election for a constitutional convention would be held, the constitution would be ratified with a popular vote, followed by another election for a permanent government. Critically, following President Bush's decision and with the approval of the Governing Council, the November 15 Agreement also called for a system of regional caucuses of "notables" to select the Transitional Government.[148]

Bremer's decision to abandon the seven-step plan also occurred after a rise in violence led some officials in Washington to push for a rapid transfer of authority to Iraqis in October 2003. President Bush, however, backed Bremer's plan for an extended transition on October 29, and Bremer continued to push for an extended transition on his return to Iraq as late as November 6. Bremer only abandoned the extended transition plan when it was clear that the Shia would not accept an unelected constitutional convention rather than because of the upswing in violence.[149]

By November 2003 the CPA had managed to create a modicum of effective Iraqi central government through the Governing Council and development of the ministries (I score effectiveness as 1 out of 3). Accountability remained weak as senior Iraqi leaders were appointed by the CPA, and the rule of law remained in flux given the absence of established constitutional documents (I score 0 out of 3 for both accountability and the rule of law). I therefore score Iraq's central governing institutions at this stage as 1 out of 9, implying a limited improvement in the first stage of reform.

Stage 2: Building Iraqi Interim Institutions, November 2003–June 2004

For the remainder of its tenure, the CPA would seek to implement the November 15 plan. As with the seven-step plan, the November 15 Agreement did not threaten the nationalist goals of the main Iraqi groups, because it could have led to a variety of outcomes for Iraq's institutions and reflected the country's ethnic balance.[150] The CPA did increase its attempts after November 2003 to undermine corruption, including through adding inspector generals to ministries and establishing the Commission on Public Integrity. In practice, these efforts posed little challenge to the patron-client networks of the major parties represented in the Governing Council.[151]

Nevertheless, Sistani continued to organize public opposition. Sistani was opposed to selecting a transitional government through a caucus system, which he called "treasonable." Instead, he insisted on direct elections prior to the CPA's planned transfer of sovereignty in June 2004.[152] The CPA resisted Sistani's objections, which it found to be "moving the goalposts" by adding a requirement for a directly elected assembly beyond the insistence of the elected constitutional convention. Nevertheless, by early 2004, the CPA had recognized Sistani's influence and organized a UN mission, led by Lakhdar Brahimi, to investigate the feasibility of early elections. After examining the situation in Iraq, Brahimi agreed with the CPA's assessment that earlier elections were not feasible and also opposed the caucus system, which he described as "totally alien to Iraqis."[153] Instead, he recommended that the CPA transfer authority to an appointed caretaker government and hold elections for a transitional government, which would also write the constitution. Although another modification of the CPA's plan, this one was more minor and was accepted by Sistani and the CPA.[154]

The CPA used its resources to implement this plan, despite efforts by various factions to shift the development of Iraqi's governing institutions to suit their interests. One challenge was the negotiations over the Transitional Administrative Law (TAL), the interim constitution that would govern Iraq after the CPA left and would serve as a model for the subsequent Iraqi constitution. Kurdish officials sought to ensure maximum autonomy, which other Iraqis opposed for fear that it would split up the country. Shia Islamists sought the greatest inclusion of Islamic law into the constitution, which was opposed by the more secular Iraqis. Some Shia, in part based on Sistani's concerns, also opposed a provision that two provinces could veto the constitution. After extended negotiations, the CPA managed to finesse and compromise across these demands, and the TAL was signed on March 8, 2004.[155] The TAL drew from liberal, Western standards in establishing a structure for Iraq's interim and transitional governments and instituting basic standards of human rights for Iraq. Critics, however, saw the document as not reflecting Iraqi traditions.[156] But the signing and eventual incorporation of elements of the TAL into the subsequent constitution does indicate how the CPA used its resources to engage in persuasion and thereby replace existing institutions.

Throughout the spring of 2004, the CPA faced violent attacks by both Shia and Sunnis, which Allawi describes as a "nationwide insurrection against the occupation."[157] In April 2004 two crises threatened to derail the political process—the seizure of Najaf by the Shia Mahdi Army, led by Sadr, and fighting between US Marines and Sunni insurgents in Fallujah following the killing of US security guards. These events demonstrated the fragility of the Coalition's control over Iraq and the importance of quickly transferring authority to an Iraqi government. The CPA did successfully deescalate both events through a combination of the use and threat of military force and the political balancing of opposing groups, demonstrating effective use of its resources. But conflicts with both the Sadrists and Sunni insurgents persisted following the CPA's tenure.[158]

Reliable public opinion data on attitudes toward the CPA appear to have first become available in November 2003. As shown in table 3.3, these surveys indicated that the CPA was not particularly popular. Support for Iraqi institutions was significantly higher than for the CPA or Coalition forces, although support for all of these entities declined over early 2004. All things being equal, the domestic opposition theory expects some improvement in public opinion due to the CPA's movement toward Iraqi independence. However, other factors likely encouraged distrust of the CPA, especially declining security. Strikingly, Iraqis became more convinced over the course of 2004 that the departure of the Coalition would leave them safer.[159]

TABLE 3.3. Results of Public Opinion Surveys

Confidence in	November 2003 (%)	January 2004 (%)	March 2004 (%)	April 2004 (%)	May 2004 (%)
Coalition Provisional Authority	47	32	14	9	11
New Iraqi ministries	63	54	42	31	39
Governing Council	63	51	41	23	28
Coalition forces	N/A	28	13	7	10

Source: "Public Opinion in Iraq," 37.

After November 2003, the CPA also accelerated its ministerial capacity-building efforts, recognizing that "the primary risk to the achievement of the CPA's vision . . . is the lack of a coordinated, well-trained and well-managed civil service."[160] Despite the increased intensity and spending $490 million for governance activities by the end of the occupation, Iraqi administrative capacity remained poor. Indeed, the CPA intended for 206 advisers to remain in the ministries after June 2004.[161] Further, whatever the CPA's efforts, corruption networks were reported to be reestablished within the ministries during or soon after the CPA's tenure. For example, Ali Allawi documents how networks within various ministries, built in part on prewar networks, funneled hundreds of millions of dollars abroad in late 2004.[162]

In May 2004 Brahimi, the UN envoy, led a process to select the Interim Government, which would govern Iraq after the departure of the CPA. The Interim Government was appointed on June 2, 2004, and was led by a Sunni president (Ghazi al-Yawer) and a Shia prime minister (Ayad Allawi), with ministers drawn largely from the Governing Council and existing leadership. The CPA originally intended to transfer sovereignty on June 30, 2004, but because of fears of violence, the transfer was moved up to June 28.[163] Following the CPA's tenure, Iraq continued along the political process that the CPA had put in place. The Interim Government oversaw elections on January 30, 2005, and ruled until the elected Transitional Government took over in May 2005. Iraq's constitution was ratified on October 15, 2005, and the first permanent government was elected in December 2005 and took power in May 2006.[164]

The CPA did achieve a moderate improvement from November 2003 to June 2004, from a score of 1 to 3 out of 9, as coded below, by putting in place basic but imperfect central governing institutions in Iraq. While these institutions did improve governance and create a basis for the subsequent democratic elections, they also set the stage for ethnic conflict and instability over the next several years:

- Effectiveness (1 out of 3): There was an Interim Government in place, but security and other basic services remained problematic, and the United States and other foreign personnel continued to substitute for many functions.[165] This compared poorly with the fairly stable governance and service provision in Jordan, for example, which also relied on foreign assistance.[166]
- Accountability (1 out of 3): Upon the CPA's departure, there was a democratic process in place for writing the constitution and selecting a government. However, the Sunni boycott of the January 2005 elections undermined the participation of Sunnis in the constitution-writing process. Over time, the small participation of Sunnis in government hurt Iraq's democratic future.[167] Still, Iraq's neighbors also faced significant challenges in ensuring the participation of minorities in government.[168]
- Rule of Law (1 out of 3): The writing of the TAL, along with other government regulations, ensured that there were laws in place over the central government. However, as the above examples of corruption show, compliance with law within the central government on the CPA's departure was poor, even in comparison with corruption reported in Iraq's neighbors.[169]

Conclusions: Central Governing Institutions in Iraq

The CPA had mixed success in building representative institutions in Iraq. According to the change in score, the CPA brought Iraq's institutions from a score of 0 to 3 out of 9, a moderate success. While the CPA faced major opposition prior to November 2003, by June 2004 it had established basic central governing institutions. The above account shows how the occurrence of domestic opposition best explains the varied success of the CPA. Although my theory does not predict that Sistani would organize an elite boycott even though the CPA sought to recognize Shia nationalist goals, it does explain why the boycott was effective. The CPA's commitment to democratic values made it compromise, while a more autocratic occupation could have potentially ignored Shia concerns.[170] Further, the domestic opposition theory also explains how Iraqi politicians were able to shape the central governing institutions to protect their patron-client networks, even in the absence of a threat to these networks. Given its limited resources and short tenure, it is unlikely that the CPA could have realistically unwound the existing patron-client networks in Iraq.

International resources and path dependence also explain some of the observed events. The CPA's mandate and other resources enabled it to complete a political process that created democratic government in Iraq. At the same time, resource gaps, including insufficient troops and bureaucratic challenges, undermined CPA efforts at capacity building, substitution, and imposition. The path dependence theory also sheds light on how preexisting institutions determined what the CPA could realistically achieve. The severe degradation of the Iraqi state after 1991 was likely a determining reason for the problems facing the central government in 2004. However, avoiding Shia opposition from Sistani was a more feasible problem for the CPA to address than its own lack of resources or preexisting conditions in Iraq.

CONCLUSION: LESSONS FROM CREATING CENTRAL GOVERNMENTS

In both Kosovo and Iraq, apparently well-meaning foreign interveners sought to build democratic central governing institutions that would persist after their departure. Both missions had some success, showing that it is possible for highly resourced foreign actors to rapidly improve a central government, although problems remained in both cases.

The two case studies above show that the threat posed by foreign demands to political objectives of domestic groups was critically important in determining the level of success. In Kosovo, so long as UNMIK did not threaten Kosovo's independence, Kosovo Albanians supported its efforts, and UNMIK made progress. In Iraq, even though the CPA's demands did not threaten Shia nationalist goals, the details of the CPA's plan did influence Sistani's decision to oppose the reform. Both interventions also show how the democratic values of foreign actors constrained them and forced them to change their demands in the face of widespread and recurring public opposition. Both interventions also arguably achieved greater success when they accommodated elites' preexisting patron-client networks. Elites were able to shape institutions to preserve their networks, which undermined accountability and the rule of law, but did not fundamentally challenge the success of the broader effort.

Any foreign intervener seeking to build new democratic institutions will likely face the same two-step process as UNMIK and the CPA: they will need to first establish an appointed government and then gain local buy-in for a plan to establish a permanent, elected government. UNMIK and the CPA faced the greatest opposition in proposing a plan for the permanent government, and future interveners will likely face the same challenge. These two case studies show that while there are no easy or straightforward choices for foreign reformers building central governing institutions, selecting demands that do not threaten nationalist goals or otherwise provoke opposition is most likely to enable success.

NOTES

1 Another example is Timor-Leste, where public opposition also compelled a UN mission to compromise on its demands. Radin, "Domestic Opposition," 121.
2 This chapter draws in part on my article analyzing efforts by these missions to achieve their preferred electoral time line. See Radin, "Domestic Opposition."
3 Although historically Serbs represented a majority of the population of Kosovo and the territory was important in the Serbian nationalist discourse, by the 1990s 82.2 percent of the population was Albanian in 1991, while only 10.9 percent were Serbs and Montenegrins. Judah, *Kosovo: What Everyone Needs to Know*, 59.
4 Daalder and O'Hanlon, *Winning Ugly*.
5 See UN Resolution 1244 (June 10, 1999), https://unmik.unmissions.org/united-nations-resolution-1244; and Phillips, *Liberating Kosovo*, 115–16.
6 Daalder and O'Hanlon, *Winning Ugly*, 179–80.
7 UN Resolution 1244 (1999), para. 10, 11; see also UN, "Report of the Secretary-General on United Nations Interim Administrative Mission in Kosovo," July 12, 1999, S/1999/779, https://reliefweb.int/report/albania/report-secretary-general-un-interim-administration-mission-kosovo-12-jul-1999.
8 Brand, "Development of Kosovo Institutions," 8–9. See also UN, "Report of the Secretary-General on United Nations Interim Administrative Mission in Kosovo," para. 35–42.
9 See, e.g., Walter Mayr, "The Slow Birth of a Nation," *Spiegel Online*, April 24, 2008, http://www.spiegel.de/international/world/confusion-and-corruption-in-kosovo-the-slow-birth-of-a-nation-a-549441.html.
10 Dobbins et al., *Europe's Role in Nation-Building*, 243, 246, 259.
11 One official explained, "We looked at the civilian structure in Bosnia and said whatever happens, don't do that again in Kosovo." O'Neill, *Kosovo*, 37.
12 See Brand, "Development of Kosovo Institutions," 9–10.
13 Judah, *Kosovo: War and Revenge*, 286–96; and Peter Finn, "Gunman Kills Serb in Café in Kosovo," *Washington Post*, December 21, 1999.
14 "EULEX Detains Self-Confessed Political Killer," *B92*, December 1, 2009, https://www.b92.net/eng/news/crimes.php?yyyy=2009&mm=12&dd=01&nav_id=63417. See also Perritt, *Kosovo Liberation Army*, 153.
15 Brand, "Development of Kosovo Institutions," 10–11.
16 See Judah, *Kosovo: What Everyone Needs to Know*, 54–57; and Skendaj, *Creating Kosovo*, 38–39.
17 Skendaj, *Creating Kosovo*, 39.
18 Although not without controversy, as the lawyers refused to implement the Serb law in force at the time and UNMIK eventually reverted to the legal code in force in the territory in 1989. O'Neill, *Kosovo*, 79–81.
19 Ramet, *Three Yugoslavias*, 293–307.
20 Skendaj, *Creating Kosovo*, 39–40.

21 King and Mason (*Peace at Any Price*, 53) cite estimates that six hundred to eight hundred Serbs were killed in Kosovo in the first post-conflict year, but in discussions others contest that this level of violence occurred. Discussion with foreign officials and analysts, 2009–2010, Prishtina and New York. Judah writes, "Many [Serbs] left because they were frightened, many because they did not want to live in an Albanian-dominated territory, and many because they were simply intimidated out of their flats. . . . Especially at the beginning, murders were common, but these declined to virtually none by 2007." Judah, *Kosovo: What Everyone Needs to Know*, 98.

22 On the Kosovo Serbs' reactions to UNMIK, see Petersen, *Western Intervention in the Balkans*, 170–71, 186; and Tim Judah, *The Serbs: History, Myth and the Destruction of Yugoslavia*, 3rd ed. (New Haven, CT: Yale University Press, 2009), 354–57.

23 Howard Clark, *Civil Resistance in Kosovo* (London: Pluto Press, 2000), 84–119.

24 Perritt, *Independence for Kosovo*, 89; and interviews with local analysts, Pristina, winter 2010.

25 Skendaj, *Creating Kosovo*, 42.

26 Perritt, *Independence for Kosovo*, 89.

27 Michael Dziedzic, Laura Rozen, and Phil Williams, "Lawless Rule versus Rule of Law in the Balkans," *USIP Special Report* 97, December 2002, 10. See also Radoslava Stefanova, "Fighting Organized Crime in a UN Protectorate: Difficult, Possible, Necessary," *Southeast European and Black Sea Studies* 4, no. 2 (May 2004): 261. Interviews with local analysts, Pristina, winter 2010.

28 Interviews with local and international officials and analysts, Pristina, winter 2010. See also "Time to Go Straight: The EU and America Are No Longer Prepared to Tolerate Graft in Kosovo," *Economist*, March 18, 2010; and Matthew Brunwasser, "Trial Opens for 7 Kosovars in Organ-Trafficking Ring," *New York Times*, October 4, 2011.

29 Perritt, *Kosovo Liberation Army*, 152–53.

30 Kelmendi and Radin, "UNsatisfied?," 1003.

31 ICG, "Starting from Scratch in Kosovo" *Europe Report*, no. 83 (December 13, 1999): 11.

32 King and Mason, *Peace at Any Price*, 120.

33 Brand, "Development of Kosovo Institutions," 10.

34 UNMIK Regulation No. 1999/1, July 25, 1999, 1.1–2, http://www.unmikonline.org/regulations/1999/reg01-99.htm.

35 Brand, "Development of Kosovo Institutions," 11.

36 Barbara Crosette, "Kosovo Rebels' Political Chief Call for U.N. Representation," *New York Times*, September 17, 1999, A3.

37 Brand, "Development of Kosovo Institutions," 11; and Perritt, *Kosovo Liberation Army*, 154.

38 Brand, "Development of Kosovo Institutions," 12.

39 A *New York Times* article noted, "Ms. Albright and Prime Minister Tony Blair of Britain, who both visited Kosovo—'made it very clear to Thaci that he had to deal with Kouchner and the United Nations.'" Scott Erlanger, "After Slow Start, UN Asserts Role in Running Kosovo," *New York Times*, August 11, 1999.

40 ICG, "Kosovo Report Card," 27–30.

41 Brand, "Development of Kosovo Institutions," 12–25.

42 Skendaj, *Creating Kosovo*, 55.

43 National Democratic Institute (NDI), "Kosovar Voices: Divisions, Coexistence, Democracy Focus Groups and In-Depth Interviews" (2000), http://web.archive.org/web/20110108101917/https://www.ndi.org/files/1085_ksv_focgrp.pdf.

44 ICG, "Kosovo Report Card," 24.

45 Brand, "Development of Kosovo Institutions," 30–31; and Tansey, *Regime-Building*, 124–25.

46 Kosovo Albanian officials argued that Kosovo had a constitution in 1974, and Kosovo legal experts developed their own draft of a constitution. Tansey, *Regime-Building*, 127; and Brand, "Development of Kosovo Institutions," 31.

47 Tansey, *Regime-Building*, 127–29.

48 King and Mason, *Peace at Any Price*, 121. The ICG reports that "PDK was the most outspoken critic of the Constitutional Framework." ICG, "Kosovo: Landmark Election," Europe Report no. 120 (November 21, 2001): 10–11.

49 Sources differ as to whether local authorities signed the constitutional framework. According to Tansey, the Albanian leadership was never asked to sign and would not have if they had been. According to Brand, Rugova and Haradinaj signed the constitutional framework, but Thaçi refused. UNMIK's record of Regulation 2001/9 contains only Haekkerup's signature. See Brand, "Development of Kosovo Institutions," 31; Tansey, *Regime-Building*, 129; and UN, "On a Constitutional Framework for Provisional Self-Government in Kosovo," UNMIK/REG/2001/9, May 15, 2001, http://www.unmikonline.org/regulations/2001/reg09-01.htm.

50 UN, "On a Constitutional Framework for Provisional Self-Government in Kosovo," chaps. 2 and 12.

51 Phillips, *Liberating Kosovo*, 125.

52 ICG, "Two to Tango," 6–9.

53 ICG, 10–20.

54 Skendaj, *Creating Kosovo*, 152.

55 Michael Steiner, "First Things First: Step by Step in Kosovo," *New York Times*, July 24, 2002.

56 Perritt, *Independence for Kosovo*, 75, 81–82; Phillips, *Liberating Kosovo*, 138–40; and Radin, "Domestic Opposition," 108.

57 These benchmarks were "i) functioning democratic institutions, ii) the rule of law, iii) freedom of movement, iv) sustainable returns and the rights of communities, v) economy, vi) property rights, vii) dialogue, viii) Kosovo Protection Corps." See UNMIK Press Release, "Address to the Security Council by Michael Steiner," April 24, 2002.

58 UNMIK, "Kosovo Standards Implementation Plan," March 31, 2004, http://pbosnia.kentlaw.edu/symposium/resources/KSIP%20final%20draft%2031%20March%202004b.htm.

59 Perritt, *Independence for Kosovo*, 75.

60 ICG, "Two to Tango," 18; and Tansey, *Regime-Building*, 138–39.

61 For example, the standards included the investigation of organized crime; that there be "legal, financial and administrative mechanisms . . . to tackle economic crime in both the public and private sectors, including seizure of illegally-acquired assets"; and "There is fair distribution of municipal and ministerial resources to all communities." "Standards

for Kosovo," December 10, 2003, 8, 10, https://www.securitycouncilreport.org/atf/cf/%7b65BFCF9B-6D27-4E9C-8CD3-CF6E4FF96FF9%7d/Kos%20Standards.pdf.

62 Skendaj, *Creating Kosovo*, 80.

63 Skendaj, 155–60.

64 In a 2006 report, a Kosovo think tank noted that lawyers in Kosovo made laws without policy research—"the smart ones copy only one foreign law and the less smart ones combine laws from several countries, often from different legal traditions." Ilir Dugolli, "Laws without Policy—Waste, Dead Letter and Futility," KIPRED, Policy Brief Series, Paper no. 4, Prishtina, November 2006, http://www.kipred.org/repository/docs/Laws_Without__Policy_-Waste,_Dead_Letter_and_Futility_618084.pdf. See also Skendaj, *Creating Kosovo*, 66–67, 82–87.

65 Skendaj, *Creating Kosovo*, 72–73.

66 ICG, "Collapse in Kosovo," *Europe Report*, no. 144 (April 22, 2004): 10. See also Perritt, *Independence for Kosovo*, 71.

67 Early Warning Surveys, UNDP, copies with author.

68 ICG, "Two to Tango," 6–9; Skendaj, *Creating Kosovo*, 136–39, 152; and ICG, "Kosovo's Ethnic Dilemma: The Need for a Civic Contract," *Europe Report*, no. 143 (May 28, 2003): 8–11.

69 ICG, "Collapse in Kosovo," 15–31.

70 ICG, 16.

71 The diplomat further explained, "Every single UN office in Kosovo was attacked. One hundred and eighty UN cars were burned. UNMIK's initial cables described the events as a revolt against the UN. Then UN headquarters changed it into a story of ethnic violence." Phillips, *Liberating Kosovo*, 144. See also Radin, "Domestic Opposition," 111.

72 Perritt, *Independence for Kosovo*, 79.

73 UNSC, "Report on the Situation in Kosovo," S/2004/932 (November 30, 2004), 3–20, http://www.securitycouncilreport.org/atf/cf/%7B65BFCF9B-6D27-4E9C-8CD3-CF6E4FF96FF9%7D/kos%20S2004%20932.pdf.

74 Quoted in Perritt, *Independence for Kosovo*, 81.

75 See "Standards for Kosovo (with priority Standards indicated)," 5, copy with author; and UNSC, "Report of the Secretary-General on UNMIK," S/2005/88, February 14, 2005, Annex 1, https://unmik.unmissions.org/sites/default/files/s-2005-88.pdf.

76 Interview with former member of the Standards Implementation office, Pristina, January 2010. UNMIK/PISG, "Kosovo Action Plan for the Implementation of European Partnership 2006," August 2006, copy with author.

77 Note, for example, that the UN report in October 2005 recommending the commencement of final status negotiations did so in spite of the gaps in Kosovo's fulfillment of the standards. See UNSC, "A Comprehensive Review of the Situation in Kosovo," S/2005/635, October 7, 2005, http://pbosnia.kentlaw.edu/kai-eide-report-N0554069.pdf; and Perritt, *Independence for Kosovo*, 129, 184–86.

78 Phillips, *Liberating Kosovo*, 148–55; and Perritt, *Independence for Kosovo*, 82–83.

79 ICG, "Kosovo: Towards Final Status," *Europe Report*, no. 161 (January 24, 2005): 6.

80 Perritt, *Independence for Kosovo*, 84, 208.

81 Tansey, "Evaluating the Legacies of State-Building," 141; and Phillips, *Liberating Kosovo*, 150–51.

82 UNSC, "Report of the Secretary-General on United Nations Interim Administrative Mission in Kosovo," S/2006/707, September 1, 2006, 3; and interview with former member of the Standards Implementation office, Pristina, January 2010.

83 Skendaj offers a telling example: Throughout the mid 2000s, a UK-funded program sought to create senior civil service permanent secretaries. The 2004–2007 AAK appointed supporters to become permanent secretaries within some key ministries. Following the 2007 elections in which the PDK gained control of government, Thaçi ended the DFID program and instead backed a US-led program following American standards of political appointees, which enabled PDK to install political appointees from their own party. Skendaj, *Creating Kosovo*, 86.

84 Quoted in Perritt, *Independence for Kosovo*, 228.

85 Franklin De Vrieze, "Building Parliamentary Democracy in Kosovo," *Security and Human Rights* 19 (2008): 123–27; and interviews with former Kosovar official, UNMIK official, Pristina, December 2009, January 2010.

86 ICG, "Kosovo: No Good Alternatives to the Ahtisaari Plan," *Europe Report*, no. 182 (May 14, 2007): 8–9.

87 See "Comprehensive Proposal for the Kosovo Status Settlement," February 2, 2007, https://www.kuvendikosoves.org/common/docs/Comprehensive%20Proposal%20.pdf.

88 ICG, "Breaking the Kosovo Stalemate: Europe's Reasonability," *Europe Report*, no. 185 (August 21, 2007): 6. Another report noted that the "Ahtisaari Proposal represents maximum concessions that could be extract from Kosovo's Albanian 90 per cent majority in favour of a beleaguered Serb minority that is roughly 7 per cent of the population." ICG, "Kosovo: No Good Alternatives to the Ahtisaari Plan," 8.

89 Perritt, *Independence for Kosovo*, chap. 14–16.

90 ICG, "Kosovo Countdown: Kosovo Countdown: A Blueprint for Transition," *Europe Report*, no. 188 (December 6, 2007): 19.

91 ICG, "Kosovo's Fragile Transition," *Europe Report*, no. 196 (September 25, 2008): 18–20. See also Joseph Marko, "The New Kosovo Constitution in a Regional Comparative Perspective," *Review of Central and East European Law* 33 (2008): 442–43.

92 The 2009 European Commission Progress Reports for Serbia and Kosovo indicated that Kosovo had basic gaps in its legal framework, while Serbia's legislation could have been brought more into line with European standards. European Commission, "Kosovo 2009 Progress Report," October 14, 2009, 6–11; and European Commission, "Serbia 2009 Progress Report," October 14, 2009, 6–11.

93 Skendaj, *Creating Kosovo*, 63–65, 73–74.

94 Skendaj, 63–64; and Paul Lew, "Kosovo Election Fraud Undermine PM's Victory," *Guardian*, December 13, 2010, https://www.theguardian.com/world/2010/dec/13/kosovo-election-fraud-claims.

95 Perritt, *Independence for Kosovo*, 222–30.

96 A 2010 ICG report observed that "department chiefs receive[d] phone calls apparently from advisers to two separate ministers seeking information about specific investigations in which their family members or party associates were allegedly involved." ICG, "The Rule of Law in Independent Kosovo," *Europe Report*, no. 204 (May 19, 2010): 6; see also Andrew Radin, "Analysis of Current Events: 'Towards the Rule of Law in Kosovo: EULEX Should Go,'" *Nationalities Papers* 42, no. 2 (2014): 186–90.

97 In explaining international failure to build central government capacity in Kosovo, Skendaj blames coordination failures and cites the ability of local actors to play different international actors against one another. Skendaj, *Creating Kosovo*, 96.

98 While there were ongoing challenges in the central government, including boycotts of parliament and oversight issues, Kosovo's central government continued to improve relative to its neighbors. See European Commission, "Kosovo 2016 Report," November 9, 2016, pp. 6–13, https://ec.europa.eu/neighbourhood-enlargement/sites/near/files/pdf/key_documents/2016/20161109_report_kosovo.pdf.

99 Skendaj, *Creating Kosovo*, 9, 96.

100 Note also that the CPA's occupation was eventually legitimized by UN Security Council Resolution 1483, issued May 22, 2003.

101 Dobbins et al., *Occupying Iraq*, 1–9, 34–44; Bensahel et al., *After Saddam*, xvii–xxiii; and Bremer, *My Year in Iraq*, 1–13.

102 Bremer, 12.

103 Bremer explains in his memoir, "We're not going to rush into elections because Iraq simply has none of the mechanisms needed for elections—no census, no electoral laws, no political parties, and all the related stuff we take for granted." Bremer, 19. Larry Diamond, who both worked for and criticized the CPA, explained that the desire to delay elections "was not merely a political judgment that imminent elections would favor Islamist parties—though that concern existed—but the principled belief that for elections to be fair, a level playing field would have to be established for the competing parties." Diamond, *Squandered Victory*, 80. See also Dobbins et al., *Occupying Iraq*, 42–43; and Radin, "Domestic Opposition," 114–15.

104 Bremer, *My Year in Iraq*, 12.

105 Bremer, 13.

106 Dobbins, *Europe's Role in Nation-Building*, 243–44. Indeed, James Dobbins provided an early report to Bremer recommending additional troops to meet a "standard of 20 per thousand resident," which were not forthcoming. Bremer, *My Year in Iraq*, 10.

107 Government Accountability Office (GAO), "Rebuilding Iraq: Status of Funding and Reconstruction Efforts," July 2005, 6, https://www.gao.gov/new.items/d05876.pdf; Dobbins, *Europe's Role in Nation-Building*, 243–44; and Dobbins et al., *Occupying Iraq*, 254–57.

108 See, inter alia, Dobbins et al., Occupying Iraq, 98, 243–54; Bremer, *My Year in Iraq*, 113–14; and Cooley, *Logics of Hierarchy*, chap. 6.

109 Lisa Blaydes, *State of Repression*, chap. 3.

110 See Sassoon, *Saddam Hussein's Ba'th Party*, 3–14; and Charles Tripp, *A History of Iraq* (Cambridge: Cambridge University Press, 2002), 224–55.

111 Blaydes, *State of Repression*, chap. 3; and Allawi, *Occupation of Iraq*, 28–37.

112 Allawi, *Occupation of Iraq*, 115–16. For details of Iraq's security and intelligence services, see also "Comprehensive Report of the Strategic Advisor to the DCI on Iraq's WMD," vol. 1, Central Intelligence Agency, September 30, 2004, https://www.cia.gov/library/reports/general-reports-1/iraq_wmd_2004/.

113 Dobbins et al., *Occupying Iraq*, 43.

114 Allawi, *Occupation of Iraq*, 116–17; and Bensahel et al., *After Saddam*, 68–70.

115 Bremer, *My Year in Iraq*, 18. Emphasis in original.

116 Blaydes, *State of Repression*, 314.

117 Fanar Hadad, "Shia-Centric State Building and Sunni Rejection in Post-2003 Iraq," Carnegie Endowment for International Peace, January 7, 2016, https://carnegieendowment.org/files/CP261_Haddad_Shia_Final.pdf. Hadad also describes a "spectrum" of "Shia-centric state building," which, "at its most basic . . . involves ensuring that the central levers of the state are in Shia hand . . . and that Shia identities are represented and empowered." At the other end of the spectrum is "attempting to endow the state with a Shia identity" (5).

118 Allawi, *Occupation of Iraq*, 137–38.

119 The Sadrists, for example, claimed common cause with Sunnis, unlike the more Islamist Supreme Council for the Islamic Revolution in Iraq faction. Allawi, 137.

120 Allawi, chap. 11 and 13; ICG, "Iraq's Shiites under Occupation," September 9, 2003, 7–21; and Hadad, "Shia-Centric State Building."

121 Abbas Kadhim, "Forging a Third Way: Sistani's Marja'iyya between Quietism and Wilayat al Faqih," in *Iraq, Democracy and the Future of the Muslim World*, ed. Ali Paya and John L. Esposito (New York: Routledge, 2010), 66–80, 73, 76. Nir Rosen quotes representatives of Shia religious leaders in Najaf in April 2003 explaining the potential for opposition to Coalition rule: "The *marja* has no relationship with the political, it does not need the chair of the country and it does not aspire to politics, but if the political system is against Islam, then we will fight it. No Muslim can be ruled by a non-Muslim." Rosen, *In the Belly of the Green Bird*, 24–25.

122 Allawi, *Occupation of Iraq*, 137–41.

123 Radin, "Domestic Opposition," 115; Kenneth Katzman, *Kurds in Post-Saddam Iraq* (Washington, DC: Congressional Research Service, 2010); and interview with CPA official, July 22, 2013.

124 David Siddhartha Patel, "ISIS in Iraq: What We Get Wrong and Why 2015 Is Not 2007 Redux," Brandeis University Crown Center for Middle East Studies, *Middle East Brief*, no. 87 (January 2015): 6.

125 Blaydes, *State of Repression*, 314.

126 Allawi writes that "rejection of the terms of the new politics—especially the apparent ascendancy of sectarian consciousness amongst the Shi'a—was a common denominator in the thinking of all Sunni Arabs." Allawi, *Occupation of Iraq*, 136.

127 Blaydes, *State of Repression*, 317–18.

128 For example, Sunnis would boycott the 2005 elections in large part because they expected the results to exclude them from the government. Subsequent Sunni protests

in 2012–13 explicitly sought a greater role in government for Sunnis. Allawi, *Occupation of Iraq*, 389–90. See also ICG, "Iraq's Uncertain Future: Elections and Beyond." *Middle East Report*, no. 94 (February 25, 2010): 1–7; and Kamal Naama and Raheem Salman, "Iraqi Sunnis Stage Big Anti-government Rallies," *Reuters*, December 28, 2012.

129 There is little reference to corruption in Bremer's account prior to November 2003 or in the CPA archives, with the exception to discussion of corruption under the prior regime, and a study on anticorruption by the State Department's Future of Iraq project. See Bremer, *My Year in Iraq* and a list of CPA archived documents available at http://www.esd.whs.mil/Portals/54/Documents/FOID/Reading%20Room/CPA_ORHA/Archives_of_the_CPA.xls.

130 If this assessment is incorrect, and the CPA's demands did indeed threaten the Shia nationalist goals, then the domestic opposition theory does explain the public opposition that occurred and offers even greater explanatory power.

131 Interviews with CPA officials, November 2012 and July 2013.

132 Bremer, *My Year in Iraq*, 85–87.

133 Bremer, 94–103.

134 Bremer, 87–101.

135 Bremer, 149.

136 Allawi, Occupation of Iraq, 120.

137 GAO, "Rebuilding Iraq: Resource, Security, Governance."

138 Allawi, *Occupation of Iraq*, 203.

139 In particular, the seven steps were (1) creating the Governing Council, (2) naming a preparatory committee to devise a system for writing the constitution, (3) appointing Iraqi ministers, (4) writing the constitution, (5) popular ratification of the constitution, (6) the election of a government based on the constitution, and (7) dissolving the CPA and transfer authority to Iraqis. See L. Paul Bremer III, "Iraq's Path to Sovereignty," *Washington Post*, September 8, 2003; and Dobbins et al., *Occupying Iraq*, 266–68.

140 The June 26, 2003 fatwa states,

> Those forces [i.e., the Coalition] have no jurisdiction whatsoever to appoint members of the Constitution preparation assembly. Also there is no guarantee either that this assembly will prepare a constitution that serves the best interests of the Iraqi people or express their national identity whose backbone is sound Islamic religion and noble social values. The said plan is unacceptable from the outset. First of all there must be a general election so that every Iraqi citizen—who is eligible to vote—can choose someone to represent him in a foundational Constitution preparation assembly. Then the drafted Constitution can be put to a referendum. (quoted in Feldman, "Democratic Fatwa," 6)

141 As Feldman, an adviser to CPA, observed, "The fatwa was pure democratic theory. . . . Its conclusion and its reasoning were essentially indistinguishable from those of any competent international lawyer." Feldman, 6.

142 Bremer, *My Year in Iraq*, 166.

143 Feldman, "Democratic Fatwa," 7. Ayad Allawi, a relatively secular Shia member of the Governing Council and future prime minister, noted that when the preparatory committee met, "Sistani [was] sitting in the room," meaning that although Sistani was not physically present, his views were highly influential. Quoted in Dobbins et al., *Occupying Iraq*, 270; see also Bremer, *My Year in Iraq*, 210–11.

144 Noah R. Feldman and Roman Martinez, "Constitutional Politics and Text in the New Iraq," *Fordham Law Review* 75, no. 2 (2006): 894.

145 Meghan O'Sullivan and Roman Martinez, "Part I of Constitutional Strategy, Arguments against a Redline," CPA, November 4, 2003.

146 Bremer, *My Year in Iraq*, 211.

147 Bremer, 167.

148 Bremer, 224–27. See Coalition Provisional Authority, "Agreement of Political Process," November 15, 2003, http://web.archive.org/web/20031121142629/http://www.cpa-iraq.org/audio/20031115_Nov-15-GC-CPA-Final_Agreement-post.htm.

149 Bremer, *My Year in Iraq*, 210–13; Radin, "Domestic Opposition," 120; and interviews with CPA officials November 2012 and July 2013.

150 See CPA, "Agreement of Political Process," November 15, 2003.

151 Dobbins et al., *Occupying Iraq*, 280–82; and Allawi, *Occupation of Iraq*, 264–65.

152 Diamond, *Squandered Victory*, 85; and Radin, "Domestic Opposition," 118.

153 UNSC, "The Political Transition in Iraq: Report of the Fact-Finding Mission," S/2004/140 (February 23, 2004), par. 50.

154 Dobbins et al., *Occupying Iraq*, 288–89.

155 Bremer, *My Year in Iraq*, 292–307; and Allawi, *Occupation of Iraq*, 220–25, 231–32.

156 CPA, "Law of Administration for the State of Iraq for the Transitional Period," March 8, 2004, https://web.archive.org/web/20090423064920/http://www.cpa-iraq.org/government/TAL.html; and Allawi, *Occupation of Iraq*, 231–32.

157 Allawi, *Occupation of Iraq*, 266.

158 Allawi, chap. 15, 18; and Bremer, *My Year in Iraq*, 312–46.

159 These results are from in-person surveys of six Iraqi cities conducted by an Iraqi polling agency and presented in "Public Opinion in Iraq: First Poll following Abu Ghraib Revelations," June 15, 2004, 10–38, https://www.globalpolicy.org/images/pdfs/06iiacss.pdf.

160 Dobbins et al., *Occupying Iraq*, 277.

161 Dobbins et al., 277–78; and GAO, "Rebuilding Iraq: Resource, Security, Governance," 71–74.

162 Allawi, *Occupation of Iraq*, 352–56.

163 Allawi, *Occupation of Iraq*, 285–90; and Bremer, *My Year in Iraq*, 352–96.

164 For details, see Allawi, *Occupation of Iraq*, chap. 19–25.

165 Allawi, 290–93, 348–56.

166 See, for example, Sean L. Yom and Mohammad H. Al-Momani, "The International Dimensions of Authoritarian Regime Stability: Jordan in the Post–Cold War Era," *Arab Studies Quarterly* 30, no. 1 (Winter 2008): 39–60.

167 Allawi, *Occupation of Iraq*, chap. 22–23.

168 See, e.g., Freedom House, "Jordan," Countries at the Crossroads, 2004, https://freedomhouse.org/report/countries-crossroads/2004/jordan.

169 Freedom House, "Jordan."

170 As Feldman writes, Sistani's fatwa "represented . . . an epochal event in the annals of the interaction between Islam and democracy: an unelected cleric laying down the law to the United States, holding that legitimate constitutional processes required democratic underpinnings." "Democratic Fatwa," 7.

CHAPTER FOUR

DEFENSE REFORM *in* BOSNIA *and* TIMOR-LESTE

The 1995 Dayton Agreement ended the war in BiH, creating a weak central state and two political "entities": the Bosnian Serb-dominated Republika Srpska (RS) and the Federation of BiH, which was mainly Bosniak and Croat. The Dayton Agreement permitted these ethnically based entities to retain control over the militaries that had fought the war. Richard Holbrooke, the lead US negotiator, called this the "most serious flaw" of the Dayton Agreement.[1] In 2003 Paddy Ashdown, the High Representative for BiH, began an ambitious defense reform agenda to address this issue. Given the politicized ethnic division of Bosnia and the failure of other reform that challenged the authorities of the entities, the prospects for defense reform seemed grim. However, Ashdown's defense reform was a major success. By 2006 the entity militaries had been merged into a single, largely ethnically integrated military.

The first case study in this chapter on defense reform in BiH shows how that defense reform was successful for two reasons: first, because Ashdown and other international officials developed demands that did not threaten the Bosnian Serbs' nationalist goals or the ruling parties' patron-client networks, and, second, because Ashdown had particularly high resources, especially bureaucratic resources. The second case study on defense reform in Timor-Leste similarly shows the role of nationalism, patron-client networks, and bureaucratic resources in shaping the success of reform efforts. The nationalist importance of the pre-independence resistance movement, Falintil, compelled the UN Transitional Administration in East Timor (UNTAET) to establish a military for the newly independent state. However, patron-client networks associated with Falintil shaped recruitment and undermined the Timorese military after independence. A successor UN mission from 2002 to 2005 failed to improve the accountability and compliance with law of the Timorese military. The social and bureaucratic problems within the military festered and ultimately contributed to violence between factions of the police and military in 2006.

The examples of Bosnia and Timor-Leste offer broader insight for defense reform. The United States and international community frequently seek to improve the military institutions of partner or allied countries not only to help countries emerging from civil war but also to make allied and partner militaries more effective against insurgencies, terrorists, or potential foreign aggressors such as Russia, China, or Iran. The challenges and success of defense reform in BiH and Timor-Leste show that future efforts can achieve better success by selecting demands that navigate around core domestic interests while still improving military institutions and by ensuring high bureaucratic resources.

DEFENSE REFORM IN BIH, 2003–16

The defense reform in BiH under Ashdown began in 2003 and proceeded in two stages: first, the creation of a state-level Ministry of Defense with operational command of the entity militaries and, second, the merger of the entity militaries into a single, state-controlled military. This case study also explores the sustainability of defense reform by tracing the development of the BiH military to 2016, ten years after Ashdown's departure in 2006. The case study demonstrates how the threat of reform to domestic interests and the level of international resources present enabled both success under Ashdown and diminishing progress after 2006.

Context

The Dayton Agreement's division of Bosnia into the entities, combined with the ethnic cleansing of the war, enabled the wartime political parties associated with the three main ethnic groups to continue to dominate the country's politics after the war. In addition to reinforcing ethnic segregation, the divided political structure of Bosnia was highly inefficient. By one account, the Dayton constitutional structure was "one of the most complicated and wasteful systems of government ever devised."[2] Authorities were divided between the central state, the 2 entities, 10 cantons within the Federation, and 143 municipalities. A central component of the international agenda was to reform BiH institutions, including the military, to strengthen the central government and build a more ethnically integrated society.

Initial success was limited, however, in part because of inadequate international bureaucratic resources. There was a large foreign troop presence (initially 60,000, which amounted to 17.5 per capita) and high per capita spending ($277 in 2000 dollars).[3] But responsibility for implementing the Dayton Agreement was divided among several different international organizations.[4] A civilian High Representative was intended to lead and coordinate civilian peace implementation. However, the High Representative initially had little authority or ability to pursue meaningful reform.[5] In the first few years after the war, wartime ethnic parties won the initial elections and blocked the international community's agenda.[6] In response, in 1997 the international community granted the High Representative a mandate to effectively administer Bosnia through the "Bonn Powers," which included the authority to remove Bosnian officials from power and to veto or impose legislation.[7] Still, High Representatives from 1997 to 2002 had at best moderate bureaucratic resources, given continuing difficulties coordinating with the other international organizations present, which undermined reform efforts such as the development of the BiH election law.[8] Up to 2002, aside from the initial disarmament, there was little international attention on reforming the entity militaries, in part due to the limited mandate for the international military presence, the NATO-led Stabilization Force (SFOR).[9]

During his tenure as High Representative from 2002 to 2006, Ashdown, a former leader of the Liberal Democrats in the United Kingdom, continued the agenda of strengthening the Bosnian central state with more bureaucratic resources. Unlike previous High Representatives, Ashdown developed a mission implementation plan before he arrived, which specified priorities and plans to achieve them. Further, Ashdown was more able to build an international consensus before pursuing reform.[10] During Ashdown's tenure, international resources in BiH were at their highest level, and this period represents arguably the highest level of resources in any case considered in this book.

Ashdown leveraged these resources to make use of the full range of techniques suggested by the international resources theory, including pressuring politicians, removing officials from power, and imposing laws. Ashdown's actions against elected Bosnian officials led analysts to criticize him as an unaccountable "European Raj," and one Bosnian Serb observer in an interview described him as a "colonial governor" exercising a "law of violence" backed by foreign troops.[11] Ashdown's controversial approach yielded success, especially in the reform of both the military, described below, and the Bosnian tax system.[12] However, the police reform (considered in the next chapter) was not successful. As discussed below, after Ashdown's tenure ended in January 2006, the resources of the international community in Bosnia significantly declined.

From 1946 to 1992, Bosnia was part of Yugoslavia. Yugoslavia had a highly regarded military, the Yugoslav People's Army (or Jugoslovenska narodna armija, JNA), which provided an institutional legacy to the postwar BiH militaries.[13]

Given the wide respect for the JNA's capabilities and its World War II–inspired "total defense" strategy, I score the highest level of historical effectiveness of the BiH military as 3 out of 3.[14] The JNA used conscription to recruit a relatively ethnically balanced military, although in practice the JNA skewed toward Serbs and Montenegrins within the officer corps and senior leadership. In part because the ethnic balance of the military would eventually lead the JNA to side with the Bosnian Serbs and because of reports of problematic civilian oversight, I score its accountability as 2 out of 3.[15] The JNA appeared generally apolitical and under civilian command until 1990–91, when it began to move into Slovenia and Croatia to prevent their secession.[16] I therefore assess compliance with the law as 2 out of 3, leading to an overall score for the historic quality of the JNA of 7 out of 9.

After the BiH parliament declared independence in March 1992, the country descended into a war ultimately fought between three main ethnic armies: the primarily but not exclusively Bosniak (or Bosnian Muslim) Army of the Republic of BiH, the Serb Army of the RS (Vojska Republike Srpske, VRS), and the Croatian Defense Council.[17] In 1994 the Washington Agreement ended the conflict between the Bosniaks and Croats, and the Bosniak and Croat armies were merged into a single force, the Army of the Federation (Vojska Federacije Bosne i Hercegovine, VF).[18] When the war ended in 1995 the VF and VRS transitioned into the two separate entity militaries under two separate chains of command and two ministries of defense. Rohan Maxwell notes that the "VRS remained organized largely along JNA lines, with JNA weapons and doctrine," while the "VF acquired a different veneer from an extensive US bilateral training program."[19] From the perspective of some of the entity leadership, these militaries remained a final guarantee in case of renewed conflict. At the same time, the existence of the entity militaries facilitated renewed warfare, especially since the entities retained the right to declare war on one another.[20] Despite the intent in the Dayton Agreement, the state-level Standing Committee for Military Matters did little to coordinate the entity militaries.[21]

By 2002, when the reform described below began, the entity militaries were in poor shape, with an overall score of 3 out of 9.[22] Prior to 2002 one observer emphasized the poor effectiveness (scored as 1 out of 3) of the entity militaries, noting that they "provided no real security."[23] The entity militaries had large numbers of on-paper but inactive reserves, stocks of old and poorly maintained military equipment, and ill-trained conscripts.[24] Thanks to international support, the VF was seen by some as a more effective force than the VRS, given higher spending; approximately twice the personnel; and newer, Western-provided equipment.[25] The entity militaries also had problems with accountability (scored as 1 out of 3) since they pursued little integration or representation of ethnic minorities. Furthermore, oversight was poor since the entity militaries were accountable only to the entity parliaments, not the central state.[26] Funding for the entity militaries came in part from Croatia and Serbia, and corruption from military spending supported the BiH political parties.[27] There were also problems with the rule of law (scored as 1 out of 3). Audits and investigations eventually revealed that the RS defense establishment was violating an arms embargo on Iraq and had provided pensions to indicted war criminals.[28] Further, in the midst of political tension in 2001, a Bosnian Croat party urged Bosnian Croat members of the VF not to follow orders by non-Croat superiors in 2001, and some Bosnian Croat members of the military left their barracks. This raised questions about the allegiance of Bosnian Croat officers to the VF and the state.[29]

As noted earlier, postwar BiH politics broke down along ethnic lines, with the major political parties associated with one of the three major ethnic groups (Bosniak, Serb, or Croat). The most important potential opponents of the 2002–6 defense reform were the Bosnian Serbs. The Bosnian Serbs had previously used their control over the RS and ability to veto legislation within the central government to block a wide range of reforms, despite having only an estimated 34 percent of the overall population after 1995.[30] The nationalist goal of the Bosnian Serbs was ensuring the autonomy of the RS. Major Serb parties consistently referenced the protection of the RS in their public rhetoric. The legitimacy of the RS was contested by some Bosniaks and even by some representatives of the international community, especially because of the disproportionate scale of war crimes committed by Bosnian Serbs and because of continued support by the RS for the military and police structures that committed war crimes.[31] The major wartime party, the SDS, contained both hard liners with informal links to the VRS, including senior officers indicted for war crimes.[32] There were also more moderate politicians, such as Biljana Plavšić and Dragan Čavić, who were less committed to defending the illegal activities of the VRS or war criminals and to some degree opposed the hard liners for delegitimizing the RS with the international community.[33] Another Bosnian Serb party, the Alliance of Independent Social Democrats (Savez nezavisnih socijaldemokrata, SNSD), led by Milorad Dodik, was initially supported by the West as a moderate party but became increasingly nationalistic in its rhetoric.[34]

Bosniaks, who were about 44 percent of the population in 1995, had nationalist goals that included strengthening the central government and rolling back ethnic cleansing by weakening the RS.[35] As noted below, this made Bosniak elites for the most part supportive of defense reform, albeit with some fear of a premature end to reform. Bosniaks also tended to oppose special guarantees for the different ethnic groups, such as a system in which posts are specifically allocated to individuals from particular ethnic groups, also known as an ethnic key.[36] The Bosnian Croats, who made up approximately 16 percent of the postwar population, had the primary nationalist objectives of maintaining autonomy within the Croat-majority cantons of the Federation and retaining recognition for Croats within state institutions. In the context of defense reform, this meant that Croat representatives tended to an equal number of slots for each of the three ethnicities in senior positions, despite the smaller overall number of Croats, as well as maintaining visible symbols of Croat military history.[37] After a 2001 political crisis linked to the walkout by Croat soldiers mentioned above, the wartime Hrvatska demokratska zajednica (Croatian Democratic Union) party was weakened, and successor Croat parties had less strong patron-client links with the hard line members of the military.[38] Bosniak and Croat representatives would at times oppose and shape the reform, and they clearly had conflicting desires regarding ethnic keys. However, their concerns were more easily addressed, and their opposition posed less of a risk to reform than the Bosnian Serbs. The case study below mainly focuses on the potential for, but absence of, major Bosnian Serb opposition.

As outlined in table 4.1, the case study examines defense reform in three stages: the development of a state-level command and control, the elimination of the entity militaries, and the development of the military after Ashdown's departure. By tracing the development of the BiH military from 2006 to 2016, the third stage of the reform considers a hypothesis in the path dependence theory predicting that any improvements achieved from a reform will recede after international resources have substantially declined.

Stage 1: Defense Reform Commission, 2003–4

Ashdown used the 2002 scandal of the RS-based Orao company exporting arms to Iraq to initiate the first stage of defense reform in BiH. An investigation into the exports of Orao revealed that an RS army unit was conducting surveillance on the international community. In response, Ashdown decided to remove the RS president from power, using the Bonn Powers, and to "institute of a series of reforms that would, in effect, begin the process of abolishing the two entity armies and combining them into one state-controlled army."[39] Beyond improving the quality of governance in BiH, a senior international official highlighted the goals of eliminating the potential for the entity militaries to fight each other in a future war and reducing the influence of Croatia and Serbia on BiH's foreign policy.[40] Ashdown also worked with NATO officials to make use of Bosnian politicians' stated interest in joining the Partnership for Peace (PfP), a NATO program that enabled countries to participate in peacekeeping operations and was intended to prepare potential NATO candidates to pursue membership. NATO requirements for what BiH would have to accomplish to join PfP were integrated into the mandate of the Defense Reform Commission (DRC) in May 2003. The main articulated demands were the establishment of state command and control of the entity

TABLE 4.1. Development of Defense Institutions in Bosnia and Herzegovina

Stage	Threat of OHR's demands	Form of opposition	Resources	Relative success	Quality of institution at the end of the stage (out of 9)
Highest level of development before the intervention (JNA)	—	—	—	—	7
Quality of institutions at beginning of intervention (June 2001)	—	—	—	—	3
1. Creation of state command and control (May 2003–December 2004)	None	None	High	Moderate	5
2. Elimination of entity militaries (January 2005–December 2006)	None	None	High until January 2006, medium thereafter	Limited	6 in 2006
3. Implementation (December 2006–16)	None	None	Medium	Limited	7 by 2016

Note: JNA = Jugoslovenska narodna armija (Yugoslav People's Army); OHR = Office of the High Representative.

militaries, democratic oversight at both the state and entity levels, and interoperability between the two entity militaries.[41]

As implemented, these demands took into account Bosnian political constraints and posed little threat to Bosnian Serb nationalist goals or the patron-client networks of the ruling Bosnian Serb party. The Serb nationalist goal of autonomy rested primarily on the existence and political autonomy of the RS. Some international efforts to reform Bosnia's institutions did threaten the autonomy of the RS, including the police restructuring effort discussed in the next chapter. By contrast, command and control over the RS military—the VRS—was not necessary for the autonomy of the RS. Because the VRS had become weaker than the Federation's army, the VF, its effectiveness as a military formation under operational control of the RS was arguably less important to the RS's autonomy than the VRS's role as a symbol of Bosnian Serb identity. I therefore judge that state control, oversight, and interoperability over the RS military did not pose a key threat to the Serb nationalist goals, at least so long as these changes did not undermine RS autonomy in some other way, such as by setting precedents that ethnically based institutions were illegitimate or that the state could unilaterally take away RS authorities. The reform also did not threaten the patron-client networks of Čavić, the RS president from 2003 to 2006, since, as noted above, he did not share the same wartime networks as the hard line members of SDS.[42] The domestic opposition theory therefore expects, at most, limited Serb opposition and predicts successful reform due to the presence of high international resources.

Ashdown appointed James Locher, an American official who had previously worked on US defense reform, to lead the DRC in BiH. The Bosnian participants articulated opposing views of defense reform based on their ethnicity and divergent nationalist goals, although there was some familiarity among the officers from different entity armies who had served together under the JNA.[43] Concerned about the precedent of defense reform, Serb officials insisted that the entity parliaments vote on the DRC agreement before it could be considered by the state. In their view, the state should not be able to take away defense competencies from the entities—competencies should be transferable only on the initiative of the entities.[44] Serb officials also focused on ensuring the continued symbolic recognition of the RS and the medium-term existence of the entity militaries. Croat officials sought to maintain an equal distribution of positions for the different ethnic groups, while Bosniak officials opposed the end of conscription and sought to shift the entity militaries under state control as much as possible. Sulejman Tihić, the Bosniak member of the triparty BiH presidency, at one point insisted that the reform eliminate the entity militaries. He backed down only after being assured by the United States and Turkey that defense reform would continue and that conscription would be ended only once the entity militaries were eliminated.[45] By several accounts, Locher was able to move the negotiation process forward by listening to and taking seriously the different sides' concerns and by communicating proposed solutions that met domestic actors' constraints but still secured progress in areas such as state command and control and improved oversight.[46]

Under Locher's leadership, the DRC developed a report and drafted legislation to fulfill the demands specified in the DRC mandate, which was ultimately passed in December 2003. In particular, the new legislation created state-level operational command and control through new state-level defense structures—a Ministry of Defense, Joint Staff, and Operational Command (see figure 4.1). The entities retained administrative command, meaning responsibility for manning, training, and equipping the entity militaries (the dotted lines in figure 4.1). The entities could also still call on the entity militaries to respond to natural disasters. Parliamentary oversight was significantly strengthened, both through a new Joint Committee for Defense and Security in the state parliament and through improved parliamentary oversight at the entity level.[47] As anticipated, Serb representatives blocked legal changes at the state level until the RS had approved the relevant legislation.[48]

Fully staffed and operating state-level structures to implement the new law developed slowly over the course of 2004.[49] By the end of 2004 BiH had a meaningfully improved military. Accountability improved (to a score of 2 out of 3) due to the greater oversight role by entity and state parliaments. The rule of law also improved (to a score of 2 out of 3) due to the stronger legislation at the state level and the declining tolerance of malfeasance by the entity militaries.[50] Military effectiveness did not improve as much (leaving a score of 1 out of 3). Although the Bosnian defense establishment was placed under a single operational chain of command, "in reality," as one observer noted, "nothing changed in [the entity

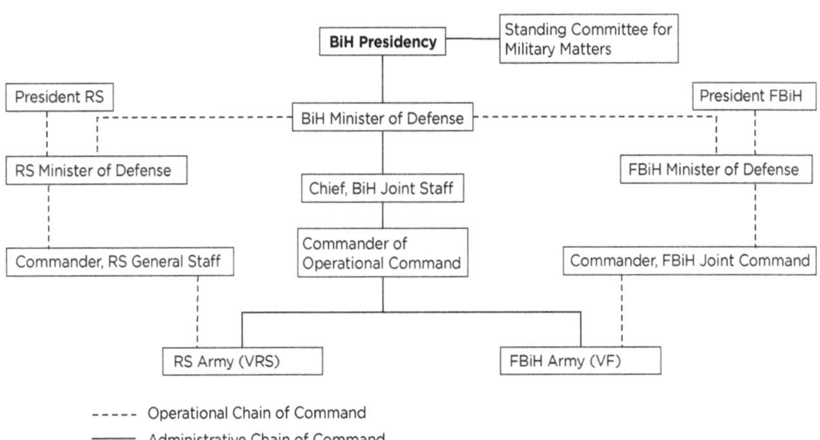

FIGURE 4.1. Proposed Chain of Command in Bosnia and Herzegovina, September 2003

Source: Adapted from Defense Reform Commission, Office of the High Representative, Bosnia and Herzegovina, "The Path to Partnership for Peace." Sarajevo, September 2003, 11. http://www.ohr.int/archive/drc-report/pdf/drc-eng.pdf.

Note: BiH = Bosnia and Herzegovina; FBiH = Federation of BiH; RS = Republika Srpska; VF = Vojska Federacije Bosne i Hercegovine (Army of the Federation of BiH); and VRS = Vojska Republike Srpske (Army of the RS).

militaries'] daily operations."[51] There was some downsizing of about one-third of the active force, and the entity militaries were able to deploy a multiethnic platoon to Iraq. However, a great deal of spending still went to conscription, and only 60 out of 150 positions within the state bodies had been filled, in part due to BiH's civil service law.[52] One senior international official also observed that the RS engaged in "foot-dragging resistance," especially on pay and personnel issues. This shows how limited private opposition can to some degree slow reform even when there is little threat to core interests.[53] Overall, the reform improved BiH's defense establishment from a score of 3 to 5 out of 9, a moderate success. This success appears to come in part from the presence of international resources, including the mandate of the DRC and presence of OHR. But the most important factor leading to success was that OHR's demands were formulated and implemented to avoid threatening RS autonomy. Unlike other reform efforts, where the international community used their leverage to pursue wider political change, OHR focused on achieving incremental objectives and made necessary compromises to achieve its demands.

Stage 2: Defense Reform, January 2005–December 2006

In June 2004 NATO declined to invite Bosnia to join the PfP. The problem was not that BiH had not met NATO standards, although some flaws in BiH's structures remained. Instead, NATO officials explained that BiH had failed to cooperate fully with the international war crimes tribunal by failing to capture the indicted war criminals Radovan Karadžić and Ratko Mladić.[54] In late 2004 it was found that before 2003 (and before the first stage of the defense reform, above), the RS had been paying Mladić a pension and the VRS had been hiding him. In December 2004, as a result of the RS's failure to apprehend war criminals, Ashdown announced a process to address "systematic weaknesses of the RS' security institutions." He removed nine RS officials, started the police restructuring effort (discussed in chapter 5), and initiated a new stage of defense reform requiring "the transfer of the functions currently carried out in the Entity MoDs [Ministries of Defense] to the BiH MoD."[55] The international community's demands therefore became the elimination of the entity militaries and their merger into a single state military. While the goal of creating a single state military had long been in the minds of international officials working on prior stages of defense reform, one participant noted that the "goals increased" during the second stage.[56]

Although the international community's demands had grown, the threat to nationalist goals and patron-client networks of the Serbs (as well as the other major ethnic groups) remained low. The Bosnian Serbs sought to protect the existence of the RS and gain ethnic recognition for Serbs in the new military. So long as the international community recognized the legitimacy of the Serbs' political rights and the authority of the RS, the autonomy of the RS could be preserved even as its military was eliminated. Similarly, the patron-client dynamics had not changed from the first stage—Čavić and his successor, Dodik, lacked patronage links with the VRS, although there was some political challenge from the elimination of the RS Ministry of Defense and military commands.[57] International resources remained high, as Ashdown was at the height of his influence. He had also demonstrated the ability to use several of the techniques suggested by the international resources theory, including removing officials from power, imposing laws, and using EU and NATO conditionality. The domestic opposition theory therefore predicts continued limited opposition and successful reform.

There was some Serb opposition during the second stage of reform, including the resignation of the RS prime minister in response to Ashdown's removal of RS officials and a January 2005 statement from the RS Parliament voicing a preference for demilitarization over the elimination of the VRS and RS Ministry of Defense.[58] By the account of international participants in the reform effort, however, once the negotiations began, they proceeded more smoothly, without frequent appeal to nationalist issues.[59] In mid-to-late 2005 the DRC drafted two laws—one creating the single, unified Armed Forces of Bosnia and Herzegovina (AFBiH) and the other creating an all-volunteer force—and issued a second report. The laws were passed in September 2005, in part thanks to the support of RS president Čavić, whom one international official commended for his personal engagement in enhancing lawmakers' understanding of the new legislation.[60] Accounts of the passage of the law also recognized the supporting influence of international officials in pushing through the legislation.[61]

A key challenge of the negotiations was how to recognize the political rights of the ethnic groups in the new military—and thereby avoid threatening Serb nationalist goals—without undermining either state control or the right of anyone in BiH to serve in the military. To resolve this challenge, the DRC's international co-chair, Raffi Gregorian, proposed a regimental system modeled on the British Commonwealth. Under this system, the Bosnian military was organized into three brigades, each composed of three infantry battalions and supporting elements. Three regiments were also created, each carrying the military traditions of the ethnically based armies. Three infantry battalions, one from each brigade, were associated with each of the regiments. However, the responsibility of the regiments was solely limited to military tradition (according to Rohan and Maxwell "such things as dress uniforms, ceremonies, awards and museums"), and they had no operational authority over the infantry battalions.[62] Noninfantry forces, including artillery, signals, engineering, and military police, formed multiethnic regiments, and the command elements of the brigade were also not assigned to the ethnic regiments. The result was an overall ethnically integrated Bosnian military, albeit with infantry battalions that retained some association with one of the three main ethnic groups.[63]

The AFBiH was established on January 1, 2006. Largely as a result of passing the defense reform, BiH was granted entry into the PfP in December 2006. The new laws significantly improved the accountability of the Bosnian military by creating a single, more ethnically integrated force (increasing accountability to a score of 3 out of 3). One international official noted that infantry units were no longer ethnically based since anyone could join any units, and some recruits joined battalions that were not their own ethnicity for geographic convenience.[64] Still, as a Bosniak official observed, infantry battalions were about "nine-tenths the 'right' ethnicity."[65] There was little change in military effectiveness due to the new legislation (leaving a score of 1 out of 3), and there appeared little major change in compliance with the law (leaving a score of 2 out of 3).[66] Hence, the quality of the BiH military improved from a 5 to a 6 out of 9, a noticeable improvement in slightly less than a two-year period.

Stage 3: Pursuing and Sustaining Reform as Resources Diminish, 2006–16

In January 2006 Ashdown departed as High Representative and, at the same time, international resources declined. While subsequent High Representatives maintained the same legal authority, they were either unwilling (in the case of Christian Schwarz-Schilling) or unable (in the case of Miroslav Lajčák) to use the Bonn Powers as effectively as Ashdown had. The change in policy and decline in bureaucratic resources led to the weakening of the effective mandate so that BiH in practice had a train-and-equip mandate, as defined in chapter 2.[67] The international troop presence also declined as the NATO SFOR transitioned in 2004 to the European Union peacekeeping force, EUFOR, with approximately 6,300 personnel in 2004 and about 2,000 in 2010.[68] Given these shifts, the international community would overall have moderate resources for the remainder of the reform effort.

Nevertheless, the international community, including the United States, continued to pursue defense reform. The path dependence theory expects some backsliding of BiH defense institutions in this period. This did not occur, although reform did slow as resources declined. Nevertheless, defense reform in BiH continued to make some progress, as the domestic opposition theory expects, given a continued low threat to nationalist goals and patron-client networks.

The BiH military achieved a key political objective by deploying forces—staff officers in 2009; an infantry platoon in 2010; and, later, military police—to support the NATO mission in Afghanistan.[69] Still, observers highlighted three problems in the AFBiH that revealed both its underlying ineffectiveness and the continuing challenges of ethnic division.

First, the AFBiH struggled with building a personnel structure to enable military effectiveness. The 2006 legislation intended to make the AFBiH more efficient by reducing the size of the force and the reserves. The international community effectively reduced opposition, albeit not corruption, by ensuring that the main ethnic groups were not competing with one another for slots in the new force.[70] Downsizing from the two entity militaries into one unified military also left a disproportionate number of older soldiers in the ranks. Despite repeated international efforts, this problem persisted; in 2015 NCOs were an average of forty years old and soldiers were an average of twenty-seven years old. Observers also expressed concern that the need to maintain ethnically "tagged" positions undermined operational effectiveness, including by leaving gaps in some billets.[71]

A second lingering problem was the disposition of defense property. In 2006 the entities owned nearly all defense property, both immovable (i.e., real estate) and movable (e.g., equipment). The creation of the AFBiH established a process for the assessment and reallocation of existing property from the entities to the central state. However, there remained disagreement about how to reallocate military property that had belonged to the former Yugoslavia. Serb politicians from the RS tended to claim that such property—in particular, immovable property—should remain the property of the entities, while Bosniak personnel argued that it should belong to the central state.[72] This dispute over the ownership of defense property became a major impediment to BiH's future. In 2008 OHR included the resolution of the defense property issue as a condition for its closure and the end of international supervision in BiH. In 2010 NATO invited BiH to join the Membership Action Plan, a precursor to membership, but only if the immovable defense property issue was resolved. Through at least the end of 2017 Serb officials rejected permitting the state to register Yugoslav-era defense property within the RS, which delayed BiH's progress toward NATO membership and the closure of OHR.[73]

Third, there are differing views about whether defense reform really prevented the military from being used in a future war. A Bosnian Serb politician argued in 2009 that the reform effort had significantly reduced that possibility. A Bosniak official, by contrast, argued that even further integration would not prevent the military from being used in a future conflict. This official highlighted the past example of the JNA, which had been more carefully structured to integrate the different ethnic groups but was then co-opted by Bosnian Serbs during the war.[74] International observers tend to be reluctant to say that the military could not be used in a conflict, given that there were "sufficient arms for another major war locked in a basement."[75] While these statements admit that there is some potential for elements of the AFBiH to be used in a future war, they also indicate that no reform effort can fully prevent that possibility. The defense reform did, however, diminish the ethnic homogeneity of the defense forces and eliminate entity control, thereby reducing the ease with which the country could return to war.[76]

Overall, based on these improvements, I give the Bosnian military in 2016 a total score of 7 out of 9:

- Effectiveness (2 out of 3): There was a single chain of command under the state and an ability to contribute small forces to NATO missions but little other military capability. Bosnia's military was smaller per capita than those in Slovenia and Croatia and, hence, potentially more economically sustainable.[77]
- Accountability (3 out of 3): Although challenges remained, the BiH military had a high degree of ethnic integration compared with the region and has oversight institutions in place. Still, some degree of ethnic identification and tension remained.[78]
- Rule of Law (2 out of 3): While obedience to law had improved, lingering challenges with the defense property issue remained.

Over the course of 2006–16, BiH achieved a one-point improvement (from 6 to 7), implying limited success over the ten-year period.[79]

Conclusion: BiH Defense Reform

Interlocutors in BiH describe the defense reform both as one of the most difficult and most successful reforms. Overall, from 2003 to 2016 the international-led reform of the Bosnian military improved four points, which represents high success over the entire course of the reform. The domestic opposition theory offers the best explanation for the reform's success. Foreign officials avoided provoking strong domestic opposition by selecting demands that did not threaten nationalist goals or the ruling elites' patron-client networks. In particular, the international advisers made compromises and creative demands that improved institutions without threatening core interests, including preserving the entity militaries during the first stage of reform, proposing the regimental system during the second stage, and maintaining an explicit ethnic balance in the AFBiH.

International resources were also essential. Ashdown's initiative and the Bonn Powers were needed to create the DRC, for example. While Gülner Aybet emphasizes the role of NATO conditionality in achieving reform, conditionality was not sufficient to compel the Bosnian Serbs to address the challenge of defense property.[80] Rather, the overarching level of international resources present under Ashdown's tenure, especially bureaucratic capacity, enabled OHR to encourage defense reform. Indeed, after Ashdown's departure, diminished bureaucratic capacity slowed reform. Even with high international resources, if Ashdown had threatened nationalist goals or patron-client networks, reform would not have proceeded as effectively, as shown by the domestic opposition to police reform during the same period (discussed in the next chapter).

The development of the BiH military offers little support for the path dependence theory. The Yugoslav military did in some ways set the stage for the development of the entity militaries and then the BiH military. The overall quality score of the BiH military in 2016 was the same as the historical highest quality of the JNA. However, the AFBiH was very different from the JNA, as the higher score for accountability and lower score for effectiveness indicates. Foreign reform led to a major break from the past structures—the AFBiH was restructured based on a British regimental model and focused on supporting NATO operations rather than defensive partisan warfare. Indeed, the rapid improvement of the entity militaries into a more accountable state-controlled military is contrary to the expectations of the path dependence theory, as is the sustainability of the BiH military after the decline in international resources in 2006.

An alternative explanation for the success of defense reform is that defense is a unique institution because of the interests, culture, and ability of military officers. Aybet claims that Bosnian military professionals understood foreign demands and pushed reform more effectively than their civilian counterparts would have.[81] One participant in the reform similarly claimed that senior officers supported defense reform in BiH because they preferred a smaller and more professional military over the existing entity militaries in order to gain the respect of their regional and NATO colleagues.[82] While military officers' support for reform may have helped facilitate the process, defense reform was ultimately a political choice, approved by the RS Assembly. The domestic opposition theory underscores the importance of tailoring foreign demands to avoid provoking opposition.

A second alternative argument, from Ric Bainter, argues that Serb representatives had difficulty opposing reform because they were unable to point to another country or model where two militaries existed.[83] However, Bosnian officials in interviews repeatedly emphasized the uniqueness of BiH's institutions. The behavior of Serb officials in police restructuring (in the next chapter) demonstrates that Serb officials would have found a way to block defense reform if they believed it threatened RS autonomy, even at the cost of delaying NATO integration or risking embarrassment in front of other professionals. The absence of a threat to nationalist goals was necessary for the Bosnian Serbs to agree to reform.

DEFENSE REFORM IN TIMOR-LESTE

In Bosnia, the international community recognized and sought to address the problems with the countries' two separate militaries. In Timor-Leste, defense reform was never a priority. UNTAET built many institutions in the country from scratch. However, UNTAET only belatedly established a military, the Falintil-Forcas Defensa Timor Lorosae (F-FDTL), after facing elite public opposition, motivated by the nationalist resonance of the guerrilla movement that opposed Indonesian occupation. After UNTAET departed in 2002, successor missions continued to pay little attention to the defense force and failed to create a bureaucracy overseeing the F-FDTL. This failure later contributed to a wave of violence between elements of the Timorese police and military in 2006. While patron-client networks did to some degree explain elites' reluctance to build the defense institution, the lack of bureaucratic resources was perhaps most responsible for the failure of UN-led defense reform.

Context

Timor-Leste was a former Portuguese colony in Southeast Asia, which was occupied by neighboring Indonesia starting in 1975. The country strongly resisted Indonesian occupation and eventually voted for independence in June 1999, after which pro-Indonesian militias engaged in widespread violence. A UN-mandated, Australian-led military force, the International Force East Timor, was launched to reestablish security in the territory in September 1999. UN Resolution 1272 in October 1999 then established UNTAET to take over from International Force East Timor and administer the country pending formal independence.[84]

Overall, UNTAET had high resources, especially compared to the small size of Timor-Leste. UNTAET's mandate gave it full executive power to administer the country.[85] The mission had large numbers of personnel (9,150 authorized troops and 1,640 civilian police) and financial resources ($1.3 billion to fund UNTAET and $518 million on reconstruction) relative to a local population of approximately 900,000 in 1999.[86] Defense-specific material resources were also significant. Among other donors, Australia provided A$26 million over five years for training and construction; Portugal provided training, uniforms, and two patrol boats; and the United States provided infantry weapons.[87] UNTAET's legal and material resources were so extensive that observers described the intervention as a "laboratory" to test whether the United Nations could effectively engage in state building in a society that many UN officials saw as a *terra nullius*, or empty land.[88]

UNTAET, however, faced planning problems and policy choices that meant it had only moderate bureaucratic resources for defense reform. Indonesia had opposed planning for a potential mission to prepare for Timor-Leste's independence prior to the results of the referendum. As a result, planning for UNTAET began only after the referendum, and the hurried planning team was told to "take the Kosovo plan and reconfigure it to fit East Timor."[89] Copying the UNMIK plan led to a mandate for UNTAET to administer the country and the creation of a hierarchical, pillar-based structure centralizing authority under a SRSG. Critics questioned the choice to copy the plan from Kosovo given the different political context—it was not clear that Timor-Leste really needed an international administration.[90] Furthermore, internal disagreements within the headquarters in New York led the Department of Peacekeeping Operations to disregard existing internal knowledge within the United Nations about the politics of Timor-Leste.[91] In addition to incorrectly perceiving Timor-Leste as a *terra nullius* without persistent preexisting institutions, the United Nations adopted a flawed view of the umbrella Timorese resistance organization, the Congresso Nacional de Reconstrução de Timor (National Congress for Timorese Reconstruction, CNRT), as another political faction in the conflict rather than a legitimate local authority.[92] Similarly, the United Nations also failed to appreciate the nationalist resonance of the guerrilla resistance movement, Falintil. Resources were noticeably lower for defense reform than other priorities both under UNTAET and subsequent missions. One article explains that "in terms of defence force development, the UN essentially absconded."[93] UNTAET initially did not intend to create a military, while the follow-on missions focused primarily on the police and only begrudgingly offered support for reform of defense institutions, as detailed below.

No country is truly a *terra nullius*, and, indeed, the institutional and political legacy of Falintil and the resistance movement would play an important role in the development of the Timorese military. Falintil was founded in August 1975 as the armed wing of the then Marxist party Fretilin. Falintil reached its apex in 1975–79, when for a brief time it engaged in conventional combat with the Indonesian military. Despite little success, this indicates some historical military effectiveness, for a score of 1 of 3. After many of the senior leadership of the organization were killed, Falintil transformed into a guerrilla organization with little military effectiveness but powerful political resonance as a symbol of Timorese resistance.[94] Falintil also had strong ties to the population since it was supported by a larger covert political organization.[95] Given this connection to the population, I score accountability as 1 out of 3, even in the absence of formal representative structures. Overall, the peak historical quality score for Falintil was 2 out of 9 (I score compliance with the law as 0 out of 3, given the absence of a formal constitution after 1975).[96] By the late 1990s Falintil had significantly weakened, although many former fighters retained an allegiance to the organization. Falintil agreed to canton itself for the referendum, meaning it remained within the military encampment at Aileu. After the referendum in September 1999 there were approximately 1,000–1,300 Falintil personnel present at Aileu.[97] I rate Falintil as having the same approximate quality—2 out of 9—since in 1999 Falintil retained some military effectiveness and an ongoing close connection to the population.

The key Timorese nationalist goal was the achievement of independence. Unlike Bosnia, Kosovo, and Iraq, there were not multiple competing nationalist goals held by different groups. Few supporters of integration with Indonesia remained, and the vast majority of the population and elites shared the same nationalist goal.[98] Furthermore, the political parties and leaders who contested Timor-Leste's postwar politics emerged from the factions of the resistance movement who had pursued independence. The leaders and parties campaigning in the postwar elections focused their appeals on their wartime achievements and role in the resistance struggle.[99]

Although Timorese leaders nearly all campaigned on their role pursuing independence, there were important personal and ideological divisions. One faction was led by Xanana Gusmão, who emerged as the leader of Falintil in the early 1980s and was later imprisoned by Indonesian authorities. Gusmão built a national pro-independence coalition by incorporating the competing Timorese political parties that had fought a brief civil war following Timor-Leste's declaration of independence in 1975.[100] Gusmão's coalition-building led him to disassociate Falintil from Fretilin in 1987, an action that provoked violent opposition from more hard line Fretilin elements within Falintil.[101] After the war, Gusmão retained strong patron-client networks within Falintil and its leadership—as Edward Rees writes, "by 1999 the FALINTIL command structure consisted almost entirely of Gusmao loyalists."[102] Gusmão was also one of UNTAET's primary interlocutors, giving him an effective ruling position in the post-referendum period.[103]

While Gusmão had split from Fretilin, the party remained popular and became the most powerful political party after 1999. Fretilin abandoned its Marxist ideology in 1982 and became a broader, more conservative party with authoritarian tendencies.[104] The patron-client networks of the party and its leadership dated back to Fretilin's declaration of Timorese independence in 1975 and Fretilin's resistance during the war. After 1999 the party drew on a wide range of leadership, including both resistance leaders and returned exiles from Angola, Mozambique, and Australia. Fretilin also developed a strong network throughout the country, reinforced—by one account—through threats of violence.[105] One notable leader of Fretilin was Rogerio Lobato, the first defense minister of Timor-Leste from the 1975 period, who was a longtime friend of the Fretilin leader and first prime minister, Mari Alkatiri. Lobato was a steadfast opponent of Gusmão in part due to

Gusmão's decision to split Falintil from Fretilin.[106] Lobato built on the grievances of Falintil veterans who were not included within the F-FDTL by recruiting them into the police, which came under his personal control after he became the minister of internal administration.

Below, I describe two stages of defense reform, summarized in table 4.2. The first stage occurred under UNTAET from 2000 to 2002 and involved the creation

TABLE 4.2. Development of Defense Institutions in Timor-Leste

Stage	Threat of UN demands	Form of opposition	Level of resources	Relative success	Quality of institution at the end of the stage (out of 9)
Highest level of development before the intervention (Falintil during insurgency)	—	—	—	—	2
Quality of institutions at beginning of intervention (late 1999 / early 2000)	—	—	—	—	2
1. UNTAET's intent to not create Timorese military	NGs and PCNs	Public	Medium	None	2
2. Establishment of F-FDTL under UNTAET (June 2000–May 2002)	None	None	Medium	Limited	3
3. Defense reform by successor missions (2002–6)	None	None	Low	None, violence	2

Note: F-FDTL = Falintil-Forcas Defensa Timor Lorosae; NG = nationalist goal; PCN = patron-client network; UNTAET = UN Transitional Administration in East Timor.

of F-FDTL. The second stage, from 2002 to 2006, describes how successor missions failed to improve F-FDTL and supporting defense institutions and how this failure contributed to the 2006 violence.

Stage 1: Formation of the F-FDTL under UNTAET, October 1999–May 2000

In October 1999, when UNTAET was first established, it intended to disband Falintil and leave Timor-Leste without a military.[107] A UN report in July 2000 explained that "it was not originally envisaged that East Timor would have armed forces, except for security personnel associated with the police. Initially, CNRT supported this view, bearing in mind the country's limited resources."[108] UNTAET's misperception that CNRT and its armed wing Falintil represented but one of several political factions, rather than a coalition with broad Timorese support, also appears to have informed this decision.[109]

The policy of not creating a military threatened Timorese nationalist goals and ruling elites' patron-client networks. Falintil had tremendous nationalist resonance as the "custodians of independence" as well as close patron-client links with Timorese elites, especially Gusmão.[110] In part due to limitations on donor organizations providing humanitarian support for armed groups, the physical condition of Falintil members in Aileu became very poor, with reports of malaria and tuberculosis spreading in the camp. Gusmão stated that by June 2000 the group was "almost in a state of revolt," and he began to seek a change in UN policy.[111] Gusmão may have been motivated to pursue the creation of a military because of his patron-client networks. In an interview with the author, for example, one Fretilin official explained that while Gusmão preferred that there be no military, the Falintil commander, Taur Matan Ruak, insisted that one be formed.[112]

Whatever the source of Gusmão's decision to support the creation of a military, the United Nations was responsive. The July 2000 UN report explained that "CNRT has changed its position and now advocates the establishment of a national security force, initially based on members of FALINTIL."[113] As former UN officials explained in retrospect, it was "impossible to deny a military to a newly independent county," and "at the end of the day, the Timorese wanted a defense force, that's why F-FDTL was created."[114] Gusmão's public opposition shifted UNTAET's position, even without the presence of major demonstrations. UNTAET was likely more sensitive to Timorese opposition because it had already acceded a few months earlier to Timorese demands for a greater role in the UNTAET and an accelerated time line for independence.[115]

Stage 2: Forming the F-FDTL under UNTAET, June 2000–May 2002

In June 2000, in response to Timorese demands, UNTAET decided to pursue a Timorese defense force and commissioned a study to develop options for the force. While Falintil had preferred a defense force of five thousand with an air force and navy, UNTAET and CNRT ultimately agreed on a defense force of fifteen hundred active-duty soldiers and fifteen hundred reservists, with a modest navy. Given Timor-Leste's small gross domestic product, it simply could not afford a larger military. UNTAET also accepted Falintil's importance and recognized that it would "form the core of the new force."[116] UNTAET revised demands consisted of the creation of F-FDTL out of Falintil, the disarmament and demobilization of Falintil members who were not incorporated into the new force, and the creation of necessary civilian oversight structures for F-FDTL.[117]

By accepting the incorporation of Falintil into a new military, UNTAET diminished the threat to nationalist goals. Further, because the selection of members of the force was largely made by the existing leadership of Falintil, who were loyalists of Gusmão, the revised policy posed little threat to the patron-client networks of the ruling local leadership, namely Gusmão.[118] The Fretilin leadership, by contrast, were not included in the selection process, and former Falintil members who were opponents of Gusmão were more likely to be excluded from F-FDTL.[119] Since Fretilin was not in government at the time of recruitment, it was less capable of obstructing the development of F-FDTL, although Fretilin leaders' patron-client networks did subsequently shape the development of other institutions—namely, the police. Given the low threat to core domestic interests and moderate international resources, the domestic opposition theory predicts some success in this stage.

The F-FDTL was formally established in a ceremony in February 2001. Of the veterans of Falintil, 650 were selected to become part of the F-FDTL, while approximately 1,300 entered the Falintil Reinsertion Assistance Program, a World Bank and International Organization for Migration–funded demobilization, disarmament, and reintegration program.[120] One Timorese official observed in retrospect that it was "odd" that UN funds limited the size of the force, especially considering the UN's vast resources and given that personnel who were not selected later became disgruntled and more likely to engage in protest.[121] Former Falintil members who entered the F-FDTL were formed into the 1st Battalion. New recruits, under twenty-one years of age at the time of selection and primarily from the western part of Timor-Leste, formed the 2nd Battalion. The new force was trained and equipped with international assistance, although observers questioned the discipline of the force and the education and training of the officers. For example, one interviewee explained that F-FDTL would simply "break their people out of jail" after they were arrested by the police.[122] Roque Rodrigues, an early Fretilin member and adversary of Lobato, was selected to become the senior civilian defense official. UNTAET, however, failed to develop a functional defense ministry since Rodrigues was the only civilian charged with overseeing the F-FDTL and initially had no staff or resources.[123]

Upon its creation the F-FDTL faced immediate challenges in its effectiveness and the rule of law. As Desmond Ball notes, F-FDTL was "likely to be wrongly organized for any of the more conceivable contingencies," such as Indonesian military action or cross-border militia activity, especially since F-FDTL would be stationed in the eastern part of the country.[124] Further, the Constitution specified that the military would be responsible for external defense and "shall not intervene in political matters."[125] However, some interviewees described the F-FDTL's vision of its role as similar to the militaries of Indonesia and other Southeast Asian countries, where the military is often seen as a better-armed, more effective police force that is ultimately responsible for addressing serious internal security challenges. One former defense adviser further explained that F-FDTL "just doesn't take the constitution seriously" and sees its "role far more broadly" than just external security.[126] Still, there was some public support for a F-FDTL role in internal security. For example, one Timorese survey respondent in 2003 explained, "In my opinion the main task of F-FDTL is to provide security for the people [of] East Timor from the Eastern to Western end of the country. . . . F-FDTL should be responsible to counter internal and external threats."[127]

Another problem was that the narrow selection of the F-FDTL encouraged and enabled Lobato, the Fretilin leader and former defense minister, to develop competing security forces by recruiting disgruntled Falintil veterans. Lobato rallied veterans who had not been included in F-FDTL during the 2001 election campaign and created the Association of Ex-Combatants, which had links with armed "political security groups."[128] After Lobato organized protests that included some two thousand to three thousand Falintil veterans at the same time as Timor-Leste's declaration of independence in May 2002, Lobato was appointed minister of internal administration. By one account, the Fretilin government, which had been elected in 2001, decided Lobato "was a lesser threat inside the government than outside of it."[129] He thereby gained leadership over the national police, the Polisia Nasional Timor-Leste (PNTL, National Police of Timor-Leste), to which he recruited Falintil veterans who had not joined the F-FDTL.[130] While Lobato's actions did not directly undermine the F-FDTL, they are an example of how elites can use patron-client networks to undermine state institutions.

Overall by my scoring, UNTAET achieved moderate success in creating a military in Timor-Leste since, at independence in May 2002, I score the F-FDTL's quality as 3 out of 9:

- Effectiveness (1 out of 3): F-FDTL had only minimal military capabilities, with some light infantry and a small navy, and limited ability to address real external security threats.
- Accountability (1 out of 3): Although F-FDTL had substantial public support, the selective recruitment of the force by allies of Gusmão undermined its representativeness to the broader population, and the absence of civilian staff undermined oversight.
- Rule of Law (1 out of 3): UNTAET had created a legal framework for the establishment of the F-FDTL. However, the legal basis of the F-FDTL did not reflect the organization's vision of itself as a guarantor of independence, and compliance with law by the F-FDTL was also questionable, as the next section shows in more detail.

The lingering flaws in the military were somewhat disappointing considering UNTAET's overall resources. There seemed little good reason for UNTAET's unwillingness to devote more resources to defense. One article explains, "In essence, the UN transitional administration demurred from playing an active role in the force's development, and, most egregiously, in the force's oversight, despite being the legal governing entity in the territory for more than two and a half years."[131] Nevertheless, over the next four years, follow-on UN missions continued to do little to address the continuing problems within the F-FDTL.

Stage 3: The Failure to Strengthen the F-FDTL and the Resulting Violence, 2002–6

After Timor-Leste gained independence on May 20, 2002, two UN successor missions had ostensible responsibility to pursue reform of F-FDTL: the UN Mission in Support of East Timor (UNMISET) from May 2002 to May 2005 and, thereafter, a small political mission called the UN Office in Timor-Leste. However, neither mission devoted significant attention to the military or addressed the growing fissures that eventually contributed to the outbreak of violence in 2006.

UNTAET's immediate successor, UNMISET, had an effective train-and-equip mandate. UNMISET focused primarily on the PNTL and benefited from fairly substantial material resources (albeit fewer than UNTAET), including a peak of 4,476 military personnel and 771 UN police in August 2002.[132] UNMISET's police development efforts were heavily criticized and made little progress due to a combination of private obstruction by Lobato and bureaucratic failings by the mission, including poor planning and the inappropriate application of foreign models.[133]

There were fewer resources available for defense reform. Australia and other donors continued to train the F-FDTL, but international efforts to develop oversight structures were scattershot. The internationally staffed Office of Defense Force Development, first created under UNTAET, was formally separate from UNMISET and had limited influence. Advisers rotated frequently, and the office had little coordination with UNMISET. According to one report, for example, this defense office had to negotiate with UNMISET for "basic office support such as telephone lines and access to the UN hospital."[134] Interviewees noted that a general distaste for the military among UN advisers contributed to the lack of investment in defense reform.[135] After the UN Office in Timor-Leste took over in May 2005, resources further diminished since that mission had no peacekeeping force, had only an observer mandate, and included only about ten military advisers.[136]

The United Nations' demands for F-FDTL after 2002 consisted of strengthening it and transferring responsibility for internal (i.e., military support to the civil authorities) and external security from the peacekeeping force to the F-FDTL.[137] These demands posed no threat to Timorese nationalist goals because they recognized the authority of the F-FDTL. At the same time, since F-FDTL remained an important national symbol, Timorese officials were hesitant to criticize it, which prevented actions that might have improved the F-FDTL's accountability or compliance with the law.[138] There was also little threat to the ruling elites' patron-client networks since increasing the F-FDTL's authority did not undermine the ability of the ruling elite to stay in power. Given UNMISET's low resources and the absence of a threat to Timorese core interests, the domestic opposition theory predicts limited domestic opposition after 2002, with some minimal improvements in the F-FDTL.

In practice, from 2002 to 2006 international efforts did little to improve civilian command and control, parliamentary oversight, or legal and policy guidance over F-FDTL. Rodrigues, the secretary of state for defense, continued to have no staff and was not perceived as an effective or responsive administrator. As one international interviewee put it, he was "incompetent and dangerous" due to his failure to address simple complaints by F-FDTL soldiers related to issues such as leave, housing, and food.[139] Despite international plans for a civilian defense staff, by January 2004 only four junior civil servants had been hired, and strategic documents guiding the development of the F-FDTL were not released until July 2006.[140] The relevant parliamentary committee was, by one account in 2004, "ill-prepared and powerless to effectively monitor the security sector."[141] The legislation underlying the F-FDTL specified general guidelines of the authority of the president, prime minister, government, and Ministry of State for Defense without providing specific regulations.[142] Rees attributes the delays in establishing a civilian staff to Rodrigues's "considerable trust" in the F-FDTL leadership and the strong politicization of the F-FDTL.[143] In interviews with the author, some senior Fretilin officials reluctantly admitted flaws in the military's ability to secure the border but by and large blamed insecurity on the recruitment of Indonesian-era personnel into the police. One official observed that there were "not so many problems in the military."[144]

Nevertheless, the F-FDTL's weak accountability and compliance with law was visible in its frequent involvement in internal security. For example, in January 2003 the F-FDTL responded to protests in Atsabe (Emera District) by arresting between fifty-nine and ninety people without charges. All of these individuals were later freed, and the incident was criticized by Amnesty International.[145] This incident also contributed to Lobato's decision to create heavily armed police units within the PNTL, including the police reserve unit and the rapid response unit. These units developed a poor relationship with the F-FDTL for several reasons, including Lobato's reported effort to selectively recruit from the western part of the country to counter the perceived favoritism of the F-FDTL toward easterners; F-FDTL's vision of itself as the foremost provider of security; and an existing general suspicion of the PNTL because it recruited officers from the Indonesian police.[146]

Problems with the conditions of service in F-FDTL festered through 2003–6, leading to increasing protests by F-FDTL members, especially younger recruits from the western part of the country. Because of Timor-Leste's extremely poor road network, F-FDTL members from western Timor-Leste had difficulty taking leave and returning to the eastern base in Lautem in a timely way. As a result of this problem, in December 2003, 42 soldiers, primarily westerners, were discharged due to absenteeism. A presidential commission in August 2004 raised further concerns about bias against westerners in promotion decisions and poor housing and food as well as the lack of an established defense bureaucracy.[147] But the F-FDTL leadership did little to address these issues. Housing and food further worsened after October 2005 after a US-funded logistics contract was cut. In January 2006 159 soldiers filed a petition asking President Gusmão for relief in response to alleged discrimination against westerners in the military. Throughout early 2006 the number of soldiers seeking redress from the government increased. A group of about 400 soldiers met with Gusmão in February 2006. In March, the F-FDTL commander, Taur Matan Ruak, dismissed 593 soldiers after they failed to return from leave. While Gusmão urged the F-FDTL to respond to the petitioners' concerns, the F-FDTL leadership claimed that political parties were encouraging the petitioners, and it did not heed their concerns.[148]

The petitioners began to engage in protests, leading to a heavy-handed response by elements of the police and military and escalating into major conflict between the F-FDTL and the PNTL in May 2006. After several protests by the petitioners in March failed to shift the situation, the petitioners began larger demonstrations in front of the main government building on April 24, 2006.[149] On April 28 the protests escalated further, which led to the deployment of several different security units, although only a few personnel were from the trained riot police or F-FDTL military police. The protesters quickly overran the police and entered the main government building. Thereafter, according to the UN Commission of Inquiry, Lobato, who opposed the petitioners, arrived at PNTL headquarters "wearing a flak jacket and in a highly agitated state, yelling 'kill them all.' "[150] Lobato signed out automatic weapons and two thousand rounds of ammunition, which were then apparently used to arm his civilian supporters. After the protesters dispersed from the government building, there were skirmishes between the protesters and the police and F-FDTL. Five people were killed and approximately one hundred houses were destroyed.[151]

Over the next month conflict between several factions escalated. Maj. Alfredo Reinado, the head of the military police, deserted on May 3 with several military police officers and members of the riot police. Reinado reportedly asserted that he did not "want to be a part of the [army] that shot westerners," although international observers questioned this account.[152] Despite efforts to defuse the situation, Reinado's group skirmished with the F-FDTL in late May. Reports circulated that the police supported the petitioners against the F-FDTL and that Timorese leaders had armed several groups of civilians, although the exact lines of conflict were unclear. According to a UN report, by this point the relationship between the PNTL and F-FDTL had devolved into "mutual suspicion."[153] A violent altercation in Dili developed into a pitched gun battle on May 25 between the PNTL and F-FDTL at the PNTL's headquarters. After PNTL personnel agreed to surrender, F-FDTL soldiers fired on a column of unarmed PNTL escorted under a UN flag, killing 8 and injuring 27.[154] Soon thereafter, the PNTL largely abandoned its posts in Dili, undermining the enforcement of law within the city, and approximately 150,000 persons became internally displaced. On May 24, 2006, Timor-Leste officially requested international support from Australia, New Zealand, Malaysia, and Portugal. All four countries soon deployed military and police to help reestablish security in Dili.[155]

The 2006 crisis revealed the serious flaws within the F-FDTL and the failure of the international effort to improve the F-FDTL's quality. An August 2006 UN report assessing the causes of the conflict noted, "Institutional failures in PNTL and F-FDTL are at the core of the recent crisis," adding that, following the crisis, the "F-FDTL ceased to be a fully functioning national force."[156] The report also identifies flaws within the F-FDTL that contributed to the crisis, which I rely on to code the quality of the F-FDTL before the crisis:[157]

- Effectiveness (1 out of 3): The F-FDTL was clearly weakened by the dismissal of more than one-third of the overall force in 2006. While retaining some minimal combat power to intervene in internal conflicts, its ability to provide external security remained in question. Further, the August 2006 UN report notes that "the extremely weak institutional development" of the Ministry of Defense had limited the ability of the government to devote resources to the military.

- Accountability (0 out of 3): The dismissal of the petitioners, many of them westerners, had undermined the representativeness of the military. According to the August 2006 UN report, "Legislation and internal procedures for the regulation of the force and the Ministry itself are almost entirely lacking, resulting in inadequate civilian oversight of the force."
- Rule of Law (1 out of 3): The F-FDTL shooting of the police indicated serious problems in discipline. The August 2006 UN report observes "a failure to develop a legal framework governing [the F-FDTL's] activities."

Even compared to the problems facing the neighboring Indonesian military—including weak civilian control, impunity, political interference, and corruption—the absence of structures to maintain the accountability and the rule of law of the F-FDTL are striking.[158] From 2002 to 2006, the F-FDTL had receded from a score of 3 to 2 out of 9, indicating the failure of defense reform during the period.

As a result of this failure and the 2006 violence, the UN created a new mission, the UN Integrated Mission in Timor-Leste, with a mandate to conduct an overarching review of the security sector, exercise policing authority while it sought to retrain the PNTL, and provide new advisers to the defense forces.[159] This mission initiated a new reform effort, separate from the one initiated under UNTAET, which I do not assess in detail. As in the previous UN-led efforts, defense reform received less attention than policing. Nevertheless, there was significant improvement in the quality of the military, largely due to local initiative. In 2007 Gusmão became the prime minister as well as the minister of defense and security. He took advantage of growing oil and gas revenues to pay off the petitioners and veterans and expand the size of the F-FDTL without resolving problems of oversight and accountability. The UN Integrated Mission in Timor-Leste departed in 2012, although foreign observers still expressed concerns about the dysfunction in the navy, disciplinary issues, and the lack of strategy or legal structure for the use of the military in internal security.[160]

Conclusion: Timor-Leste Defense Reform

Overall, the score of the Timorese defense institutions remained the same from 1999 to 2006, a 2 out of 9, although the rule of law improved while accountability declined. The result is a disappointment considering the international resources present in Timor-Leste. UNTAET did make some contribution by standing up F-FDTL and providing a basic legal framework, but it and its successor missions did far too little to establish effective oversight and accountability structures. This failure was part of the reason for the outbreak in violence in 2006, although a range of other factors also played a role, including the poor development of the PNTL under Lobato's leadership and the underlying antipathy between the F-FDTL and PNTL. The inability or unwillingness of the United Nations or other international actors to confront the problems facing the F-FDTL offers a clear demonstration of the need for greater attention to defense institutions in post-conflict societies.

None of the three theories can fully explain the trajectory of the F-FDTL's development, but each offers some insight, especially the international resources theory. The domestic opposition theory can explain why UNTAET did eventually create the F-FDTL, and it correctly predicts that international resources were important when there was little threat to nationalist goals or patron-client networks. The reluctance of local elites to identify flaws in the defense force may have contributed to the problems in the F-FDTL, but domestic opposition in response to international demands does not appear to be the driving factor of the failure of reform. Path dependence can explain both the decline in the quality of the F-FDTL as international resources decreased after 2002 and the persistence of weak oversight structures. The international resources theory best explains the failure of the international community to prevent violence in Timor-Leste by highlighting how poor attention to the military, even amid large-scale efforts to build the police force, inhibited the development of oversight structures.

CONCLUSION: LESSONS FROM DEFENSE REFORM

The different processes of defense reform in BiH and Timor-Leste demonstrate two lessons for future defense reform efforts and institution-building efforts in general. First, following the predictions of the domestic opposition theory, the perceived impact of foreign demands on domestic politics shapes potential opposition and the success of reform. In BiH, the development of demands that did not threaten Serbian nationalist goals or the ruling elites' networks enabled success. In Timor-Leste, the United Nations had to establish a military given nationalist opposition and a possible threat to the leadership's patron-client networks. Both reforms likely achieved greater success because they did not challenge the patron-client networks of ruling elites. Astute navigation of domestic politics therefore appeared to be a key condition for progress on defense issues in both societies.

The second lesson is the importance of bureaucratic resources. In the case of the F-FDTL, poor planning and a failure to focus on defense reform contributed to violence in 2006. Conversely, Ashdown was more successful than his predecessor and successor High Representatives primarily because of good bureaucratic management. It appears that modest bureaucratic resources are necessary to make any progress in defense reform and that such resources may be more important than other types of resources.

Preexisting institutions also played a role in determining the structure of defense institutions and the potential for reform, but they did not determine or limit the potential for reform. In Timor-Leste, despite UN views that the country was a *terra nullius* without preexisting institutions, the history and popularity of Falintil shaped the new defense force. In BiH the conditions and history of the entity militaries also shaped the unified AFBiH, including through the continued need for a specified ethnic distribution in senior positions or operations abroad. There was mixed support for the prediction that the quality of a reformed institution would decline as international resources decreased: improvements in the BiH military were sustainable, whereas the F-FDTL declined in quality after 2002. In both BiH and Timor-Leste, the overall quality of defense institutions at the end of the reform was scored the same as the institutions' highest historical quality, even though the form of these institutions had become quite different.

Defense reforms in BiH and Timor-Leste also had different outcomes from other reform efforts in the same societies, pointing to the importance of studying efforts to build specific institutions separately. In BiH defense reform was one of the more successful international efforts, compared with disappointing results in police reform (the next case study) and constitutional reform.[161] In Timor-Leste the poor results of defense reform contrasted with UNTAET's general success in establishing effective central governing institutions. The outcome of defense reform was also important for the overall political development of these societies, especially Timor-Leste, where weak defense institutions facilitated violence. The potential impact of failed defense reform indicates how important it is for foreign reformers to ensure that there are sufficient resources and attention devoted to defense institutions in the future.

NOTES

1 Richard C. Holbrooke, *To End a War* (New York: Random House, 1998), 361.

2 Quoted in Toal, O'Loughlin, and Djipa, "Bosnia-Herzegovina Ten Years after Dayton," 61.

3 Dobbins et al., *Europe's Role in Nation-Building*, 259.

4 The NATO-led Implementation Force, later renamed the Stabilization Force (SFOR), was deployed to implement the military elements of the agreement. On the civilian side, the Organization for Security and Cooperation in Europe was responsible for elections, the United Nations High Commission for Refugees for refugee return, and the European Union for economic reconstruction.

5 As Cousens and Cater write, "The High Representative had, at best, the leverage of the bully pulpit—to consult, inform, cajole, liaise, even hector, but not to direct, allocate, or spend, let alone to hold accountable." Cousens and Cater, *Toward Peace in Bosnia*, 37–42. See also Bieber, *Post-War Bosnia*, chap. 3–4.

6 One example is the ethnic elites' opposition to refugee return. See Toal and Dahlman, *Bosnia Remade*, chap. 6.

7 Bieber, *Post-War Bosnia*, 84–85; and ICG, "Ensuring Bosnia's Future," 4–5.

8 Radin, "Limits of State Building," 84–97.

9 A 2001 SFOR article, for example, highlighted SFOR's role only helping the entity militaries community. Peter Fitzgerald, "The Armed Forces in Bosnia and Herzegovina," *SFOR Informer* No. 127, November 28, 2001, https://www.nato.int/Sfor/indexinf/127/p03a/t0103a.htm. See also Maxwell and Olsen, *Destination NATO*, 24–25.

10 Ashdown, *Swords and Ploughshares*, 224–31; and interviews with international officials, Sarajevo, Summer 2009, October–November 2009.

11 See Knaus and Martin, "Travails of the European Raj"; William Bain, "In Praise of Folly: International Administration and the Corruption of Humanity," *International Affairs* 82, no. 3 (2006): 525–38; and Chandler, "State-Building in Bosnia."

12 Radin, "Limits of State Building," 129–35.

13 Gaub, *Military Integration after Civil Wars*.

14 See Robert Clinton Herrick, "The Yugoslav People's Army: Its Military and Political Mission," September 1980, Masters' thesis, Naval Postgraduate School, http://www.dtic.mil/docs/citations/ADA092586.

15 Maxwell, "Bosnia-Herzegovina," 183.

16 Thomas S. Szayna and Michele Zanini, "The Yugoslav Retrospective Case," in *Identifying Potential Ethnic Conflict*, ed. Thomas Szayna (Santa Monica, CA: RAND, 2000), 83–85; and Ramet, *Three Yugoslavias*, 370–71.

17 Steven L. Burg and Paul Shoup, *The War in Bosnia-Herzegovina: Ethnic Conflict and International Intervention* (Armonk, NY: M. E. Sharpe, 1999), chap. 4.

18 Branka Magas and Ivo Zanic, *The War in Croatia and Bosnia-Herzegovina, 1991–1995* (New York: Routledge, 2013), 193–94.

19 Maxwell, "Bosnia-Herzegovina," 183.

20 Interviews with Bosniak official and Bosnian Serb politician, Sarajevo and Banja Luka, November 2009.

21 Maxwell and Olsen, *Destination NATO*, 24–25.

22 The challenges facing the entity militaries are especially striking in comparison with neighboring Croatia, which had already initiated a major military reform effort that included downsizing its force, removing wartime leaders, and rewriting defense legislation to pursue NATO accession. See Dreisbach, "Preparing for Peace."

23 Interview with senior international official, Sarajevo, November 2009.
24 Interview with senior international official, Sarajevo, November 2009; and Maxwell and Olsen, *Destination NATO*, 24–26.
25 Short, "Orao Affair," 46.
26 Aybet, "NATO Conditionality in Bosnia and Herzegovina," 27.
27 Interview with senior international official, Sarajevo, November 2009; and Dudley, "Civil–Military Relations in Bosnia and Herzegovina," 126–30.
28 Maxwell and Olsen, *Destination NATO*, 21–31; Ashdown, *Swords and Ploughshares*, 248; and OHR, "Statement by the High Representative, Paddy Ashdown."
29 Dudley, "Civil–Military Relations in Bosnia and Herzegovina," 126.
30 Bieber, *Post-War Bosnia*, 29.
31 Bieber, 76–79; Toal and Dahlman, *Bosnia Remade*, 293–96; ICG, "The Wages of Sin: Confronting Bosnia's Republika Srpska," *Europe Report*, no. 118 (October 8, 2001); and interviews with analysts and international officials, Sarajevo, June 2008.
32 For example, it was discovered in 2004 that prior to the defense reform the VRS had paid and allegedly hid General Ratko Mladić, who had been indicted by the International Criminal Tribunal for the former Yugoslavia. See DRC, "AFBIH: A Single Military Force for the 21st Century," Sarajevo, September 2005, 187–88 https://www.jfcnaples.nato.int/systems/file_download.ashx?pg=1440&ver=1.
33 Berg, "From Weakness to Strength," 156. See also the distinction between Bosnian Serb "Euro-nationalism" and "paleo-nationalism" proposed by Toal, O'Loughlin, and Djipa, "Bosnia-Herzegovina Ten Years after Dayton," 70.
34 Gerard Toal, "'Republika Srpska Will Have a Referendum': The Rhetorical Politics of Milorad Dodik," *Nationalities Papers* 41, no. 1 (2013): 166–204.
35 Interviews with international and SBiH officials, Sarajevo, summer 2008, fall 2009. See also Bieber, *Post-War Bosnia*, 41; and Carrie Manning, "Elections and Political Change in Post-War Bosnia and Herzegovina," *Democratization* 11, no. 2 (April 2004): 74–75, 77.
36 Maxwell, "Bosnia-Herzegovina," 183.
37 Ric Bainter, "Elephant in the Room," 248–49; and Maxwell, "Bosnia-Herzegovina," 184.
38 Dudley, "Civil–Military Relations in Bosnia and Herzegovina," 126; and ICG, "Bosnia's Alliance for (Smallish) Change," *Europe Report*, No. 132 (August 2, 2002): 2, 6.
39 In fact, the RS president, Mirko Šarović, would resign before Ashdown had planned to remove him from office. Ashdown, *Swords and Ploughshares*, 280–82. Quote from Ashdown, 278. See also Short, "Orao Affair," 51–59.
40 Interviews with international officials, Sarajevo, October–November 2009.
41 Maxwell and Olsen, *Destination NATO*, 29; and OHR, "Decision Establishing the Defence Reform Commission," May 9, 2003, http://www.ohr.int/?p=65835&print=pdf.
42 Berg notes that Čavić "became convinced that the military was a liability" and publicly criticized the senior leadership of the VRS for showing "greater loyalty to Belgrade than Banja Luka." "From Weakness to Strength," 156.
43 Gaub, *Military Integration after Civil Wars*, 109.
44 Bainter, "Elephant in the Room," 250.

45 See Bainter, 248. Interviews with OHR officials, Sarajevo, September–October 2009.

46 Maxwell and Olsen, *Destination NATO*, 34–36. See also Locher and Donley, "Reforming Bosnia and Herzegovina's Defense Institutions."

47 DRC, "Path to Partnership for Peace," 8–20; and Maxwell and Olsen, *Destination NATO*, 39.

48 Bainter, "Elephant in the Room," 250.

49 Maxwell and Olsen, for example, note that international personnel supporting the defense reform process decreased since there was initially no formal mechanism after the passage of legislation to secure formal international support. Maxwell and Olsen, *Destination NATO*, 41–42.

50 See Maxwell and Olsen, 44–46; and Locher and Donley, "Reforming Bosnia and Herzegovina's Defense Institutions."

51 Bainter, "Elephant in the Room," 251.

52 Maxwell and Olsen, *Destination NATO*, 44–46; and Aybet, "NATO Conditionality in Bosnia and Herzegovina," 29.

53 Interview with senior international official, Sarajevo, November 2009.

54 Aybet, "NATO Conditionality in Bosnia and Herzegovina," 27–29; and interview with OHR official, Sarajevo, fall 2009.

55 OHR, "Statement by the High Representative, Paddy Ashdown"; and Ashdown, *Swords and Ploughshares*, 294.

56 Interview with senior international official, Sarajevo, November 2009.

57 Berg, "From Weakness to Strength," 157; and Maxwell and Olsen, *Destination NATO*, 48.

58 Maxwell and Olsen, *Destination NATO*, 46–48.

59 Interview with international official, Sarajevo, fall 2009. See also Bainter, "Elephant in the Room," 251–52.

60 Interview with international official, Sarajevo, fall 2009.

61 Maxwell and Olsen, *Destination NATO*, 48–49; and DRC, "AFBIH."

62 Maxwell and Olsen explain, there was "a Bosnian Croat regiment (1st 'Guards' Infantry Regiment); a Bosniak regiment (2nd 'Rangers' Infantry Regiment); and a Bosnian Serb regiment (3rd 'RS' Infantry Regiment)." Maxwell and Olsen, 75–76.

63 Maxwell and Olsen, 69–78; and DRC, "AFBIH."

64 Interview with senior international official, Sarajevo, November 2009.

65 Interview with Bosniak official, Sarajevo, November 2009.

66 Maxwell and Olsen observed that after reform the AFBiH structure "contained little operational capability," in part due to "aging, poorly maintained materiel," and wide geographic distribution of personnel. Maxwell and Olsen, *Destination NATO*, 69. See also Maxwell, "Bosnia-Herzegovina," 188–91.

67 See ICG, "Ensuring Bosnia's Future"; and Leroux-Martin, *Diplomatic Counterinsurgency*, 35–67.

68 European Union, "EU Military Operation in Bosnia and Herzegovina (Operation EUFOR ALTHEA)," updated April 2010, http://www.europarl.europa.eu/meetdocs/2009_2014/documents/sede/dv/sede230610factsheeteuforalthea_/sede230610factsheeteuforalthea_en.pdf; and Dobbins et al., *Europe's Role in Nation-Building*, 151–52.

69 Maxwell and Olsen, *Destination NATO*, 72–73.
70 Maxwell, "Bosnia-Herzegovina," 186.
71 See Maxwell, 184; and discussions with US officials and advisers, April 2017.
72 Maxwell and Olsen, *Destination NATO*, 65.
73 OHR, "Agenda 5+2," no date, http://www.ohr.int/?page_id=1318; NATO, "Membership Action Plan," June 12, 2017, https://www.nato.int/cps/de/natohq/topics_37356.htm; and Council of Europe, "Honouring of Obligations and Commitments by Bosnia and Herzegovina," December 15, 2017, 15–16, http://website-pace.net/documents/19887/3258251/20181215-+rapport-BosnieHerzegovine-EN.pdf/babe97e7-e41a-4d98-a541-b5b9d12677b9.
74 Interviews with Bosnian Serb politician, Bosniak official, international official, Sarajevo and Banja Luka, November 2009.
75 Interviews with international officials, Sarajevo and Banja Luka, November 2009.
76 See also Maxwell, "Bosnia-Herzegovina," 192.
77 Maxwell, 188–90.
78 Maxwell notes "unofficial parallel chains of influence" associated with the different ethnic groups. Maxwell, 188–89.
79 In Croatia, note also reports of a reduction in corruption, limited military effectiveness beyond contributing to foreign missions, and problems with duplicative organizations. See Dreisbach, "Preparing for Peace"; and "Croatian Defense Reforms and Issues of National Security: Interview with Military Analyst Igor Tabak," Balkanalysis.com, October 31, 2010, http://www.balkanalysis.com/croatia/2010/10/31/croatian-defense-reforms-and-issues-of-national-security-interview-with-military-analyst-igor-tabak/.
80 Aybet, "NATO Conditionality in Bosnia and Herzegovina," 23. The ICG makes a related argument that the success of defense reform "stem[s] from NATO having a strong mandate to begin the reforms; NATO giving no hint it would leave before the job was finished; and the NATO inducement (at least the PfP portion) being far closer to hand than the promise of eventual EU membership." "Ensuring Bosnia's Future," 15–17.
81 Aybet, "NATO Conditionality in Bosnia and Herzegovina," 23, 31–32.
82 Interviews with international officials, Sarajevo, summer 2008 and fall 2009.
83 Bainter, "Elephant in the Room," 243–50.
84 Paulo Gorjao, "The Legacy and Lessons of the United Nations Transitional Administration in East Timor," *Contemporary Southeast Asia* 24, no. 2 (2002): 313–15; and John R. Ballard, *Triumph of Self-Determination: Operation Stabilise and United Nations Peacemaking in East Timor* (Westport, CT: Praeger Security International, 2008), 84–96.
85 UNTAET's mandate was "(a) To provide security and maintain law and order throughout the territory of East Timor; (b) To establish an effective administration; (c) To assist in the development of civil and social services; (d) To ensure the coordination and delivery of humanitarian assistance, rehabilitation and development assistance; (e) To support capacity-building for self-government; (f) To assist in the establishment of conditions for sustainable development." UNSC Resolution 1272 (1999), para. 1–2.
86 Nassrine de Rham-Azimi and Li Lin Chang, eds., The United Nations Transitional Administration in East Timor (UNTAET): Debriefing and Lessons: Report of the 2002 Tokyo Conference (Boston: Martinus Nijhoff, 2003), 109–10.

87 Ball, "Defence of East Timor," 179–80.
88 See Traub, "Inventing East Timor," 74.
89 Suhrke, "Peacekeepers as Nation-Builders," 7–8.
90 Samantha Power writes that Lakhdar Brahimi declined to become SRSG of the mission on these grounds. She writes that he told Kofi Annan "I know nothing about Kosovo or Timor, but the one thing I'm absolutely certain of is that they are not the same place," and joked to Sergio Vieira de Mello, the eventual SRSG, "Sergio, instead of you being the dictator and Gusmão your adviser, why don't you make Gusmão the dictator and you be the adviser?" Power, *Chasing the Flame*, 300, 302.
91 Suhrke, "Peacekeepers as Nation-Builders," 6–10.
92 Suhrke, 6–10, 13; and Goldstone, "UNTAET with Hindsight," 85.
93 Hood, "Security Sector Reform in East Timor," 61. See also Ball, "Defence of East Timor," 179–80; and Rees, *Under Pressure*, 12–14.
94 Edward Rees writes that after 1987 "the mass of the population had been disconnected from the remaining leadership [of Falintil] and was inactive (or indifferent) to the resistance, or simply trying to stay alive." Upon Kay Rala Xanana Gusmão's capture in 1992, Falintil was estimated to have "a mere 150 men and some 60 weapons," although the movement is reported to have significantly expanded in the late 1990s. Rees, *Under Pressure*, 43–44.
95 Hughes, *Dependent Communities*, 39–41.
96 To be sure, there were extensive problems with the accountability and compliance with law of other militaries in the region, such as the politicization, extralegal violence, and lack of civilian control within the military in Indonesia. Freedom House, "Indonesia," Freedom in the World, 1999, https://freedomhouse.org/report/freedom-world/1999/indonesia.
97 Rees writes, "When discussing FALINTIL it is important to note that the definition of who constitutes FALINTIL is a confused and highly manipulated subject. Many of those who claim to be 'veterans of the resistance' in 2004 were less than 18 years old in 1999. Thousands of men and women served in FALINTIL from 1975 to 1979 but never again after that, and many joined after 1979, or even after 1992." Rees, *Under Pressure*, 48n145.
98 Francisco da Costa Guterres notes that after the referendum, "pro-Indonesian elites ceased to exist in East Timor because many of them left East Timor and currently live in West Timor, Indonesia." Guterres, "Elites and Prospects of Democracy in East Timor," 246.
99 Tanja Hohe writes that "party programmes were a minor aspect of the election campaign" and, instead, "the historical resistance fight was a detailed and elaborated feature of the campaign." Hohe, "'Totem Polls.'"
100 Niner, *Xanana*, 111–19; Rees, *Under Pressure*, 37; and Damien Kingsbury, *East Timor: The Price of Liberty* (New York: Palgrave Macmillan, 2009), 48–58.
101 Rees, *Under Pressure*, 40.
102 Rees, 41–43, 45.
103 See, e.g., Goldstone, "UNTAET with Hindsight," 89–90.
104 See Sven Gunnar Simonsen, "The Authoritarian Temptation in East Timor: Nation-building and the Need for Inclusive Governance," *Asian Survey* 46, no. 4 (2006): 575–96;

and Dennis Shoesmith, "Timor-Leste: Divided Leadership in a Semi-Presidential System," *Asian Survey* 43, no. 2 (2003): 231–52.

105 Tanja Hohe explains that "[Fretilin] started to spread its presence throughout the country, establishing structures on all administrative levels." Guterres writes that during the 2001 campaign, "leaders of FRETILIN even demanded that the people vote for them or risk being wiped out." Hohe, "'Totem Polls,'" 72–73; see also Guterres, "Elites and Prospects of Democracy in East Timor," 197, 230.

106 Guterres, "Elites and Prospects of Democracy in East Timor," 219.

107 The secretary-general's report that served as a planning document for UNATET called for UNTAET to "take measures to disarm and demobilize armed groups" but did not specifically mention Falintil or any future military for East Timor. UN, "Report of the Secretary-General on the Situation in East Timor," October 4, 1999, S/1999/1024, para. 75.

108 UN, "Report of the Secretary-General on the United Nations Transitional Administration in East Timor," July 26, 2000, S/2000/738, para. 58.

109 Sérgio Vieira de Mello, the head of UNTAET, reportedly believed that supporting Falintil would intimidate voters who had preferred autonomy. Power, *Chasing the Flame*, 311–12.

110 Interview with UN official, Dili, August 2010. See also Hughes, *Dependent Communities*, 115; and Rees, *Under Pressure*, 45–47.

111 Hughes, *Dependent Communities*, 115–16; Rees, *Under Pressure*, 44–47; and Ball, "Defence of East Timor," 176.

112 However, these details are disputed—another Fretilin official claims that Timor-Leste did not follow a "Costa Rica" model of having no defense force because Gusmão and Fretilin both opposed it. Interviews with Fretilin officials, Dili, August 2009.

113 UN, "Report of the Secretary-General," July 26, 2000, S/1999/738, para 58.

114 Interview with former UN officials, Dili, August 2009 and August 2010.

115 Radin, "Limits of State Building," 282–86; and Joel C. Beauvais, "Benevolent Despotism: A Critique of UN State-Building in East Timor," *NYU Journal of International Law & Politics* 33 (2000): 1124–27.

116 Ball, "Defence of East Timor," 177–79.

117 See Rees, *Under Pressure*, 13; and UNTAET, "On the Establishment of a Defense Force for East Timor," Regulation 2001/1, January 31, 2001, http://mj.gov.tl/jornal/lawsTL/UNTAET-Law/Regulations%20English/regenglish.htm.

118 Edward Rees also explains, "The Falintil Commanders who were admitted to the F-FDTL form a cadre of Gusmao and Taur Matan Ruak loyalists. . . . [The] FRETILIN leadership, the Central Committee, and the party rank and file were never included in the process that determined the orientation of the defence force." Rees, *Under Pressure*, 48.

119 Rees, 49.

120 Rees, 12–13, 47; and Michael Geoffrey Smith and Moreen Dee, *Peacekeeping in East Timor: The Path to Independence* (Boulder, CO: Lynne Rienner, 2003), 81.

121 Interview with Timorese official, Dili, August 2009.

122 Interview with a former UN official, Dili, August 2010; Ball, "Defence of East Timor," 180; and Rees, *Under Pressure*, 28–32.
123 Rees, 7, 11–12.
124 Ball, "Defence of East Timor," 181–82; see also Rees, *Under Pressure*, 14–15.
125 Constitution of the Democratic Republic of East Timor (2002), §§ 146–48, https://www.constituteproject.org/constitution/East_Timor_2002.pdf?lang=en. See also Rees, *Under Pressure*, 6–11.
126 Interview with former defense adviser, August 2010.
127 Rees, *Under Pressure*, 15–16.
128 Rees, 50; and ICG, "Resolving Timor-Leste's Crisis," *Asia Report* 120 (October 10, 2006): 4–5.
129 ICG, "Resolving Timor-Leste's Crisis," 5.
130 Niner, *Xanana*, 226; and Rees, *Under Pressure*, 51–52.
131 Hood, "Security Sector Reform," 71.
132 UN, "UNMISET," website (2005), sections "Facts and Figures" and "Mandate" (2009), https://peacekeeping.un.org/mission/past/unmiset/index.html.
133 Wilson, "Smoke and Mirrors," 75–81; and Hood, "Security Sector Reform," 65–67.
134 Hood, "Security Sector Reform," 71; and Rees, *Under Pressure*, 13–14.
135 Interviews with UN officials, Dili, August 2010.
136 UN News Center, "UN Peacekeeping Mission in Timor-Leste Comes to an End," May 19, 2005, https://news.un.org/en/story/2005/05/138432-un-peacekeeping-mission-timor-leste-comes-end.
137 In particular, the United Nations identified the challenge of militia on the border with Indonesia. See UN, "Report of Secretary-General to the Security Council," April 17, 2002, S/2002/432, para. 87–95.
138 For example, as one UN official explained about the post-2006 period, Timorese politicians were "not going to encourage real reform of [the F-FDTL] . . . that might weaken the connection between them and the F-FDTL." Interview with former UN official, Dili, August 2010.
139 Interviews with former UN officials, Dili, August 2010. See also Rees, *Under Pressure*, 11–12.
140 Rees, *Under Pressure*, 11. See also Defence 2020, "Strategic Blueprint for the Development of the Armed Forces of Timor-Leste 2005–2020," July 2006, copy with author.
141 Hood, "Security Sector Reform," 72–73.
142 Democratic Republic of Timor-Leste Government, "Organic Structure of the Falintil—East Timor Defense Force (Falintil-FDTL)," Decree-Law NO. 7/2004, May 5, http://mj.gov.tl/jornal/lawsTL/RDTL-Law/RDTL-Decree-Laws/Decree-Law-2004-7.pdf.
143 Rees, *Under Pressure*, 11.
144 Interviews with Fretilin officials, Dili, August 2009, August 2010.
145 James Scambary, "Anatomy of a Conflict: The 2006–2007 Communal Violence in East Timor," *Conflict, Security & Development* 9, no. 2 (2009): 270.
146 Rees, *Under Pressure*, 23–24, 52–53; Wilson, "Smoke and Mirrors," 82–86; Hood, "Security Sector Reform," 64; ICG, "Handing Back Responsibility to Timor-Leste's

Police," *Asia Report*, no. 180 (December 3, 2009): 3; and interviews with Fretilin member of parliament and adviser, Dili, August 2009.

147 ICG, "Resolving Timor-Leste's Crisis," 6; and "On the Findings of the Independent Inquiry Commission (IIC) for the FALINTIL-F," August 24, 2004, https://www.etan.org/et2004/august/22/24onthe.htm.

148 ICG, "Resolving Timor-Leste's Crisis," 6–7.

149 ICG, 7–8.

150 UN, "Report of the Independent Special Commission of Inquiry for Timor-Leste" [hereafter, Report of the Commission of Inquiry], October 2, 2006, S/2006/822, 26.

151 Report of the Commission of Inquiry, 24–29.

152 According to the ICG, Reinado did not witness the east-west violence he claimed to have seen. ICG, "Resolving Timor-Leste's Crisis," 9–10. See also Report of the Commission of Inquiry, 29–31.

153 Report of the Commission of Inquiry, 33–37, quote on 33.

154 See Report of the Commission of Inquiry, 33–37. See also ICG, "Resolving Timor-Leste's Crisis," 11–13.

155 See UN, "Report of the Secretary-General to the Security Council," August 8, 2006, S/2006/638, para. 10. The statistics on the violence are from Report of the Commission of Inquiry, 42.

156 UN, "Report of the Secretary-General," August 8, 2006, para. 56.

157 All quotes are from UN, "Report of the Secretary-General," August 8, 2006, p. 17.

158 Freedom House, "Indonesia," Countries at the Crossroads 2006, https://freedomhouse.org/report/countries-crossroads/2006/indonesia; Freedom House, "Indonesia," Freedom in the World, 2006, https://freedomhouse.org/report/freedom-world/2006/indonesia; and Human Rights Watch, "Too High a Price: The Human Rights Cost of the Indonesian Military's Economic Activities," June 20, 2006, https://www.hrw.org/report/2006/06/20/too-high-price/human-rights-cost-indonesian-militarys-economic-activities.

159 UN, "Report of the Secretary-General," August 8, 2006, para. 56–70. See also ICG, "Resolving Timor-Leste Crisis," 18–19; and interviews with senior UN officials, Dili, Summer 2009 and 2010.

160 ICG, "Timor-Leste: Stability at What Cost?," *Asia Report*, no. 246 (May 8, 2013): 24–27.

161 See Sofia Sebastián, "Leaving Dayton Behind: Constitutional Reform in Bosnia and Herzegovina," FRIDE, November 2007, http://fride.org/download/wp46_dayton_bosnia_herzegovina_en_nov07.pdf.

CHAPTER FIVE

POLICE REFORM *in* BOSNIA *and* IRAQ

In July 2004, while Ashdown, the High Representative in Bosnia, began the second stage of defense reform discussed in the previous chapter, he also began an effort to reform the structure of policing in BiH. Unlike the defense reform, which took measures to respect the legitimacy of Bosnian Serb self-governance, the police reform seemed explicitly intended to undermine the autonomy of the majority Serb entity, the Republika Srpska (RS). Ashdown insisted on creating policing districts that crossed the boundary of the RS, a policy that provoked near-universal opposition by Bosnian Serb elites, who were also backed by popular sentiment. Ashdown had high resources and sought to compel Serb elites to meet his objectives, including by threatening to block progress toward EU accession. In the end Serb public opposition forced Ashdown to back down, as he could not overrule the clear preference of the elected Bosnian Serb officials. Ashdown's failure to achieve police reform was compounded by his successors, who also caved in response to local opposition. The record of police restructuring appeared to delegitimize OHR, which was unable to achieve major reform in BiH after 2007.

Police restructuring in BiH, the first case study in this chapter, offers a clear example of how threats to nationalist goals can sink even the most powerful international interventions. A comparison of police restructuring and the BiH defense reform case in chapter 4 shows how careful selection of demands to avoid domestic opposition can enable success. While the first case study in this chapter focuses on the role of nationalist goals, the second case study, police reform in Iraq, explores the role of patron-client networks in motivating and enabling opposition.

Beginning in 2003 the Coalition sought to develop Iraq's police. The Coalition's demands focused on increasing the number of police to temporarily improve security and enable a transition to Iraqi control. Iraqi parties also sought to gain control over the Ministry of Interior (MoI), and, after 2005, Shia parties and militias co-opted the MoI and used elements of the police to commit extralegal violence. The domestic opposition theory explains why Shia private opposition was effective and was particularly intense in regions of Iraq where Coalition forces most actively sought to build nonsectarian police forces. At the same time, private opposition by Shia parties appeared to be more motivated by a desire for political control and preexisting antipathy toward Ba'athism than it was by the threat of the Coalition demands, especially since the Coalition's focus on increasing the number of police posed little threat to Shia networks. Increasing Coalition resources might have helped to build a better Iraqi police force. However, the Coalition would have faced intensified opposition if it had posed a greater threat to Shia networks. It is also unlikely that the Coalition could have deployed additional sufficient resources to more credibly improve the police, given the size of Iraq and the already high costs of the intervention.

POLICE REFORM IN BIH, 2003–7

The police restructuring effort in BiH offers a clear example of why reform efforts that threaten nationalist goals are unlikely to achieve success, whatever the resources of the international community. From 2003 to 2006 Ashdown failed to compel the Bosnian Serbs to agree to restructure the police, despite leveraging the full gamut of techniques identified by the international resources theory. Thereafter, international resources declined as other High Representatives took over for Ashdown, but Serb public opposition continued to derail reform as international demands threatened nationalist goals.

Context

Ashdown's police restructuring reform followed on an earlier effort by the UN International Police Task Force mandated by the 1995 Dayton Peace Agreement. The United Nations had focused, with some success, on improving the quality and efficiency of the entity-level police in BiH.[1] Still, Ashdown argued that additional reform to restructure the police was necessary to address the lingering problem of politicization. He explained in an interview that "it was impossible to have on the one hand a police force that was confined to, let's say the Republika Srpksa, that was not also controlled by the Republika Srpska politicians."[2] As I explain below, police restructuring was also seen as one step in a broader agenda toward making the central state more efficient and effective. However, from the perspective of the Bosnian Serbs, police restructuring weakened the autonomy of the RS and cast doubt on the basic terms of the postwar settlement. Much of the disagreement over the reform was effectively a debate over the reform's intent and meaning.

Overall, Ashdown had high resources to pursue police restructuring. As detailed in chapter 4, these resources included an executive mandate from the Bonn Powers that permitted him to remove politicians and veto or pass laws if necessary; substantial troops and financial resources; and, most critically, an unparalleled ability to coordinate within and across the various international organizations present in BiH. In part because he was dual hatted as the EU special representative, Ashdown was better able to leverage the European Union to encourage reform. Most critically, Ashdown collaborated with the European Commission, the executive branch of the EU, to ensure that police restructuring was made a condition for BiH to make progress toward EU accession. Given the draw of the EU for BiH's economic future, EU conditionality ought to have been a powerful incentive to persuade Bosnian elites to accept reform. It also offered a positive inducement, a "carrot," compared with the more coercive "stick" of the Bonn Powers that emerged from the Dayton Agreement.[3] Ashdown also worked with the EU Police Mission (EUPM), a smaller police capacity-building mission that was created in January 2003 after the closure of the UN International Police Task Force.[4]

Although the postwar Bosnian police may have drawn in part on the police institutions of former Yugoslavia, the war and subsequent reform efforts largely replaced them.[5] During the war, the ad hoc, mainly ethnically based political structures linked to the warring groups established their own policing structures, which grew to a total size of about forty-five thousand. These wartime police forces operated outside of the rule of law and in some cases were accused of major atrocities and war crimes.[6] After the war, the Dayton Agreement made policing the responsibility of the entities, preserving the wartime policing structures. The UN International Police Task Force and other international efforts up to 2003 reduced the number of police through a certification process; recruited small numbers of minority police; and provided training, infrastructure, and advice.[7] These efforts did not challenge entity control over policing or the resulting multiplicity of police organizations. In 2004 there were fifteen different police forces in Bosnia, including the RS police, the Federation police, police forces for each of the Federation cantons, the State Investigation and Protection Service (created in 2002), the State Border Service (created in 2000 and later renamed the Border Police), and the Brčko district police force. There was no apparent formal structure to coordinate across these various police forces.[8]

When the reform began in 2004, the quality of the Bosnian police was hurt by the country's complex political structures, but police effectiveness was perceived to be generally comparable to other countries in the region (I score as a 2 out of 3). There was a low crime rate, high expenditures and staffing, and some gaps in some desirable police roles.[9] Accountability was more problematic (I score it as 1 out of 3). The police forces of BiH were generally dominated by the ethnic group that had a majority of the population in a given territory.[10] In particular, the RS police was dominated by Serbs, while the police in the cantons of the Federation were generally disproportionately composed of the majority ethnic group in the canton. For example, one canton of the Federation had no Croat police officers, while in another the police were 99.2 percent Croat.[11] The police thereby reinforced the segregated structure of the country and put minority populations at risk, especially when the police played a direct role in perpetrating or permitting violence against returning minority refugees.[12] With respect to the rule of law, observers expressed particular concern about politicization (I score as 1 out of 3). The political elite at various levels of government—almost always representing the majority ethnic group—exercised political control over the police. The RS police had also failed to arrest war criminals and had a history of complicity with war crimes.[13] Overall, the police in BiH had a score of 4 out of 9 in 2004. This was also the highest relevant historical level of development for the BiH police (for the purpose of evaluating the path dependence theory), given the divergence between the former Yugoslav police and the postwar police.

With some exceptions, Bosnian Serbs were the main potential opponents of the police reform and are the focus of this case study. As detailed in chapter 4, the key Serb nationalist goal was the autonomy of the RS. Bosnian Serbs believed that to retain RS autonomy, the RS needed to maintain control of policing within the entity and Serb officials in the state government needed to maintain a veto on critical issues.[14] For the first stage of police restructuring, from 2004 to 2005, the RS government was led by the SDS and Dragan Čavić. During the second stage, from 2006 to 2007, the SNSD took power, led by Milorad Dodik. As noted in chapter 4, Čavić did not have strong patron-client links within the security services, at least compared with other SDS politicians. Dodik was widely accused of corruption, especially through kickbacks on state-funded construction, although it is not clear how developed his networks within the RS security forces were when he came to power.[15] The major Bosniak parties consistently sought to strengthen the state and weaken the entities. They therefore supported police restructuring but were frustrated by the international community's willingness to compromise in the face of Serb objections. The Bosnian Croats also largely accepted restructuring, so long as it did not impinge on their prerogatives in the cantons of the Federation or undermine Croat participation in the state government.[16]

TABLE 5.1. Development of the Police in Bosnia and Herzegovina

Stage	Threat of OHR's demands	Form of opposition	Resources	Relative success	Quality of institution at the end of the stage (out of 9)
Quality of institutions at beginning of reform / highest level of development (2004)	—	—	—	—	4
1. Restructuring under Ashdown (July 2004–January 2006)	NGs	Public	High	None	4
2. Restructuring under Schwarz-Schilling and Lajčák (2006–7)	NGs	Public	Medium	None	4

Note: NG = nationalist goal; OHR = Office of the High Representative.

The following case study examines police restructuring during two stages shown in table 5.1: Ashdown's tenure from July 2004 to January 2006 and the tenure of successor High Representatives from 2006 to 2007.

Stage 1: Police Restructuring under Ashdown, July 2004–January 2006

In July 2004 Ashdown launched the restructuring effort by using his authority as High Representative to create the Police Restructuring Commission (PRC). Ashdown's overarching goal, as mentioned above, was to shift authority over policing from the entities toward the central state, thereby reducing the politicization of police. In part due to the political sensitivities of the Bosnian Serbs, there was little prior articulated need for restructuring policing. Nevertheless, in coordination with Ashdown, EU officials identified three principles for police restructuring that had to be met for Bosnia to proceed toward EU accession by beginning negotiations for a Stabilization and Association Agreement (SAA). These principles required that the central state have authority over policing; that there be no political interference in policing; and that "the size, shape and number of local police areas within the new BiH Police Service" be guided by technocratic policing criteria, "not by political considerations."[17] Although innocuous in tone, this third principle would prove to be the most problematic since it was interpreted by international officials to mean that the police organizations under state control had to cross the inter-entity boundary line (IEBL), the border between the RS and Federation. According to Gemma Collantes-Celador, Ashdown effectively "hijacked" the ongoing technical efforts by the EUPM and other donors and "press[ed] for a remaking of Bosnia in a certain political image."[18]

These demands were articulated into a concrete proposal by the PRC, led by Wilfried Martens, which issued its final report in December 2004. The PRC considered several challenges to effective policing other than district structure, but all of the three proposed options included regions that crossed the IEBL, despite the strong objection of Serb participants (see one proposed district map in figure 5.1).[19]

International demands, reflected in the EU's principles and articulated through the PRC report, threatened the Serb nationalist goal of RS autonomy in several ways. A first concern was the proposal to shift policing from the RS to the state. If the RS could have exercised political authority over the state body overseeing policing within the RS, a shift to state control could have been feasible. A second challenge to RS autonomy was the cross-IEBL districts, which would have undermined the boundary between the entities, and possibly the existence of the entities. A third issue was that restructuring would serve as a precedent for subsequent unilateral weakening of entity authority.[20] International demands posed less of a threat to the patron-client networks of the ruling party since, as noted earlier, Čavić had weaker ties within the security services and since the impact of the high-level restructuring on lower-level officers was uncertain. Given the reform's threat to Serb nationalist goals, the domestic opposition theory predicts public opposition—including popular rejection, public protests, and consistent elite opposition.

Indeed, that was what occurred. Thomas Muehlmann writes, "The Serb side—government, opposition, and civil society representatives—unanimously protested" the OHR-backed PRC report including cross-IEBL policing districts.[21] Serb politicians described police restructuring as an attempt to undermine the RS. Čavić, the RS president at the time, responded to international demands by noting that "the RS is a result of a four-year fight of the Serb people . . . not a gift of the international community" and threatened a secession referendum.[22] Dodik noted that "the principal aim of police reform was to change the internal structure of BiH," and Mladen Ivanić, a relatively moderate Serb leader, speculated that "the idea was to abolish the RS police and thereafter the entity."[23]

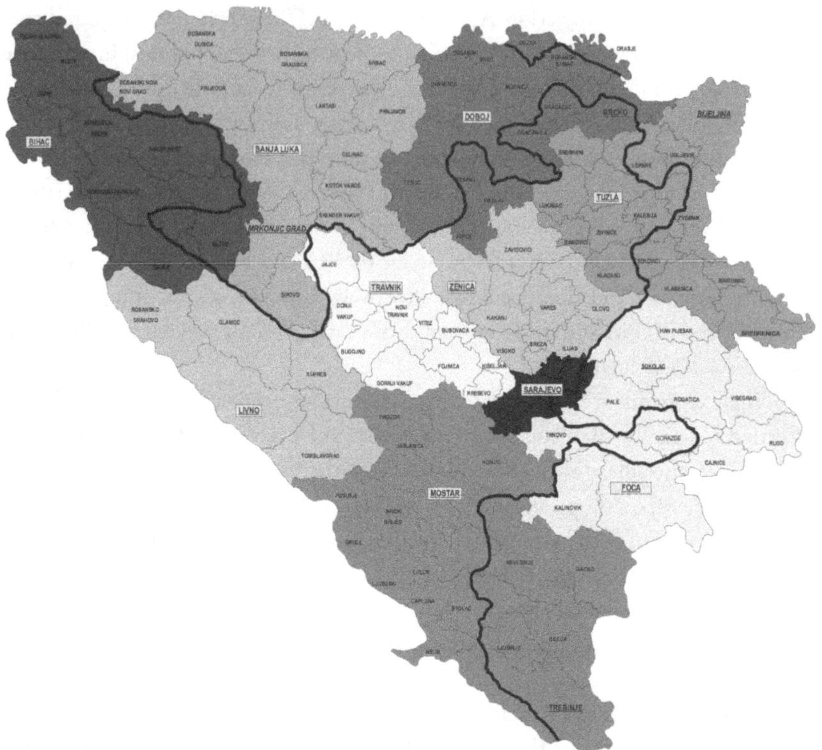

FIGURE 5.1. Bosnia and Herzegovina Police Districts Proposed by the Police Restructuring Commission

Source: Adapted from "Final Report of Work of the Police Restructuring Commission of Bosnia and Herzegovina," December 2004, 38, http://www.ohr.int/ohr-dept/presso/pressr/doc/final-prc-report-7feb05.pdf.

Note: The IEBL is the dark black line, the different shaded regions are the proposed districts, and the light gray lines indicate the municipal boundary lines.

OHR attempted to bolster public sentiment for restructuring by describing the reform as intended to create "an efficient police service, accountable to the community" and "not about abolishing the entities, or the Entity Ministry of Interiors [*sic*]."[24] The Serb population was initially divided about the necessity of the reform in July 2005, with a majority questioning the effectiveness of current structures and about 47 percent supporting some sort of cross-IEBL districts. However, Serb opposition to the reform grew over the course of 2005 (see table 5.2), and there was a series of rallies and demonstrations, including a ten-thousand-person rally in Banja Luka in May 2005.[25] Elite and mass opposition appeared to be mutually reinforcing.

TABLE 5.2. Bosnian Serb or Republika Srpska Resident Responses to Surveys on Police Restructuring

		July 2005 (%)	October 2005 (%)	June 2007 (%)
Do you think that the current structures are effective in fighting crime?	Yes	35	—	47.1
	No	59	—	46.0
	Don't know/ No answer	6	—	6.8
In your opinion, do we need to reform our police if we are to join the EU?	Yes	48.5	—	30.7
	No	51.2	—	56.6
	Don't know		—	12.7
In your opinion, for an effective fight against criminals, police areas should . . .	Cross the IEBL	28.5	21.0	—
	Cross the IEBL at 2–3 places defined by policeman	18.1	21.0	—
	Not cross IEBL	38.2	48.2	—
	Do not know/other	15.3	9.8	—
Do you think that a unified police would work better than the current entity structure?	Yes, totally	—	—	6
	In general yes	—	—	8
	In general no	—	—	16
	Absolutely not	—	—	55
	Don't know/Refusal	—	—	15

Source: Surveys were conducted by Prism Research and reported in Lindvall, "Limits of the European Vision," chap. 10.

Note: IEBL = inter-entity boundary line.

The unity of Bosnian Serbs in opposition to the reform is notable given the high international resources available. Ashdown leveraged powerful tools to overcome Serb opposition, including threatening to block Bosnia's integration in the European Union. In a speech to the RS parliament in April 2005, Ashdown exhorted Serb officials, "Do you really believe maintaining political control of your police is more important than this country's entire European future? . . . When you decide on Police reform, you will decide whether you join Serbia and Montenegro on the path to Europe—or whether you and the rest of BiH remain cut out, cut off, and left behind."[26] Based on the noncompliance with war crimes prosecution, OHR also engaged in a punitive "death by a thousand cuts" attack on the SDS, by, for example, requiring all financial transactions to go through a single supervised account.[27]

Given international pressure, as Čavić explained to a newspaper in May 2005, "the government would either have to face the reprimands of the international community or the sanction of the public."[28] Ultimately the fear of public sanction was more pressing than international reprimand. In protest of international demands, several senior Bosnian Serb politicians resigned, including the RS prime minister and the state minister of foreign affairs, Ivanić.[29] Dodik, the leader of the SNSD, explained that "a Serb politician accepting [the police reform] conditions would not be concerned about surviving the elections, but to keep his life, literally."[30] Dodik, whom the United States had previously supported as a moderate, would go on to run "a nationalist populist campaign for the first time in his fifteen-year political career" and win the election in part based on his opposition to police restructuring.[31]

After months of deadlocked negotiations in 2005, with the RS National Assembly (RSNA) continuing to reject agreements that included cross-IEBL districts, the international community backed down. As Ashdown noted, while he disagreed with Serb elites about the willingness of the population to accept reform, "they were the power structures that people voted for and no steps could be taken without the agreement of the RS assembly, the RSNA."[32] In October 2005 Ashdown and the EU accepted a two-page agreement drafted by Čavić as fulfilling its requirements. The RSNA later approved the agreement—which included the three EU-specified principles but did not mention the IEBL—and proposed that police restructuring occur in accordance with the entity constitutions.[33] With this agreement, Ashdown declared victory, later explaining that Serb leaders had verbally committed to cross-IEBL districts.[34] Because of the agreement, the EU began negotiating the SAA, the next step in the process of BiH's accession to the European Union. However, in practice, the October 2005 agreement only delayed the issue by leaving the question of how the police would be restructured to a subsequent "technical" body, the Police Restructuring Directorate.

In effect, the international community had achieved little—merely an agreement to kick the can down the road. The quality of the police remained the same, implying no success in spite of Ashdown's use of the full range of techniques suggested by the international resources theory.

Stage 2: Police Restructuring, 2006–7

After Ashdown stepped down as High Representative in January 2006, two subsequent High Representatives continued to pursue police restructuring. The first,

Christian Schwarz-Schilling, a former German diplomat, rejected Ashdown's more aggressive approach to compelling Bosnian politicians to pursue reform, explaining, "Bosnia and Herzegovina must be fully sovereign. That means I must step back." Unlike Ashdown, Schwarz-Schilling was also viewed as an ineffective leader, with a reputation for falling asleep in meetings, and he was replaced in July 2007 by Miroslav Lajčák, a Slovak diplomat.[35] Lajčák adopted a more aggressive approach and was more willing to use the Bonn Powers to secure reform. However, he faced declining available troops and a diminishing international consensus. Russia began to work more in support of the Bosnian Serbs, and some EU member states questioned whether the police reform principles Ashdown had proposed were really necessary or in alignment with EU standards.[36]

Over the course of 2006 and early 2007, Bosnia's police did seem to improve by some accounts. EUPM officials noted that its "benchmarking" system led to "general police improvement" and that EU conditionality in particular was effective in standing up and improving the state-level police force and a border service.[37] The ICG also observed improved compliance with war crimes prosecution and increasing public trust in policing.[38]

But the effort to restructure the police made little progress. OHR weakened its demands somewhat, dropping the requirement for cross-IEBL districts while still insisting that the central state have authority over policing within the entities. Serb representatives in the technical negotiations with the Police Reform Directorate continued to oppose restructuring. However, Dodik, whose SNSD party had replaced SDS to lead the RS government in January 2006, reportedly yielded to international demands in March 2006 by making an offer that would place the RS police under state control.[39] But Bosniak politician Haris Silajdžić, of the Stranka za Bosnu i Hercegovinu (Party for BiH), rejected the offer. Silajdžić appeared to be concerned that the reform would have preserved the RS police, which some Bosniaks viewed as a genocidal organization; that the RS would retain control of its police through the state; and that the international community had failed to implement its own principles.[40]

Bosniak opposition added new complexity to the problem and revealed how diminishing international resources under Schwarz-Schilling hurt the prospects for reform. By one account, Raffi Gregorian, the deputy High Representative and lead negotiator on police restructuring, claimed that greater international pressure on Silajdžić could have secured progress, observing, "No one [in the international community] said . . . 'No, God damn it, that is not an acceptable answer, Haris Silajdžić! Take the deal! Because Rehn [the EU Commissioner] is coming tomorrow and he will sign the SAA if you agree to this.' No one pressured him."[41]

In July 2007 Lajčák took over as High Representative from Schwarz-Schilling and attempted to pursue a more aggressive approach, but his police restructuring efforts were even less successful due to Serb public opposition. Shortly after Lajčák took over, OHR drafted a protocol to complete police restructuring, which accounted for the prior negotiations by not insisting on cross-IEBL districts. Dodik rejected the protocol. Negotiations stalled into mid-October, despite Lajčák's attempt to leverage an EU deadline.[42]

Due to Dodik's opposition, OHR decided that instead of attempting to use EU accession as a carrot to convince the Serbs to accept police restructuring, it should instead use the Bonn Powers under the Dayton Agreement as a stick to impose costs for noncompliance.[43] The first step in this plan was enacted on October 19, 2007, when Lajčák imposed a change in the decision-making rules of the Cabinet of Ministers, the state-level cabinet, to prevent members from blocking its activities through absenteeism. Lajčák also instructed the Bosnian presidency to amend the parliamentary rules of procedure. OHR saw these measures as just the first step in a larger plan to impose costs on the Bosnian Serbs to encourage them to accept reform. Philippe Leroux-Martin, an OHR lawyer who played a role in drafting the changes, notes that his boss speculated that OHR's leadership did not "fully realize what's ahead"—namely, Serb public opposition.[44]

OHR's imposition of rules on the state parliament made the reform a proxy for the Bosnian Serbs' ability to veto state decision-making and thereby threatened Serb nationalist goals. In itself, the specific content of the October 19 decision would not have prevented the Bosnian Serbs from overruling actions at the state level.[45] However, from the Serb point of view, if OHR had its way, the international community would have gained the ability to unilaterally shift additional authorities to the state level. Dodik had previously been willing to accept police restructuring in March 2007, so his opposition might appear to be opportunistic. Dodik and other Serb politicians did probably exaggerate the threat for political gain. But they also likely perceived a real threat to the RS's autonomy from OHR's imposition.

After Lajčák's decision was announced, Dodik immediately threatened to remove all Serb officials from the state government. On October 29, 2007, there were large demonstrations against the measures in Banja Luka, the capital of the RS.[46] These protests were facilitated by Serb public sentiment—a majority of Serbs already believed that police restructuring was unnecessary and undesirable (see table 5.2). Further, more than three hundred thousand people signed a petition opposing Lajčák's measures.[47] The RSNA rejected Lajčák's decision. It called on the Peace Implementation Council, which acted as OHR's supervisor, to close OHR since it had exceeded its authority under the Dayton Agreement. The Peace Implementation Council Steering Board, which included the major Western powers, backed OHR in an October 31 statement, arguing that "certain political leaders have overreacted to [OHR's] measures in order to create a political crisis."[48] Russia, however, added a footnote expressing its concern with OHR's approach, signaling its support of

Dodik. Despite Western pressure, Nikola Špirić, the chair of the Council of Ministers and a close political ally of Dodik, resigned in protest on November 1. He explained, "Bosnia and Herzegovina is absurd. If the international community supports the High Representative and not the institutions of Bosnia and Herzegovina, then it doesn't matter if I am the head of that state, or Bart Simpson."[49]

Over the course of November, Dodik and his allies continued to oppose OHR. Serb officials proposed changes to Lajčák's decisions and made statements highlighting the illegitimacy of OHR. In one op-ed, Dodik wrote, "The citizens of BiH are simply extras in an eternal film entitled: 'I am your OHR and you shall have no other gods before me.'"[50] On November 5 the RSNA threatened the use of "all legal and democratic means," likely meaning holding a referendum on Serb independence, if Bosnian state organizations overruled the political entities or main ethnic groups.[51] While the United States and United Kingdom stood firm behind Lajčák, many EU officials and some EU member states, including France and Germany, "thought that [Lajčák] had gone too far already." OHR officials were also internally divided, with some senior advisers seeking a compromise.[52]

In late November OHR realized that it could not counter Serb opposition, in large part due to growing concern about the democratic legitimacy of OHR's actions and resulting division within the international community. For example, a November 26, 2007, op-ed by Ian Bancroft in the *Guardian* agreed with the Serb concern that OHR's actions "stifled the development of representative elected bodies and a democratic culture."[53] According to Leroux-Martin's account, in late November Lajčák determined and EU officials agreed that "the international community no longer enjoyed the power to enforce decisions in Bosnia."[54]

In December 2007 Lajčák issued an "authentic interpretation" of his October 19 decision, which undermined the original decision and indicated OHR's willingness to negotiate its decisions with Bosnian leaders.[55] OHR and the EU accepted an earlier agreement on police restructuring proposed in November 2007. The agreement did little to actually change the structure of policing. As one EU official noted, the agreement "was a means to the SAA."[56] It created new state-level coordinating structures that would gain control of local police structures only after constitutional reform, which had been repeatedly blocked in BiH, including in April 2006.

The quality of BiH's police was largely unchanged from 2006 to 2007, achieving a score of 4 out of 9, although there was some improvement unrelated to restructuring:

- Effectiveness (2 out of 3): As one senior EU official noted, despite the failure of police restructuring, the Bosnian police "at the end of the day are not so bad."[57] Public attitudes about the effectiveness of the police appeared to improve, as did homicide rates compared with Croatia and Serb.[58] There remained challenges from the multitude of police organizations and problems with investigating and prosecuting organized crime.[59]

- Accountability (1 out of 3): Police forces remained linked with the ethnic majority groups in different regions of BiH, reinforcing segregation. There were some improvements in minority refugee return during the period of police restructuring, but this did not appear to fundamentally change the accountability of the local power structures to minority populations.[60]
- Rule of Law (1 out of 3): While the RS's cooperation with the International Criminal Tribunal for the former Yugoslavia improved, an EU progress report still noted problems with "political interference by Entity and cantonal politicians" and widespread "petty and serious corruption."[61]

Conclusion: Police Restructuring in Bosnia

Police restructuring in Bosnia was a failure and a missed opportunity. The quality of policing did not change over the course of 2004 to 2007, despite high international resources during Ashdown's tenure. Further, the failure of police restructuring seemed to have weakened the international mission in Bosnia.[62] At the urging of EU member states, in February 2008 OHR issued the conditions BiH would have to achieve for OHR to close. A decade later, despite continued efforts by OHR and the rest of the international community these conditions were still not achieved, and OHR remained open, with foreign reporting noting a recurring cycle of intensified international demands, domestic opposition, and stalemate.[63]

The failure of police restructuring does provide an instructive lesson for future efforts. Police restructuring fits the general predictions of the path dependence theory, as preexisting institutions remained. But the domestic opposition theory offers the best explanation for the process and outcome of the reform effort. By insisting on creating policing districts that crossed the IEBL, Ashdown threatened Serb nationalist goals, triggering public opposition that was impossible to circumvent. The case study does not follow the predictions of the international resources theory, since even with a strong mandate and bureaucratic resources Ashdown could not achieve reform that threatened the nationalist goals of the Bosnian Serbs. In the second phase of reform, Lajčák's actions also challenged the autonomy of the RS, again leading to Serb public opposition and failure. In comparison with defense reform in BiH, where the international community achieved success by avoiding Serb red lines, in the police restructuring effort the international community ignored these redlines and achieved less as a result.

COALITION DEVELOPMENT OF THE IRAQI POLICE, 2003–11

US SECRETARY OF DEFENSE DONALD RUMSFELD: When I think back to the brief I got on the police, I got the impression everything was okay, but now you're telling me they are not okay.

GEN. GEORGE W. CASEY JR.: That's because the brief you got was about the process of training them—the mechanics—and they are going well. The briefing wasn't about their performance. It didn't address loyalty issues.[64]

Following the invasion of Iraq, the US-led Coalition faced a dilemma: it needed to stabilize Iraq in the face of growing sectarian violence, but there was also strong political pressure to reduce the large Coalition military presence. The Coalition did have significant resources—it had a peak military presence of 183,000 and spent more than $8 billion on the Iraqi police—but the scale of the Coalition presence still paled in comparison to the size and complexity of Iraq.[65] The only feasible solution to this problem was for the Coalition to focus on rapidly developing the Iraqi security forces, especially the police, to create security in the country. The Coalition effort to increase the number of Iraqi police did not threaten Iraqi core interests. Still, Shia factions privately opposed the development of the police by seizing control of the MoI, recruiting militia members, and engaging in sectarian violence. Shia private opposition was to some extent a response to Coalition reform efforts, as there was more intense opposition in regions of the country where the Coalition could more credibly develop a nonsectarian police force. Nevertheless, the development of the Iraqi police was more a result of the political antipathies that emerged from Saddam Hussein's regime and the desire of Shia parties for political control. As one Iraqi police general explained, "In Iraq, there is a culture of 'he who owns the security forces, owns the politics.'"[66]

Context

After the 2003 invasion a security vacuum emerged in Iraq. The CPA took over control and sought to build the police, among other state institutions. Over the next eight years, Coalition resources to develop the police varied but were generally moderate according to the criteria in chapter 2. The CPA had a strong mandate as the occupying authority of Iraq but had few personnel focused on policing. By August 2004 only 376 US and 50 non-US police trainers or advisers were deployed, compared with the approximately 6,600 that the CPA had initially sought, and the total number of foreign military personnel was low relative to Iraq's population of approximately 26 million in 2003.[67] In 2004 responsibility for police development was transferred to the military, which increased the rate of training Iraqi police but reduced the aspirations for improving the accountability and rule of law of the police, as discussed below. Even as more Coalition personnel focused on policing—including police liaison officers and US police transitions teams—Coalition forces aspired to provide only a thin layer of supervision. After sectarian violence increased, the United States in 2007 initiated a "surge," deploying additional US troops to improve security and seeking to incorporate Sunnis into the security forces (see also changes in Iraqi and US leadership in table 5.3). Still, the number of police advisers was too small to directly supervise the Iraqi police. Throughout the Coalition presence, as noted below, observers also noted significant bureaucratic gaps, including a lack of planning for the CPA, and a short-term approach, demonstrated by the rapid rotation of US personnel.

Prior to the US-led invasion, the Iraqi police had some history of effectiveness but had a very poor human rights record. Under Saddam Hussein's regime, there were at least eight different policing agencies. Secret police agencies and party militias included some members of the MoI but were administered separately. The Iraqi MoI under the Ba'athist regime was a sizable institution, albeit smaller than the MoI in the late 2000s. In the late 1970s, when the last reliable statistics are available, the MoI grew in size from 102,422 in 1976 to 151,301 in 1978.[68] The MoI also employed approximately 22.8 percent of the total publicly employed workforce, at the time a level similar to that of Syria and higher than Jordan.[69] The various police organizations operated a highly complex bureaucracy that was able to secure the regime and provide a degree of physical security in Iraq, in part through arbitrary violence and the imposition of fear. However, the regime's ability to monitor and punish opposition varied throughout the country.[70] At the height of their capacity, I rate the police as a 5 out of 9, with a 3 out of 3 for effectiveness, given its size and capacity relative to the region; a 1 out of 3 for accountability, given the inclusion of Shia and Kurds into the security forces but the simultaneous history of repression of the Shia and Kurdish minorities; and 1 out of 3 for the rule of law, given the arbitrary application of the law, torture, and violence.[71]

After the 1991 Gulf War, Iraqi institutions weakened up through the 2003 invasion, after which the Iraqi police all but vanished. The country descended into chaos and looting, in part encouraged by the remnants of Saddam Hussein's regime. While the CPA formally dissolved other elements of Saddam Hussein's security infrastructure, including the defense ministry, intelligence agencies, and various secret police forces, the MoI and the Iraqi Police Service (IPS) were preserved. However, the CPA's policy of de-Ba'athification, meaning removing senior party members of the former regime, combined with many officials leaving their post left the police "leaderless."[72] Further, prior to the war, IPS had responsibility only for minor traffic offenses or street crime, while other institutions had primary responsibility for security and law enforcement. As one 2005 RAND report noted, "It is very doubtful that any police force would have been able to cope with the levels of violence that erupted, let alone one as weak as the IPS."[73] Initial CPA assessments similarly noted that "the Iraqi police, as currently constituted and trained, are unable to independently maintain law and order and need the assistance and guidance of Coalition Force assets (or some appropriate follow on force) to accomplish this task."[74] I therefore rate the police as effectively nonexistent at the beginning of the CPA, with a score of 0 out of 9.

This case study focuses primarily on the interaction between the Coalition and the Shia in the development of the police. Other ethnic groups also played a role in the development of security institutions in Iraq. Kurdish groups sought to maintain their own militia, the *pesh merga*, as a protection of their interests and dominance in their region. There was also a strong Sunni insurgency, including the radical Islamist al-Qaeda in Iraq. Later, with the Awakening movement, many Sunnis who had participated in the insurgency joined US-backed militias.[75] Nevertheless, as detailed below, the future of the Iraqi security forces, and with it the future of Iraq, hinged on the willingness of Shia groups to build accountable and law-abiding national security forces that incorporated Sunnis and Kurds. Shia obstruction and co-optation of the security forces—including their rejection of Sunni recruits—undermined the quality of the Iraqi police.

Drawing on the analysis in chapter 3, there were two dominant Shia nationalist goals relevant to the police: to establish a prevailing role for Shia within the MoI and police organizations and to prevent the resurgence of Ba'athism. The interpretation of these goals varied among Shia parties and militias. Some Shia parties and militias appeared to seek control of the police for political power. Others may have sought to take revenge because of past offenses by Ba'athists or to preempt a potential Ba'athist resurgence. Other individuals or groups may simply have been motivated by personal greed or corruption.[76]

In terms of their patron-client networks, the Shia parties were linked with particular militia organizations. The largest Shia party, the Supreme Council for the Islamic Revolution in Iraq (SCIRI), voiced a more sectarian identity and was associated with the Badr militia. The Mahdi Army was led by Muqtada al-Sadr, who espoused an anti-Coalition perspective, but was also more inclusive to other ethnosectarian groups in Iraq. The Islamic Dawa Party, whose leader, Nouri al-Maliki, was prime minister from 2006 to 2014, had its own associated armed groups.[77] As ruling coalition of the Iraqi government and control over the MoI shifted, as detailed in table 5.3, so did the ability of different Shia parties to control the police.

TABLE 5.3. Main US and Iraqi Leadership

Period	Lead Coalition organization for security development	Main US leader	Minister of Interior	Sect/Party affiliation
July 2003–April 2004	CPA	L. Paul Bremer	Nuri Badran	Shia / Iraqi National Accord
April 2004–June 2004	CPA (although CPATT created in May 2004)	L. Paul Bremer	Samir Shakiral-Sumaida'ie	—
June 2004–January 2005	MNSTC-I	Gen. George Casey	Faleh Al-Naqib	Sunni
January 2005–May 2006	MNSTC-I	Gen. George Casey	Bayan Jabr	Shia/SCIRI
May 2006–February 2007	MNSTC-I	Gen. George Casey	Jawad al-Boulani	Shia / Iraqi Constitutional Party
February 2007–September 2008	MNSTC-I	Gen. David Petraeus	Jawad al-Boulani	Shia / Iraqi Constitutional Party
September 2008–January 2010	MNSTC-I	Gen. Raymond Odierno	Jawad al-Boulani	Shia / Iraqi Constitutional Party

Note: CPA = Coalition Provisional Authority; CPATT = Civilian Police Advisory Training Team; MNSTC-I = Multi-National Security Training Command–Iraq; SCIRI = Supreme Council for the Islamic Revolution in Iraq.

Disentangling the activity or motivation of Shia groups was often difficult. Leading Shia officials, for example, insisted that they supported a multiethnic Iraq and condemned the violence perpetrated by radicals.[78] The extent to which Shia leaders were sympathetic to or in control of the violence remained uncertain throughout the US presence.

Below, after describing the context of police restructuring in Iraq, I describe the reform in three stages (see table 5.4): the CPA's effort to reconstruct basic policing; police reform during the tenure of Gen. George W. Casey Jr. from 2004 to 2007; and police reform during and after the 2007 "surge."

TABLE 5.4. Development of the Police in Iraq

Stage	Threat of Coalition demands	Form of opposition	Resources	Relative success	Quality of institution at the end of the stage (out of 9)
Quality of institutions at beginning of reform (April 2003)	—	—	—	—	0
Highest level of development (late 1970s)	—	—	—	—	4
1. CPA (April 2003–June 2004)	None	Public and private	Medium	Limited	3
2. Stand down to stand up Iraqis (June 2004–February 2007)	None	Private	Medium	None	2
3. Surge to US departure (February 2007–December 2011)	Sporadic threat to PCNs	Private	Medium-low	Limited	4

Note: CPA = Coalition Provisional Authority; PCN = patron-client network.

Stage 1: Development of the Iraqi Police under the CPA, April 2003–June 2004

After his arrival in Baghdad in May 2003, Bremer learned that the Iraqi police "have just disappeared, like the army," and he immediately sought to increase the number of Coalition police in Iraq, including through the deployment of additional US military police.[79] However, throughout the CPA's tenure, senior US officials resisted the idea of deploying dramatically more US or other international civilian police, including due to concerns about the availability of US police and the perceived poor quality of UN police.[80] Given the need to have sufficient police to reestablish law and order, the CPA's main demand therefore became increasing the number of available Iraqi police as quickly as possible. The CPA would pursue this goal through two general approaches: maintaining the preexisting MoI and rapidly rehiring police into it, and simultaneously pursuing the training of new police abroad.[81]

Increasing the number of police did not threaten the nationalist goals or patron-client networks of the Shia. A reconstituted police force was consistent with the Shia goal of dominance within Iraq so long as the Shia had a proportionate role in the police. Some Shia, especially those aligned by Muqtada al-Sadr, opposed the Coalition as an occupying force, but this did not appear to be a dominant perspective. The Coalition did voice a desire for police that was representative of the ethnic structure of Iraq and met the general standards of democratic societies.[82] However, in practice, as described below, the CPA did not emphasize or put major resources toward achieving these more ambitious objectives. Andrew Rathmell explains that after 2003 the MoI "was restructured with the explicit purpose of reflecting and accommodating the political power balance of post-Saddam Iraq. . . . It was clearly too politically dangerous to allow any one party to control this institution, hence the structure was designed to give the key power-brokers—the Kurds, [SCIRI], and Dawa—a share in the ministry."[83] With a low threat to Shia interests, the domestic opposition theory predicts some minimal private opposition by the mainline Shia parties and limited Coalition success in establishing the Iraqi police.

Some Shia factions, such as the one led by Muqtada al-Sadr, would engage in more intensive, violent opposition to the CPA's police reform than the domestic opposition theory anticipates. This opposition was likely due to their more radical views of the Coalition as an occupying force or to preexisting antipathies, such as a desire for revenge against former Ba'athists. Nevertheless, rather than organized Iraqi opposition, the CPA's main challenges at least at first were resource gaps, including insufficient personnel relative to Iraq's size, insufficient planning, poor administration, and training programs ill suited to achieving the Coalition's objectives.

The CPA's first priority was to reconstitute the Iraqi police by locating and rehiring former Iraqi police and by using US military police to conduct three-week training classes. But the reconstituted police were lacking in both quantity and quality. By mid-July, according to Bremer's account, there were approximately fifteen thousand police available (although a security report from the same period notes "30K Iraqi police rehired nationally"), far less than the CPA's desired sixty-five thousand to seventy-five thousand.[84] Many who were recruited reportedly lacked prior experience or did not meet age or literacy requirements.[85] A regional CPA official in August 2003 in Ramadi noted that the police were "undermanned, poorly-led, mis-armed or under-armed, and without vehicles and equipment."[86] An effort by the Coalition military to recruit thirty thousand police in thirty days, which was later extended to sixty thousand in sixty days, reinforced the quality problem. According to one account, during the recruitment drive, "no allowance had been made in the MOI budget for the management, salaries, or sustainment of such a quickly expanding force; [and] the new recruits often found themselves omitted from official salary rolls," which facilitated "bribery and corruption."[87] In a *New York Times* article, Coalition police advisers recalled that the Iraqi police at the time were equipped only with "rusty Kalashnikovs, which they cleaned with gasoline" and that there were so few foreign advisers present that they "struggled" to visit police stations once per month.[88] Indeed, throughout 2003, only about fifty police advisers were deployed, despite repeated requests for more, including by Bernard Kerik, the former New York Police Department commissioner and head of the police effort.[89]

Because of a lack of facilities in the country, the CPA developed a plan to train the Iraqi police abroad, initially in Hungary, at a planned cost of approximately $750 million per year. However, the plan to train in Hungary fell through, and the CPA instead developed a training center in Jordan, where approximately eighteen thousand police could be trained per year. Construction of the training facility in Jordan would begin in November 2003.[90] CPA officials in part blamed Kerik's lack of administrative skill for the delay, noting that "we lost several critical months under Kerik in rebuilding the police program."[91] Even once the training center got off the ground, the training it provided was short—only eight weeks. The DynCorp-hired US advisers were mainly "retired officers from small towns," according to one article, and since they spoke only English, the required translation effectively cut in half the time available for training.[92] The recruitment and vetting of Iraqi police for training were also problematic. A subsequent US government assessment noted that "only a cursory background check, if even that, was conducted before policemen were trained or entered the force," although it is unclear whether this referred to the police initially rehired in Iraq or trained in Jordan.[93]

Accounts of the Iraqi police highlight their poor preparation and vulnerability to the insurgency. Dobbins and colleagues note that "Iraqi police were often cowed by local militia forces and insurgents and were involved in criminal activity."[94] Insurgents appeared to have systematically targeted the police—Nir Rosen, for example, describes the murder of an Iraqi police colonel in February 2004 in a previously peaceful area of Baghdad.[95] As discussed in chapter 3, in April 2004, two simultaneous security challenges occurred. First, Sunni insurgents seized Fallujah and co-opted the local security forces against the Coalition military.[96] Around the same time, Shia forces loyal to Sadr also seized police headquarters in Najaf, Kufa, and Sadr City, confronting poorly equipped Iraqi security forces. One indication of the impact of low resources was a complaint by a police commander in Sadr City to an American adviser that the Iraqi police "didn't have enough weapons or men. 'There may be five thousand RPGs in Sadr City, . . . and [the police] have none. Some of the criminals even have mortars. We have five hundred policemen and only thirty bulletproof vests.' "[97]

The slow pace of police development frustrated Donald Rumsfeld, the secretary of defense. Rumsfeld pushed Bremer to permit US military forces to take control of the reform effort to boost the available resources. While Bremer initially resisted Rumsfeld's proposal, following a report by Maj. Gen. Karl Eikenberry, responsibility for police training was transferred in May 2004 to the US military, where it remained through 2011. The Civilian Police Assistance Training Team (CPATT) was created and placed under the control of the Multi-National Force–Iraq.[98] Bremer strongly resisted the shift, noting, "It would convey to the Iraqis the opposite of the principle of civilian standards, rules and accountability for the police."[99] In practice, the US military would largely rely on the same contractor as the State Department, DynCorp, so the practicalities of training did not greatly change. Even so, the emphasis shifted toward envisioning the police as a paramilitary force that could contribute to the counterinsurgency campaign rather than as a community-based police force that could enforce the law and follow democratic norms.[100]

In the spring of 2004 the CPA began protracted negotiations about disbanding the extant militias. Political parties strongly protested the elimination of their militias. Kurdish officials, for example, used nationalist rhetoric—Masoud Barzani explained that the *pesh merga* "were not a militia force like the other parties had, but a symbol of Kurdish dignity and a force that had helped liberate Iraq."[101] SCIRI officials similarly opposed disbanding the Badr Corps, noting the poor state of the Iraqi security forces. SCIRI leaders argued that "political parties and civil organizations, especially those with security experience like the Badr Corps, should carry the burden of responsibility for providing security."[102] By May CPA officials negotiated an agreement with all parties to disband and reintegrate the militias, with the exception of Sadr's Mahdi Army, which would not be included as a "recognized" militia. The CPA then issued Public Order 91 to implement the agreement.[103] However, the US Agency for International Development refused to cooperate, and Public Order 91 was not fully realized.[104] Further, it is not clear that Iraqi officials intended to follow through, given the threat to their networks. One adviser explained that the new interim prime minister, Ayad Allawi, hesitated because "the amount of political capital that would be necessary in order to really fully implement this plan was very high, and would be very complicated to do, from an Iraqi perspective."[105] While some of the militias did integrate their forces into Iraq's security forces on the basis of Public Order 91, the militias were not disbanded, and militia penetration of the security forces remained a persistent challenge.

The CPA's efforts appear to have been somewhat removed from the actual development of the Iraqi police. CPA advisers appeared to focus on discussions with other Western officials within the Green Zone, especially in the early months of the occupation. One adviser argued that the absence of Iraqi opposition during the CPA was simply because there was little Iraqi participation in governance during the CPA period.[106] Different military units also pursued different approaches for developing the police in their area. The MoI under the CPA, Nuri Badran, appeared to exercise little influence—for example, in one letter to Bremer in November 2003 Badran criticized the decision to use the Iraqi police in antiterror operations, and he began by noting that he had not been consulted on the issue.[107] In April 2004 Badran resigned when the CPA transferred authority of the police to the provinces over his objections.[108] Another factor was that many of the personnel in the ministry were hired from the nearby Sadr City, leading to what Joshua Paul describes as "bottom-up infiltration" by Sadr's militia, the Mahdi Army.[109] The separation between the policymaking of the CPA and the development of the police on the ground undermined the CPA's ability to shape the police and MoI and likely unfolded in part due to the shortage of police advisers.[110]

While the CPA had made progress over its tenure and achieved a transition to Iraqi authority in June 2004, serious problems remained. Overall, I assess the quality of the Iraqi police as a 3 out of 9:

- Effectiveness (1 out of 3): The Coalition had rapidly increased the size of the police force, but significant problems remained, including poor retention of trained officers and a focus on paramilitary training over democratic policing.
- Accountability (1 out of 3): The accountability of the police was deeply problematic. The CPA's effective sovereign control prevented Iraqi officials from exercising oversight. Statistics on the ethnic balance of the police were not available, although the accounts above indicated the increasing dominance of Shia within the security institutions.
- Rule of Law (1 out of 3): The internal procedures to ensure obedience to law appeared deeply problematic or nonexistent—some accounts noted continuing corruption and the poor screening of recruits.[111]

Stage 2: Standing Down So Iraqis Stand Up: MNSTC-I and Shia Co-optation, July 2004–February 2007

After the closure of the CPA, the Coalition redoubled its focus on building up the size of the police force to take greater responsibility. General Casey, the new commander of the Coalition military effort, hoped to speed up the development of the

Iraqi forces to contribute to the counterinsurgency mission, and with a lower priority for building a community focused police. Based on his experience in the Balkans, and in line with a hypothesis from the path dependence theory, Casey also feared that the provision of security by US forces would reduce the incentive for Iraqis to build strong security institutions.[112] Under Casey's command, then lieutenant general David Petraeus took over the Multi-National Security Training Command–Iraq (MNSTC-I), which was responsible for developing the police and other Iraqi security forces.[113] Funding for training the security forces rapidly increased, with Congress allocating $3.24 billion in FY 2004 and $5.3 billion in FY 2005.[114]

In June 2004 the Iraqi Interim Government, led by Prime Minister Ayad Allawi, took power, and Faleh al-Naqib, a Sunni Arab, took over as minister of interior. Facing increasingly well-armed radical Shia and Sunni groups and seeking to establish security in January 2005, Naqib sought to rapidly expand the size of the police and provide greater combat capabilities. One of Naqib's major priorities was the creation of paramilitary units that were loyal to him personally, outside of the normal hierarchy, including the special commando units and public order battalions. The commandos, who were led by Naqib's uncle, Adnan Thabit, primarily comprised Sunnis who had been part of the military under the previous regime but had a larger, nonsectarian political orientation.[115] US advisers saw the commandos as highly effective—as one adviser explained, unlike the other police, they "had [their] act together."[116] Although there were still reports of human rights violations, Coalition officials believed the approximately five thousand commandos could help provide security, and they were eventually provided with arms and assistance.[117]

After the January 2005 elections, a Shia political alliance came into power, with Ibrahim al-Jaafari becoming prime minister. SCIRI, a key element of the Shia coalition, made gaining control of the MoI their first priority and succeeded in appointing Bayan Jabr as minister. By one account, SCIRI, and especially the Badr militia members associated with it, saw both a "threat from the commandoes and an opportunity" to use them to consolidate power and achieve their agenda.[118] Jabr began to replace the leadership of the special police commandos and public order battalions, co-opting the same units that Naqib had used but instead ensuring that they were loyal to SCIRI and Badr. The MoI also rapidly recruited Shia—"many of them straight from the militia"—into both the existing units and into newly formed units.[119] Joshua Paul estimates that between two thousand to seventeen thousand Badr members entered the National Police, which subsumed the commandos during this period.[120]

By late 2005 and early 2006 MoI forces began to develop a reputation for brutality against Sunnis. As Robert Perito writes, during Jabr's tenure "members of the IPS and special police commando units acted as death squads, kidnapping, imprisoning, torturing, and killing Sunnis. Iraqis reported that gunmen in police uniforms routinely abducted people from their homes, cars, and—in one particularly flagrant case—a hospital bed."[121] Paul writes, "There can be little doubt that these squads were, indeed, some of the new Shia militia elements within the Commandos." He also argues that they were under the "chain of command if not actual control" of the Badr-linked senior commanders of the National Police.[122] By taking over the leadership of the MoI and recruiting militia members into the police, SCIRI and Badr hard liners were able to take control of the police, including both the commandos and regular force, and use it to pursue their agenda.

In November 2005 US forces also found that a Badr-affiliated Shia official in the intelligence section of the ministry, known as Engineer Ahmed, was operating a secret underground detention bunker where more than one hundred prisoners were held and tortured. The prisoners were primarily although not exclusively Sunnis—either they or members of their family had participated in attacks on Shia during Saddam Hussein's regime. The detention of individuals from the former regime points to Badr's motivation—it offered a means of taking revenge against the former regime and limiting the influence of members of the former regime in the new Iraq. Jabr downplayed the abuses and noted the presence of Shia prisoners in order to claim that the abuse was not sectarian.[123] Nevertheless, with escalating violence carried out by Sunni insurgents against Shia and by Shia police against Sunnis, sectarian violence rapidly spread in mixed areas, especially after the bombing of al-Askari shrine in Samarra in February 2006.[124]

The Coalition recognized the challenges with the police—for example, US Ambassador Zalmay Khalilzad declared 2006 as the "Year of the Police in Iraq."[125] However, the Coalition was unable and, to an extent, not interested to address Shia co-optation and abuses by the police, which meant that the Coalition's effort generally posed little threat to Shia networks. As the quote from Rumsfeld opening this case study emphasizes, the primary mission for the Coalition missions for the police was to increase their number, not to ensure their accountability or adherence to the rule of law. Similarly, Matthew Sherman, an MoI adviser, explains, "Gen. Petraeus' mission was to train and equip 135,000 individuals. That was done. But the accountability of those individuals is also a key component which got missed."[126] As the number of police trained and equipped rapidly increased, as shown in table 5.5, the quality of the police remained in question, as did whether they remained on duty.[127] Further, the metrics adopted to evaluate the quality of the police tended to be the same as for US infantry units—such as personnel on hand, training, and equipment availability—not statistics relevant to a community-oriented police force such as education of personnel, complaints, or arrests.[128] Even with high US spending on the police, there were still gaps in basic supplies and equipment. One adviser noted that the Iraqi police typically carried fewer than twenty rounds of ammunition due to US-imposed procedures. The result was that insurgents could

TABLE 5.5. Selected Reports on the Size of the Iraqi Police

	July 2005	October 2005	November 2006	September 2008	March 2009	June 2010
Iraqi police service (Trained and equipped)	62,000	67,500	135,000	192,028	—	297,000
Iraqi national police (Total personnel)	—	—	29,000	39,739	43,000	43,000 (Federal police)
MoI (Trained and equipped)	—	104,300	188,200	276,582	—	—
MoI (Total personnel)	—	—	—	—	486,000	464,000

Source: Department of Defense (DoD), "Measuring Stability and Security in Iraq," Reports to Congress, 2005–10, https://archive.defense.gov/home/features/Iraq_Reports/Index.html.

Note: DoD reports to Congress do not consistently use the same metrics. For example, the November 2006 DoD report explained that "it is unclear how many of the forces trained by [CPATT] are still employed by the MoI, or what percentage of the 180,000 police thought to be on the MOI payroll are [CPATT]-trained and equipped" (32). Furthermore, which forces were included within the MoI changed over time—the Facilities Protection Service, for example, were incorporated in March 2009. CPATT = Civilian Police Assistance Training Team; DoD = Department of Defense; MoI = Ministry of Interior.

adopt a standard tactic of firing on a police unit until they ran out of ammunition and then overrunning the position.[129]

The Coalition forces did face more intense opposition above and beyond the bureaucratic opposition they had encountered in the past, especially where there was the greatest effort to build a more effective and nonsectarian police. One former US officer noted that in 2005, convoys with police recruits headed to training centers would routinely be attacked by suicide bombers, in some cases resulting in heavy casualties. There was low trust between Coalition personnel and the Iraqis with whom they worked. Because of the pattern of attacks by improvised explosive devices, Coalition personnel believed there were informants within the Iraqi security forces. US police advisers themselves were sometimes targeted, including, according to one account, by Shia militias encouraged by Iran. While it was difficult to ascertain the exact reason for particular attacks, it was clear that both Sunni and Shia groups—including the Mahdi Army—sought to violently undermine Coalition efforts to develop the police.[130]

There remained few police advisers in the field relative to the size of the Iraqi police. Compared with the four thousand advisers in Kosovo for a population of only 2 million, by mid-2005 there were five hundred international police liaison officers in the field in Iraq, a country of 28 million.[131] This later increased to nine hundred advisers, and the Coalition began to deploy police transition teams (PTTs) with a mix of US military and civilian personnel. Even with 177 PTTs deployed in late 2006, these advisers were highly limited in their ability to engage across the country given security and political challenges.[132] One former adviser in Diyala Province emphasized that the US personnel could often only sporadically visit Iraqi police stations—"riding circuit"—instead of embedding personnel within those sites because of security concerns and limited number of available personnel. Prime Minister Allawi's early opposition to PTTs in local station may also have played a role.[133] The former adviser also highlighted the mixed quality of the members of the PTTs—many US military personnel assigned to PTTs were previously in other military specialties such as artillery and had received at most a few months' retraining.[134] At the ministerial level, Robert Perito writes that Coalition advisers were "confined to the top floor of the building, where they drank tea, drafted statements in English, and had no influence with the Iraqis."[135] The result was that Coalition forces and efforts could not easily observe the Iraqi police and were unable to shape the development of the police or prevent most abuses.

In May 2006 a new government took power. Nouri al-Maliki of the Dawa Party became prime minister, and Jabr left the MoI to become minister of finance. Rathmell explains that in looking for a new minister of interior, "it was evident [to the United States, United Kingdom, and Maliki's coalition] that a consolidation of Badr Corps control over the ministry would be disastrous for Iraq's internal political balance." Hence, Rathmell writes, "The compromise that was reached was to appoint a weak political figure with some reputation for administrative competence (Jawad al-Boulani) but to retain in place powerful Dawa, Badr [the SCIRI-affiliated militia] and Kurdish (KDP [Kurdish Democratic Party]) deputies."[136] Still, even after Bolani's appointment, brazen abuses by the Iraqi National Police continued despite increasing Coalition efforts to "re-blue" the Iraqi National Police, meaning replacing the leadership and retraining the rest of the force. In one striking case in November 2006, US officers found evidence that men in National Police uniforms abducted more than one hundred people from the Higher Education Ministry.[137] Given the priority of transitioning to Iraqi control, the Iraqi National Police could assert the prerogative to operate independently. And even where the Coalition sought to increase its supervision, the Iraqi police found ways to evade Coalition observation. Gordon and Trainer write that, faced with scrutiny by US military personnel, the "National Police played their trump card. Insisting they had a right to conduct independent operations, the police began to go out at night to round up Sunnis without coordinating [with US personnel]."[138]

The primary reason for the poor development of the Iraqi police appears to be Shia efforts to co-opt the police and use them to undertake extralegal violence. From 2005 to early 2007 I score a 1-point decline in quality due to growing accountability problems:

- Effectiveness (1 out of 3): While the police were increasing in number, they could not address the continuing insurgency or adequately ensure security.
- Accountability (0 out of 3): The police were captured by Shia militias and engaged in ethnic cleansing and violence against Sunnis.
- Rule of Law (1 out of 3): Although there were efforts to develop Iraq's legal system, there remained routine problems of compliance with the law, especially regarding sectarian violence.

Stage 3: The Surge and Continued Challenges in Building the Iraqi Police, 2007–11

Beginning in approximately February 2007, when General Petraeus took over command of Multi-National Force–Iraq, the Coalition began the "surge" strategy. The US sent approximately 30,000 additional troops to Iraq; Coalition forces deployed to more closely interact with Iraqis and take direct responsibility for protecting Iraqis, in contrast to the prior emphasis on transitioning to Iraqi control; and the Coalition sought to recruit Sunnis, including former insurgents, into the security forces or pro-government militias, known as the Sons of Iraq (SoI). By late 2007 more than 100,000 Sunnis had been recruited into these groups.[139] After October 2007 Coalition forces declined from their peak of 183,000 to 110,000 at the end of 2009, to 50,000 by the end of August 2010, and completely withdrawn by December 2011.[140]

Coalition demands for the police continued to focus on expanding their size and, to a degree, to create a more representative police force by recruiting Sunnis. Even at the height of the surge, based on the personnel present and the understood time line of US engagement, the US-led efforts could not realistically threaten Shia control of the police throughout Iraq. As discussed below, Shia leaders generally supported the US effort to reduce the violence by blunting insurgent activities both by Sunni extremists and Shia militias.[141] Nevertheless, certain aspects of the US strategy did threaten Shia patron-client networks and sectarian control of the police, especially the plan to hire Sunni members of the SoI into the police in mixed areas. The domestic opposition theory predicts effective private opposition by the Shia in these instances, and that is what occurred.

By mid-2007 violence in Iraq, at least against Coalition forces, had declined. Observers identified a range of reasons, including the start of Sunni cooperation with the Coalition, the greater presence of US forces, the demographic changes resulting from sectarian violence, and the departure of Coalition forces from some violent areas.[142] US forces planned to consolidate this progress by incorporating more Sunnis into the security forces, which was hoped would improve accountability and increase Sunni political support for the government.

There was significant variation, however, in how the police evolved across different regions of Iraq. For example, one article in 2008 noted the loyalty of the local police in Kirkuk, in northern Iraq, to Kurdish political factions and apparent activities against the Turkmen minority.[143] There was a major conflict in Basra among Shia-dominated forces, leading to the dismissal of hundreds of police officers as government forces fought the Mahdi Army, the militia loyal to Sadr.[144] In Sunni-dominated areas, such as Anbar, Sunni paramilitary groups were merged into the formal structure through the creation of "emergency response units" that reported to the provincial police chief and were paid by the MoI.[145] One analyst estimated that twenty thousand Sunnis were brought into the MoI and official police units in Anbar over the course of mid-2006 to 2007.[146] Prime Minister Maliki was, as Gordon and Trainer explain, "open to a modicum of cooperation with the Sunni tribes—at least in distant Anbar," where the presence of few if any Shia meant that cooperation would pose little threat to Shia control over the security forces in the rest of Iraq.[147]

Shia leaders were far less willing to incorporate Sunnis into the MoI in mixed ethnic areas for fear of ceding control over the security forces. For example, a former adviser noted that in towns closer to Baghdad than Fallujah, Sunnis tended to be recruited into US-financed SoI militias rather than the MoI.[148] One former US officer working in a fairly well-to-do, primarily Sunni area recounted resistance from "smooth-talking" MoI officials to recruiting the Sunni SoI members in 2007 and 2008. He explained that "there was enough push and pull that I left thinking there was progress, but nothing ever came through"—in his view, the Sunni police officers were "never going to be appointed."[149] This account offers one example of how officials within the MoI were able to delay police reform and undermine the development of a more multiethnic force, even at the height of the surge.

The Coalition also had limited leverage within the ministry bureaucracy, which remained divided among competing Shia groups. Rathmell, writing in 2007, for example, notes that "it is not enough to say that the ministry is 'controlled by Shiites' or even 'controlled by Daawa and SCIRI.' SCIRI, now the Supreme Iraqi Islamic Council (SIIC), has been gradually diverging from the Badr Corps since 2003. In the MoI, it is clearly Badr which has the upper hand, with senior officers having varying degrees of loyalty to SIIC's political leadership."[150] Similarly, a July

2007 *Los Angeles Times* article noted that the MoI was divided between different factions on different floors:

> The third- and fifth-floor administrative departments are the domain of Prime Minister Nouri Maliki's Islamic Dawa Party. . . . The sixth, home to border enforcement and the major crimes unit, belongs to the Badr Organization militia. Its leader, Deputy Minister Ahmed Khafaji, is lauded by some Western officials as an efficient administrator and suspected by others of running secret prisons. The seventh floor is intelligence, where the Badr Organization and armed Kurdish groups struggle for control.[151]

These parties and groups not only worked to limit the influence of Sunnis but also competed for resources and control among themselves.[152]

While the MoI faced administrative problems, including an inability to execute its budget, there was some existing capacity within the ministry.[153] Paul, for example, notes a degree of stability in the MoI because "it is in the interest of both the government and the key political players with influence over the Ministry that the Ministry be a functioning and capable body." Paul also points to areas where the minister and subordinate departments shared an interest in greater capability, such as the "Human Resources side of recruitment and training."[154]

Given the political challenges facing MoI's development, even an efficient and well-prepared Coalition force would have struggled. In practice, the Coalition police reform effort also faced greater bureaucratic and resourcing issues, as detailed in a September 2007 study led by retired General Jones. Even with the surge, the report noted that to assist the more than 230,000 police officers, CPATT "relies on just over 900 international police advisers and approximately 3,500 military personnel serving in Police Transition Teams."[155] Despite substantial US spending, the police were still reported to be underequipped, lacking more than firearms and basic vehicles. US efforts also faced significant bureaucratic challenges. By 2007 five different general officers had commanded the CPATT since it was created, which as one adviser explained meant that "we have not had four years to implement a training plan; we have implemented a one-year training plan four times in a row."[156] Young military officers also commanded the PTTs instead of the older, often retired civilian police advisers on the team. By one account, this reportedly hurt the credibility of the PTTs with Iraqis, who tended to have more respect for the older advisers.[157] At the ministerial level, as of mid-2007, the senior adviser visited the ministry at best several times a week, and "when Western officials visit the ministry they frequently wear body armor and move only under heavily armed escort."[158] This physical separation made it even harder for Coalition officials to provide advice and mentorship.

After a peak of 183,000 Coalition forces in October 2007, the troop presence in Iraq declined over the next four years, with the US military taking over the burden from other allies. The United States and Iraq negotiated a security agreement over the course of 2008 that came into effect in January 2009. It stipulated that US forces withdraw from Iraqi cities by June 2009 and that all US forces leave Iraq by the end of 2011.[159] US forces declined to 130,000 in August 2009 and fell under 100,000 by February 2010.[160] In the 2010 parliamentary elections, Maliki's party received fewer votes than Ayad Allawi's al-Iraqiyya party, a mixed Sunni/Shia coalition. Nevertheless, Maliki remained prime minister after forming a coalition with the Kurdish parties.[161]

The drawdown in forces significantly reduced the resources available for police reform. US leverage declined, as did the already limited visibility into the day-to-day activities of the Iraqi police. The number of Iraqi MoI personnel continued to rise, reaching 212,630 in January 2008 and 276,590 in December 2008.[162] At the same time there were reports that Maliki's government and other powerful Shia groups maintained control of various security agencies and continued to use the police and other security forces to carry out attacks on their opponents. A 2010 ICG report, for example, noted that while Bolani had made improvements in the ministry's finances, the police remained divided "into political fiefdoms."[163] The report also gave examples of how the police continued to be used for political ends: in August 2008, an emergency response unit in Diyala Province carried out an attack on the provincial government, and in December 2008 an internal affairs unit within the MoI "arrested two dozen ministry security officers on suspicion of belonging to an offshoot of the banned Baath Party and of planning a coup," although these officers were later released.[164]

Similarly, US pressure on the Maliki government to integrate the SoI into the security forces achieved little success. In September 2009 only 4,565 out of approximately 95,000 SoI members had transitioned into the security forces, rising to 8,748 in December 2010. Some 30,500 did transition to nonsecurity government jobs, but one observer emphasized that the such jobs were not safe or desirable for Sunnis.[165] The 2010 ICG report also noted that Awakening members in Baghdad and mixed areas were arrested or otherwise targeted by Shia-led state institutions while also continuing to face a threat from al-Qaeda. One Awakening leader explained, "We are caught between state terrorism and al-Qaeda's revenge, all in the context of an American troop withdrawal and the population's general hostility toward us."[166] The poor treatment of Awakening members by Maliki's government became one contributing factor to a larger sense of political marginalization among the Sunnis, which in turn is widely believed to have facilitated the development of the Islamic State of Iraq and Syria (ISIS).[167]

In December 2011, when US forces left Iraq, there were some improvements in the Iraqi police, especially in its effectiveness, but there remained challenges in accountability and the rule of law, leading to a score of 4 out of 9:

- Effectiveness (2 out of 3): The rising numbers and increasing effectiveness of the police likely contributed to the relative improvement in security after 2007. Most survey respondents in all but a few provinces believed that their area was calm, and a majority believed the Iraq police were controlling crime. However, the police remained more focused on counterinsurgency than community policing.[168]
- Accountability (1 out of 3): Maliki's government did exercise control over the police, albeit not through desired formal mechanisms. Sectarian violence by the police appeared to decline, although Sunnis were still not well represented in the police, nor did there appear to be mechanisms for the minority groups to hold the government accountable.
- Rule of Law (1 out of 3): While police abuses appeared to have declined, policing was believed to be widely politicized, especially as US leverage declined and Maliki consolidated control.

From 2007 to 2011 there was an improvement from 2 to 4 out of 9, a moderate success. However, the ongoing problems with the Iraqi police and development of ISIS raise concerns about the lingering problems following the Coalition mission.

Conclusion: Police Reform in Iraq

Overall, from 2003 to 2011, there was an overall 4-point improvement, which the rubric codes as a high success. However, this improvement is based on an initial score of 0, and the police present when the Coalition forces departed in 2011 remained politicized and of mixed quality, undermining the security and stability of Iraq. The record of sectarian violence by the police during the reform process is also troubling. The US-led effort to build the Iraq police was still a disappointment given the level of resources invested. This outcome likely has contributed to broader skepticism about the ability of the United States to improve security institutions abroad.

Each of the three main theories helps explain the trajectory of the Iraqi police's development. The domestic opposition theory explains why Shia opposition was more intense in some areas of Iraq but not others, and it offers insight into why Shia obstruction was so effective. However, the overall level of Shia opposition, especially from 2004 to 2007, is greater than the domestic opposition theory would expect given the low threat of the Coalition's demands to Shia patron-client networks.

Instead, the motivation for the particularly intense Shia private obstruction likely stemmed from the particular history of Iraq, as the path dependence theory predicts. Shia parties and militias were eager and able to co-opt the police because of the history of the repression of Shia Islamists under Saddam Hussein. This repression meant that there were already opposition parties and militias when the police reform began, such as SCIRI and the Badr Corps. Previous repression may have made it feasible for some Shia organizations to mobilize militias that could be recruited into the police. Furthermore, the lack of experience with democratic policing left little for the Coalition to build on. Still, given the dominance of Shia parties, the Iraqi police in 2011 did not have much in common with the pre-2003 policing structures. The final quality of the Iraqi police did receive the same score as its historical quality, 4 out of 9, as the path dependence theory predicts.

The international resources theory explains how the Coalition was able to establish some basic policing structures and make greater improvement in the effectiveness of the police after 2007. It also shows how specific gaps in resources—including too few police advisers, poor planning, and too short of a time horizon—hurt the Coalition's efforts. It was ultimately implausible for the Coalition to deploy sufficient resources to radically reform the Iraq police given the size of Iraq and the challenges facing the country. Even with the proposed—but not deployed—6,600 police advisers, the United States likely could not have effectively monitored and sanctioned bad behavior by the Iraqi police.

One implication of police reform is that the United States probably should have avoided intervening in Iraq, given the scale of the challenge and the inevitable political opposition from Iraqis. But accepting that an intervention and police reform effort were certain to occur, the Coalition could have improved its effectiveness by increasing bureaucratic resources, including by filling equipment gaps, improving planning, and having longer rotations. As the domestic opposition theory argues, it was also necessary to formulate demands that improved accountability and the rule of law without creating more intense Iraqi opposition.

CONCLUSION: LESSONS FROM POLICE REFORM

The two police reforms in both Bosnia and Iraq studied here were disappointing. In Bosnia the reform had little impact on the police, and the failure of the reform delegitimized the international community's reform efforts. Despite ongoing problems with the accountability and rule of law of the police in Iraq, the police reform did make some progress by increasing the number of Iraqi police available. Still, the Coalition effort failed to prevent ethnic cleansing by the police, the exclusion of the Sunni minority from government, and the development of ISIS.

All of the theories help explain the trends and outcomes in these reforms, but the domestic opposition theory has the greatest explanatory power. In Bosnia it explains why Ashdown failed with police restructuring, and in Iraq it explains the variable intensity of Shia opposition to reform and why Shia private opposition was so effective. The level of international resources does not explain the failure in Bosnia, where international resources were at their highest, although gaps in resources does explain part of the challenge in Iraq. Path dependence was an important factor in both societies, including the entity structure and ethnically based politics in Bosnia, and the Shia politics and nascent civil war in Iraq.

The Iraq case study also demonstrates two reasons that the police may be generally more difficult to reform than other institutions. First, patron-client networks are often strongly embedded in the police, which are often more subject to local control than militaries. The Iraqi political parties likely sought influence over the police both because of the opportunities for patronage and because of the risk and potential for the police to be used as an instrument of coercive violence. While there are many examples of police reforms that did not threaten patron-client networks, as in Bosnia, police reform may be generally more likely to threaten patron-client networks than other reforms. Police reform may also be more challenging because of the difficulty in recruiting effective international police trainers and advisers. International military forces tend to be more deployable, as with the NATO, and later EU, forces who supported reform in BiH (discussed in the previous chapter).[169]

Despite these difficulties, achieving progress with the police is possible and sometimes necessary. In the case of police reform in Georgia from 2004 to 2006, which is commonly identified as a major police reform success, there was a low threat to core political interests and considerable support from the United States. Mikheil Saakashvili, who had come to power as president at age thirty-four after the Rose Revolution, had few connections within the existing structure and was under great pressure to pursue reform. By initially focusing on the traffic police, Saakashvili also limited private opposition from entrenched stakeholders. As one former Georgian official recounted, "If you started with the unit that fights with organized crime, then you have a problem."[170] While the case of Iraq shows that achieving major success may not always be feasible, avoiding threatening core political interests will likely improve outcomes in the future. At the same time, Iraq also shows that foreign interveners must seek to build accountability and the rule of law or else risk empowering elites with destructive aims.

NOTES

1 Wisler, "Police Reform in Bosnia and Herzegovina," 142–58.
2 Phone interview with author, May 2014.
3 EU conditionality had, for example, worked in the case of the reform of Bosnia's tax system. In that instance, Ashdown writes that he "rang Chris Patten in late October and asked him if he would weigh in as Commissioner and say that these reforms were required if BiH wanted to join Europe. As always, he agreed." Ashdown, *Swords and Ploughshares*, 249. See also Dobbins et al., *Europe's Role in Nation-Building*, 150–51; and Muehlmann, "Police Restructuring in Bosnia-Herzegovina," 4–6.
4 European Union External Action Service, "European Union Police Mission in Bosnia and Herzegovina (EUPM)," June 2012, http://www.eeas.europa.eu/archives/csdp/missions-and-operations/eupm-bih/pdf/25062012_factsheet_eupm-bih_en.pdf; and Florian Bieber, "Policing the Peace after Yugoslavia: Police Reform between External Imposition and Domestic Reform," GRIPS Policy Research Center, January 2010, 10, http://www3.grips.ac.jp/~pinc/data/10-07.pdf.
5 Daniel Lindvall, for example, describes the Yugoslav structures as highly politicized—"an integral component of the political power, being directly subordinate to the Minister of Interior." "Limits of the European Vision in Bosnia and Herzegovina," 64–65.
6 Lindvall, 65; and Wisler, "Police Reform in Bosnia," 148.
7 Wisler, "Police Reform in Bosnia"; and Bieber, "Policing the Peace after Yugoslavia."
8 Wisler, "Police Reform in Bosnia," 140–41.
9 According to an EU-sponsored report, in 2001, 75 percent of the population felt very or rather safe walking alone after dark, compared with 77 percent in Switzerland and 64 percent in Poland in 2000. Bosnia had approximately 16,150 police in 2004 for about 3.72 million inhabitants, which is approximately 1 police per 230 inhabitants, compared with a European standard of 1:330. Policing accounted for 9.2 percent of public expenditures, compared with 4 percent in Hungary. ICMPD, "Financial, Organisational and Administrative Assessment," 33, 62. See also ICG, "Policing the Police in Bosnia: A Further Reform Agenda," Europe Report No. 130, May 10, 2002, 46.
10 With exceptions of the police in Brčko district, the State Border Service, and the court police, which Collantes-Celador noted were "genuinely multiethnic." Gemma Collantes-Celador, "Police Reform: Peacebuilding through 'Democratic Policing'?," *International Peacekeeping* 12, no. 3 (October 1, 2005): 367–68.
11 ICG, "Bosnia's Stalled Police Reform: No Progress, No EU," *Europe Report*, no. 164 (September 6, 2005): 17.
12 Toal and Dahlman, *Bosnia Remade*, 180–81.
13 An ICG report in 2005 explains, "Especially in the RS, police still act according to the will of their political masters, particularly when it comes to war crimes." ICG, "Bosnia's Stalled Police Reform," 2–4.
14 Toal and Dahlman, *Bosnia Remade*, 293–96; and ICG, "Bosnia's Stalled Police Reform," 2–4.

15 See Dan Bilefsky, "Bosnian Serb Leader Accused of Corruption," *New York Times*, February 24, 2009; and Berislav Jelinič, "Dodik's Agents Hiding Assassin," *Nacional*, November 10, 2008. http://arhiva.nacional.hr/en/clanak/49834/dodiks-agents-hiding-assassin.

16 Lindvall writes, "The Croats never became as intensely engaged in the police reform negotiations as the other two groups since the reform proposals were largely acceptable to them from the outset. . . . The Bosniak politicians perceived the intentions of the international community as well-meaning, designed to improve the policing system and reintegrate the police agencies that had been fragmented by the war." Lindvall, "Limits of the European Vision," 126, 129. See also Bieber, *Post-War Bosnia*, 41.

17 Christopher Patten, "Letter to Mr. Adnan Terzic, Prime Minister of Bosnia & Herzegovina," November 16, 2004, http://www.ohr.int/ohr-dept/rule-of-law-pillar/prc/prc-letters/pdf/patten-letter.pdf. See also Muehlmann, "Police Restructuring in Bosnia-Herzegovina," 4–6; and Lindvall, "Limits of the European Vision," 77–92.

18 Collantes-Celador, "Becoming 'European' through Police Reform," 239.

19 Lindvall, "Limits of the European Vision," 134–39.

20 Collantes-Celador similarly observes, "Some local stakeholders—mainly Republika Srpska—feared that it would ultimately entail a further erosion of the Entities (and ultimately their disappearance) by transferring even more competences to the State level." Collantes-Celador, "Becoming 'European' through Police Reform," 238. See also Lindvall, "Limits of the European Vision," 112–28.

21 Muehlmann, "Police Restructuring in Bosnia-Herzegovina," 8.

22 ICG, "Bosnia's Stalled Police Reform," 8.

23 Quoted in Lindvall, "Limits of the European Vision," 125.

24 OHR, "Statement at the International Agency's Joint Press Conference in Mostar," March 16, 2005, http://web.archive.org/web/20130411201031/http://www.ohr.int/ohr-dept/rule-of-law-pillar/prc/prc-statements/default.asp?content_id=34277; see also Lindvall, 92–102.

25 Grodana Katana, "Bosnian Serbs Quash Plans for United Police," *Global Voice Balkans*, August 2, 2005, http://iwpr.net/report-news/bosnian-serbs-quash-eu-plan-united-police.

26 OHR, "Speech by the High Representative, Paddy Ashdown to RSNA," April 21, 2005, http://web.archive.org/web/20060205155035/http://www.ohr.int/ohr-dept/presso/presssp/default.asp?content_id=34540.

27 Muehlmann, "Police Restructuring in Bosnia-Herzegovina," 10.

28 Lindvall, "Limits of the European Vision," 192.

29 Ivanić observed, "There was no one who was ready to accept the abolition of the entity police. In reality, none of us were ready to accept, no one had a mandate. I did not and I know that Čavić did not have any support." Quoted in Lindvall, 148; see also ICG, "Bosnia's Stalled Police Reform," 8–9.

30 Quoted in Lindvall, "Limits of the European Vision," 195.

31 ICG, "Ensuring Bosnia's Future," 19–20.

32 Lindvall, "Limits of the European Vision," 212.

33 Muehlmann writes, "The proposed agreement . . . was clearly contrary to the expressed wishes of the international community. Nevertheless, the international community, and

Ashdown in particular, had reached a point where a facesaving way out was desperately needed." Muehlmann, "Police Restructuring in Bosnia-Herzegovina," 10.

34 Phone interview with Paddy Ashdown, May 2014.

35 ICG, "Ensuring Bosnia's Future," 4–9; and OHR, "HR and His Deputies," website (n.d.), http://www.ohr.int/?page_id=1153.

36 Leroux-Martin, *Diplomatic Counterinsurgency*, 65–70; Tolksdorf, "Incoherent Peacebuilding," 68–69; and "Cracking Up," *Economist*, October 25, 2007. http://www.economist.com/node/10026370.

37 Interviews with EUPM official, Sarajevo, June 2008.

38 ICG, "Bosnia's Incomplete Transition," 11–12.

39 Interview with international official, Sarajevo, June 2008.

40 A Bosniak official explained that from Silajdžić's perspective, Dodik's proposal would mean that the police would still be effectively controlled by the RS since the "RS police would still practically be RS employees." Interview with Bosniak official, Sarajevo, July 2008. See also Lindvall, "Limits of the European Vision," 158–68.

41 Lindvall, "Limits of the European Vision," 167.

42 OHR, "OHR/EUSR: European Commission Interprets Principles," September 18, 2007, http://www.ohr.int/?ohr_archive=ohreusr-european-commission-interprets-principles; and OHR, "Press Conference Statement by the High Representative and EU Special Representative in BiH, Miroslav Lajčák after the Meeting with NGO Representatives," http://www.ohr.int/?ohr_archive=press-conference-statement-by-the-high-representative-and-eu-special-representative-in-bih-miroslav-lajak-after-the-meeting-with-ngo-representatives.

43 Interviews and correspondence with former international official, March 2013.

44 Leroux-Martin, *Diplomatic Counterinsurgency*, 20–25; see also ICG, "Bosnia's Incomplete Transition," 12–13.

45 Leroux-Martin, *Diplomatic Counterinsurgency*, 60–62.

46 ICG, "Bosnia's Incomplete Transition," 13; and Leroux-Martin, *Diplomatic Counterinsurgency*, 35–36.

47 Ian Bancroft, "An Unhealthy State," *Guardian*, November 26, 2007.

48 OHR, "Declaration by the Steering Board of the Peace Implementation Council," October 31, 2007, http://www.ohr.int/?p=38269.

49 Leroux-Martin, *Diplomatic Counterinsurgency*, 38–43.

50 Leroux-Martin, 55–60.

51 ICG, "Bosnia's Incomplete Transition," 13.

52 Leroux-Martin, *Diplomatic Counterinsurgency*, 67–68.

53 Bancroft, "Unhealthy State."

54 Leroux-Martin, *Diplomatic Counterinsurgency*, 68–70. See also ICG, "Bosnia's Incomplete Transition," 13; and Tolksdorf, "Incoherent Peacebuilding," 68.

55 Leroux-Martin, *Diplomatic Counterinsurgency*, 73–81; and OHR, "Decision Enacting the Authentic Interpretation of the Law on Changes and Amendments to the Law on the Council of Ministers of Bosnia and Herzegovina," December 3, 2007, http://www.ohr.int/?p=67105.

56 Interview with senior EU official, Sarajevo, June 2008. See also Outi Keranen, "International Statebuilding as Contentious Politics: The Case of Post Conflict Bosnia and Herzegovina," *Nationalities Papers* 41, no. 3 (2013): 360–61.

57 Interview with senior EU official, Sarajevo, June 2008.

58 In addition to a 12-point gain in Serbs who believed current structures were effective at fighting crime from July 2005 to June 2007, Bosniaks who shared this view increased slightly from 23 to 24 percent, while Croats declined to 17 percent from 20 percent. Lindvall, "Limits of the European Vision," 207, 217. On regional homicide rates, see Benjamin Petrini, "Homicide Rate Database 1995–2008," World Bank, January 2010, http://siteresources.worldbank.org/EXTCPR/Resources/407739-1267651559887/Homicide_Rate_Dataset.pdf.

59 European Commission, "Bosnia and Herzegovina 2007 Progress Report," November 6, 2007, SEC(2007) 1430, 53–54, https://ec.europa.eu/neighbourhood-enlargement/sites/near/files/pdf/key_documents/2007/nov/bosnia_herzegovina_progress_reports_en.pdf.

60 Toal and Dahlman, *Bosnia Remade*, chaps. 9–10.

61 European Commission, "Bosnia and Herzegovina 2007 Progress Report," 54. The EU framed these problems as more serious for Bosnia than for Serbia, for example. European Commission, "Serbia 2007 Progress Report," November 6, 2007, SEC(2007) 1435, 42–43, https://ec.europa.eu/neighbourhood-enlargement/sites/near/files/pdf/key_documents/2007/nov/serbia_progress_reports_en.pdf.

62 See also Toal and Dahlman, *Bosnia Remade*, 316.

63 OHR, "Agenda 5+2," 2015, http://www.ohr.int/?page_id=1318; ICG, "Bosnia's Incomplete Transition"; ICG, "Bosnia's Future"; and Leroux-Martin, *Diplomatic Counterinsurgency*, 77–81.

64 Gordon and Trainor, *Endgame*, 228.

65 This figure does not include the separate costs of funding the US military presence. SIGIR, "Iraqi Police Development Program: Opportunities for Improved Program Accountability and Budget Transparency," SIGIR 12-006, October 24, 2011, http://psm.du.edu/media/documents/us_research_and_oversight/sigir/audits/us_sigir_12-006.pdf; and Michael O'Hanlon and Jason H. Campbell, "Iraq Index," Brookings, February 26, 2009, https://www.brookings.edu/wp-content/uploads/2016/07/index20090226.pdf.

66 Quoted in ICG, "Loose Ends," 18.

67 Jones et al., *Establishing Law and Order after Conflict*, 132; and Michael Moss and David Rohde, "Misjudgments Marred US Plans for Iraqi Police," *New York Times*, May 21, 2006. See also table A.1 in the appendix. World Bank, "Population, Total, Iraq," https://data.worldbank.org/indicator/SP.POP.TOTL?locations=IQ.

68 Makiya, *Republic of Fear*, 36–38.

69 Ayubi, *Over-Stating the Arab State*, 302–3.

70 Makiya, *Republic of Fear*, ix–xv, 1–37; and Blaydes, *State of Repression*.

71 In addition to Makiya, *Republic of Fear*; Blaydes, *State of Repression*; and Ayubi, *Over-Stating the Arab State*, see also Christoph Wilcke, "A Hard Place: The United States and

the Creation of a New Security Apparatus in Iraq," *Civil Wars* 8, no. 2 (June 1, 2006): 125–26; and Sassoon, *Saddam Hussein's Ba'th Party*.

72 Rathmell et al., *Developing Iraq's Security Sector*, 42–45.

73 Rathmell et al., 42–45. See also Dobbins et al., *Occupying Iraq*, 71–75.

74 Quoted in Dobbins et al., *Occupying Iraq*, 72.

75 See Allawi, *Occupation of Iraq*, 246–48, 316–19, 414–15; Gordon and Trainor, *Endgame*, chap. 14; Dodge, *Iraq—From War to a New Authoritarianism*, 56–61.

76 See Andrew Rathmell, "Fixing Iraq's Internal Security Forces: Why Is Reform of the Ministry of Interior so Hard?," Center for Strategic and International Studies, November 2007, 10; "Gangs of Iraq: Interview with Matthew Sherman," PBS *Frontline*, October 4, 2006, https://www.pbs.org/wgbh/pages/frontline/gangsofiraq/interviews/sherman.html; and interviews with former US officials, Washington, DC, March–April 2018.

77 Allawi, *Occupation of Iraq*, 137–40; and Dodge, *Iraq*, 62–69.

78 For example, Shia officials' reactions to the news that Iraqi police were holding and torturing ex-Ba'athists in the Jadriya bunker. See Gordon and Trainor, *Endgame*, 185–88.

79 Bremer, *My Year in Iraq*, 19, 31–32.

80 Dobbins et al., *Occupying Iraq*, 73.

81 Rathmell et al., *Developing Iraq's Security Sector*, 45–46.

82 For example, CPA documents proposed instilling norms of democratic policing (such as "consider the individual citizens as the client of the police rather than the state"), vetting the police, and ensuring the police reflected the country's overall sectarian and ethnic balance. Memo from Bernard B. Kerik to Ambassador L. Paul Bremer, "Subject: Recommendations and Strategies for 'Standing Up an Interim Police Service,'" CPA, May 30, 2003, copy with author. This document, and other CPA documents cited here, are from unclassified CPA materials provided to the RAND Corporation; see Dobbins et al. *Occupying Iraq*, iii.

83 Rathmell, "Fixing Iraq's Internal Security Forces," 7.

84 Bremer, *My Year in Iraq*, 128; and "Iraq Status Update," July 2, 2003, CPA, copy with author.

85 Rathmell et al., *Developing Iraq's Security Sector*, 45–47.

86 Dobbins et al., *Occupying Iraq*, 76.

87 Sherman and Paul, "Role of Police," 234.

88 Moss and Rohde, "Misjudgments Marred US Plans for Iraqi Police."

89 Moss and Rohde; and "Iraq Police Training Program"; and attachments, August 31, 2003, CPA, copy with author.

90 Bremer, *My Year in Iraq*, 152–57, 168–69.

91 Dobbins et al., *Occupying Iraq*, 76. For his part, Kerik observed in a 2006 article, "Looking back, I really don't know what their plan was" for the development of the Iraqi police. Moss and Rohde, "Misjudgments Marred US Plans for Iraqi Police."

92 Moss and Rohde, "Misjudgments Marred US Plans for Iraqi Police."

93 Inspectors General, US Departments of State and Defense, "Interagency Assessment of Iraq Police Training."

94 Dobbins et al., *Occupying Iraq*, 79.

95 Rosen, *In the Belly of the Green Bird*, 106–8.

96 Rosen writes that he "was told by Fallujan police and soldiers that they would shoot Americans if they came in" to the city, as the US Marines planned to after the killing of US contractors. Rosen, 144.

97 Jon Lee Anderson, "The Uprising: Shia and Sunnis Put aside Their Differences," *New Yorker*, April 26, 2004, https://www.newyorker.com/magazine/2004/05/03/the-uprising.

98 Dobbins et al., *Occupying Iraq*, 69; and Perito, *Where Is the Lone Ranger When We Need Him?*, 172.

99 Memo from Paul Bremer to Secretary Rumsfeld, February 3, 2004, available at http://library.rumsfeld.com/doclib/sp/345/From%20Paul%20Bremer%20re%20Security%20Assessment%2002-03-2004.pdf.

100 Interviews with former US official and analyst, Washington, DC, March–April 2018; and "Gangs of Iraq."

101 Dobbins et al., *Occupying Iraq*, 316–17.

102 Dobbins et al., 317.

103 Allawi, *Occupation of Iraq*, 317–19.

104 Dobbins et al., *Occupying Iraq*, 319–20.

105 "Gangs of Iraq."

106 "Gangs of Iraq"; and interview with former CPA officials, 2015.

107 Letter to H.E. L. Paul Bremer from the Ministry of Interior, November 24, 2003, CPA, copy with author.

108 Perito, "Coalition Provisional Authority's Experience," 5; and Sherman and Paul, "Role of Police," 231–32.

109 Paul, "Estimation of the Internal Politics."

110 See also Joel Wing, "American Negligence in Iraq, or How the United States Failed to Plan for Securing the Country: Part One of a Two Part Interview with Jerry Burke, Former Advisor to the Baghdad Police and Interior Ministry," February 9, 2012, https://musingsoniraq.blogspot.com/2012/02/american-negligence-in-iraq-or-how.html.

111 Dobbins et al., *Occupying Iraq*, 158; and Moss and Rohde, "Misjudgments Marred US Plans for Iraqi Police."

112 Casey, *Strategic Reflections*, 38–39, 58.

113 Gordon and Trainor, *Endgame*, 88–94.

114 Jones et al., *Establishing Law and Order after Conflict*, 128; and Curt Tarnoff, "Iraq: Reconstruction Assistance," *Congressional Research Service*, August 7, 2009, 3, 10.

115 Ali Allawi (also the prime minister's cousin) explains that the new government pursued a policy for the security forces based on two premises, "the large-scale induction of professional officers" from the former regime and "to rely on the tribal and clan affiliations of the main Interim Government protagonists and flood the new Iraqi security forces with these recruits." Allawi, *Occupation of Iraq*, 319.

116 Interview with former US adviser; see also Daniel Scher, interview with Matthew Sherman, Innovations for Successful Societies, Princeton University, July 9, 2008, https://successfulsocieties.princeton.edu/sites/successfulsocieties/files/interviews/transcripts/3257/Matthew_Sherman.txt.

117 Allawi, *Occupation of Iraq*, 319; Perito, "Coalition Provisional Authority's Experience," 5; Gordon and Trainor, *Endgame*, 114, 140; and Peter Maass, "The Salvadorization of Iraq," *New York Times Magazine*, May 1, 2005.
118 Interview with former US adviser, April 2018, Washington, DC.
119 Gordon and Trainor, *Endgame*, 140–47.
120 Paul, "Estimation of the Internal Politics," 19.
121 Perito, *Where Is the Lone Ranger When We Need Him?*, 177.
122 Paul, "Estimation of the Internal Politics," 19.
123 "Gangs of Iraq."
124 Interviews with former US advisers and officers, March and April 2018, Washington, DC.
125 Jim Garamore, "Ambassador Says 2006 to Be 'Year of Police' for Iraq," American Forces Press Service, December 20, 2005, http://web.archive.org/web/20141211071743/http://www.defense.gov/news/newsarticle.aspx?id=18495.
126 "Gangs of Iraq."
127 Jones, "Report of the Independent Commission" (hereafter, Jones Report), 91.
128 Interviews with former US advisers and officers, March and April 2018, Washington, DC.
129 Interview with former US officer, March 2018, Washington, DC.
130 Interviews with former US officers and advisers, March and April 2018, Washington, DC; see also Gordon and Trainor, *Endgame*, chap. 9–11.
131 Inspectors General US Departments of State and Defense, "Interagency Assessment of Iraq Police Training," 37–44; and Dobbins et al., *Europe's Role in Nation-Building*, 246.
132 Interview with former US police adviser, March 2018, Washington, DC; and DoD, "Measuring Stability and Security in Iraq," November 2006, Report to Congress in accordance with Appropriations Act 2007 (Section 9010), 33, https://archive.defense.gov/pubs/pdfs/9010Quarterly-Report-20061216.pdf.
133 Interview with former US police adviser, March 2018, Washington, DC; and Casey, *Strategic Reflections*, 58.
134 Interview with former US police adviser, March 2018, Washington, DC.
135 Perito, "Coalition Provisional Authority's Experience," 179–81.
136 Rathmell, "Fixing Iraq's Internal Security Forces," 7; see also Gordon and Trainor, *Endgame*, 195–98.
137 Gordon and Trainor, *Endgame*, 226–27; and Jim Garamone, "Violence, Progress Coexist in Iraq, Casey Says," DoD News, October 10, 2006, http://archive.defense.gov/news/NewsArticle.aspx?ID=1533.
138 Gordon and Trainor, *Endgame*, 225.
139 Biddle, Friedman, and Shapiro, "Testing the Surge," 22–25.
140 Michael O'Hanlon and Ian Livingston, "Iraq Index," Brookings, January 31, 2012 [dated 2011 in error], https://www.brookings.edu/wp-content/uploads/2016/07/index20120131.pdf; see also Brennan et al., *Ending the U.S. War in Iraq*, 67–69.
141 See also Gordon and Trainor, *Endgame*, chap. 25.
142 Biddle, Friedman, and Shapiro, "Testing the Surge"; and interviews with US officers and advisers, March–April 2018, Washington, DC.

143 Richard A. Oppel Jr., "Kurdish Control of Kirkuk Creates a Powder Keg," *New York Times*, August 18, 2008.
144 Stephen Farrell and Qais Mizher, "Iraq Dismisses 1,300 after Basra Offensive," *New York Times*, April 14, 2008.
145 Gordon and Trainor, *Endgame*, 253.
146 Interviews with a former US adviser, March–April 2018, Washington, DC.
147 Gordon and Trainor, *Endgame*, 252.
148 Interviews with a former US adviser, March–April 2018, Washington, DC.
149 Interview with former US officer, March 2018, Washington, DC.
150 Rathmell, "Fixing Iraq's Internal Security Forces," 8.
151 Ned Parker, "Interior Ministry Mirrors Chaos of a Fractured Iraq," *Los Angeles Times*, July 30, 2007, http://articles.latimes.com/2007/jul/30/world/fg-interior30.
152 Jones Report, 90.
153 Jones Report, 90.
154 Paul, "Estimation of the Internal Politics," 24–25.
155 Jones Report, 100–101, 103.
156 Jones Report, 99.
157 Jones Report, 100.
158 Jones Report, 88.
159 Brennan et al., "Ending the US War in Iraq," 62–63.
160 O'Hanlon and Livingston, "Iraq Index," January 31, 2012.
161 Gordon and Trainor, *Endgame*, chaps. 33–34.
162 O'Hanlon and Livingston, "Iraq Index," January 31, 2012.
163 ICG, "Loose Ends," 20–21.
164 ICG, 20–21.
165 O'Hanlon and Livingston, "Iraq Index," January 31, 2012; and interview with former US adviser, March 2018.
166 ICG, "Loose Ends," 27–28; interview with former US adviser, March 2018.
167 Ehab Zahriyeh, "How ISIL Became a Major Force with Only a Few Thousand Fighters," *Al Jazeera America*, June 19, 2014, http://america.aljazeera.com/articles/2014/6/19/isil-thousands-fighters.html; Zachary Laub, "The Islamic State," Council on Foreign Relations, August 10, 2016, https://www.cfr.org/backgrounder/islamic-state; and Dan Murphy, "Iraq's Exiled Vice President Sentenced to Death as Violence Grows," *Christian Science Monitor*, September 9, 2012, https://www.csmonitor.com/World/Security-Watch/Backchannels/2012/0909/Iraq-s-exiled-vice-president-sentenced-to-death-as-violence-grows.
168 DoD, "Measuring Stability and Security in Iraq," 38, 51–53; and interviews with former US officials, Washington, March–April 2018.
169 I am grateful to Roy Licklider for helping to clarify this point.
170 Matthew Devlin, "Seizing the Reform Moment: Rebuilding Georgia's Police, 2004–2006," in *Innovations for Successful Societies* (Princeton, NJ: Princeton University, 2010), 5–8, https://successfulsocieties.princeton.edu/sites/successfulsocieties/files/Policy_Note_ID126.pdf.

CHAPTER SIX

DEFENSE REFORM *in* UKRAINE

In 2015, following the February 2014 Euromaidan protests and subsequent conflict in eastern Ukraine, the United States and other NATO members supported defense reform in Ukraine. Like the reforms detailed in chapter 3–5, Western organizations sought to make Ukraine's defense institutions more effective, accountable, and compliant with law. However, Western support for Ukraine had significantly lower resources and less leverage. Foreign advisers had no executive mandate, little credibility in offering NATO membership as a condition for reform, fewer than five hundred foreign trainers, and major constraints on material assistance, including a restriction on lethal aid. Foreign advisers also typically framed their proposed changes for Ukraine's institutions as recommendation rather than demands, given the different political context. Unlike Bosnia, Kosovo, or Iraq, Ukraine faced a real and present external threat, and its ethnolinguistic divide was also far less clearly drawn. Another difference was that Ukrainian officials led the reform agenda. Ukrainian officials specified the goal of meeting EU and NATO standards, and initiated a RAND Corporation project, which I worked on, to make recommendations to achieve those goals.

Despite these differences and strong popular support for reform, I find that the same dynamic that occurred in the other cases also occurred in Ukraine: Western reformers undermined reform by asking for changes that provoked opposition. Western recommendations were the most implemented where they posed little threat to the ruling elites' patron-client networks, such as in reorganizing command and control over the military operation in eastern Ukraine and the procurement of basic supplies such as food or fuel. By contrast, there was little progress in the more politically sensitive areas, such as weapons procurement and the military industrial complex. By avoiding recommendations that threatened these networks, Western reform could likely have achieved greater progress in improving Ukraine's institutions. The example of defense reform in Ukraine shows how the domestic opposition theory has broader applicability outside of highly resourced post-conflict cases.

The record of reform in Ukraine also offers some support for the two existing theories from the literature. As the international resource theory would expect, the low resourcing of Western efforts meant that Western organizations had little responsibility for the significant improvement in defense institutions in Ukraine from 2014 to 2018. Path dependence and preexisting institutions were also important, as structures and practices from Ukraine's past, especially Soviet-era models, reappeared in its improved institutions. Beyond the specific predictions for these theories, this case study shows the remarkable achievements of Ukraine in rapidly building a capable military to defend itself against one of the world's most capable adversaries.

CONTEXT

On February 22, 2014, Viktor Yanukovych left power as president of Ukraine after months of pro-Western protests in Maidan Square in Kyiv. The protests emerged after President Vladimir Putin of Russia pressured Yanukovych to reject the Association Agreement with the European Union out of concern that the agreement would undermine Ukraine's alignment with Russia. On February 27, 2014, Russian forces began an operation to seize the Ukrainian province of Crimea, which Russia would later annex. In the following months, with Russian support, a separatist movement developed in the Donetsk and Luhansk oblasts of eastern Ukraine. The conflict between the Russian-backed separatists and Ukrainian-aligned forces escalated into a full-blown conventional conflict in late 2014.[1]

The United States, its allies, and various Western nations supported the new Ukrainian government. They had backed the pro-reform Euromaidan movement and wanted to ensure that Ukraine was free to choose its alignment with the European Union and NATO. Ukraine's Western partners also sought to deter subsequent Russian aggression. The United States, European Union, and International Monetary Fund planned to provide some $27 billion over two years to stabilize the economy.[2] However, Western military support was politically sensitive. Western countries wanted to avoid a direct conflict with Russia, which they feared could emerge if they provided lethal assistance, supplied military advisers in the conflict area, or proceeded with Ukraine's NATO accession.[3] Western defense reform efforts were therefore slow to develop and, where they did occur, were carefully calibrated. Western efforts were also diffuse, involving separate assistance from many countries in addition to support from multilateral institutions. Western military assistance did increase over time. From February 2014 to February 2015 there was very low level of assistance, including limited nonlethal material assistance. After 2015 Western assistance increased with a greater advisory effort, enhanced US training, and some limited lethal assistance with the transfer of Javelin antitank missiles in 2018. Even at its highest level, Western assistance was paltry compared to the involvement in Iraq or the Balkan cases, especially compared with Ukraine's population of 45 million people.

Defense reform was crucial for Ukraine because of the poor quality of the Ukrainian defense establishment when the war began. Long before the conflict, upon gaining independence, Ukraine had, by one account, "the second most powerful armed forces in Europe after Russia," with 780,000 service personnel, nuclear weapons, 1,100 planes, and a wide range of tanks, armored personnel carriers, and other equipment.[4] I therefore rate Ukraine's historical military effectiveness as 3 out of 3. However, in the next twenty-five years, Ukraine's military effectiveness atrophied since Ukraine perceived little threat from its neighbors and spent very little on defense. By 2012 one report notes that only "1.2 percent of weaponry in service had been procured during the previous decade," and battalion-level live-fire exercises were few and far between.[5] When the war broke out, only 6,000 soldiers of the 41,000-strong Ukrainian army were available for use.[6] At the beginning of the war, I therefore rate Ukraine's military effectiveness as a 1 out of 3. Accountability and rule of law, by contrast, had never been strong. International assessments in 2015 (detailed below) identified the same problems as prior analyses, including an unclear division between the presidency and cabinet of ministers, weak civilian control, insufficient parliamentary oversight, unfair conscription, and corruption in procurement.[7] I therefore rate the historical and immediate pre-reform accountability and obedience to law both as 1 out of 3, meaning that when Western reform efforts began, the defense institution had a total score of 3 out of 9.

Western support for reform posed little threat to Ukrainian nationalist goals. Ukraine's main nationalist goals relevant to defense policy were ensuring military effectiveness against Russian-backed forces in Ukraine and deterring further Russian aggression. Ukraine's politics had historically been divided into two key issues: whether to align more with Russia or the West and whether to give official status to the widely spoken Russian language.[8] However, the events of early 2014, including Russia's seizure of Crimea, substantially strengthened pro-Western political sentiment throughout the country and reinforced pro-Ukrainian patriotism across the political spectrum, solidifying support for a stronger military. One article, for example, notes the "unexpected rise of a militant Russophone Ukrainian nationalism in Southern and Eastern Ukraine," despite a general trend of higher historical support for Russia in the eastern part of Ukraine.[9] Still, there was some concern about officials within Ukraine's defense establishment who remained loyal to Russia—despite Ukrainian efforts to remove them from their positions.[10]

The ruling elites' patron-client networks faced a greater threat from defense reform. One possible challenge was to the existing leadership of defense institutions who could lose status or authority due to reform. Analysts emphasize that government bureaucracy in Ukraine was highly personalized. The leaders of ministries and agencies were reported to be associated with competing political parties or political groups linked to rich and powerful Ukrainian oligarchs. Within particular ministries or agencies, staff members were often personally loyal to particular leaders, although not all of these defense officials were necessarily clearly linked to oligarchic clans.[11] Any reform would have winners and losers within these patronage systems. A second, related challenge was the possible economic impact of reform on Ukraine's leaders or oligarchs. Ukrainian media reports and foreign analysts highlighted the economic control of senior leaders of Ukraine over the defense industrial sector. For example, one 2016 article details how allies of President Petro Poroshenko gained control of the defense-related department within the Ministry of Economic Development and Trade, which managed aspects of defense procurement.[12] Similarly, a 2018 article quotes Serhiy Leshchenko, a member of parliament in Poroshenko's Bloc, observing that "money flows in defence are divided between the Poroshenko's Bloc and the Narodnyi [People's] Front, so that none of them would feel left out."[13] It is difficult to uncover to what extent personal interest or economic motives shaped elite responses to reform, especially given the denials of Ukrainian officials accused of corruption and conflicts of interests and given the fact that other issues could explain opposition, such as intellectual disagreements with Western approaches.[14] At a minimum, it is clear that defense reform could have an impact on the economic interests of powerful groups in Ukraine.

After discussing the context of the defense reform, I describe the reform of Ukraine's institutions in two stages: during the most intense fighting, from March 2014 to February 2015, when there was little international support, and after 2015, following the Minsk II agreement, when Western assistance increased (see table 6.1). This chapter draws from the analysis in the publicly released 2015 RAND report, in addition to available primary and secondary sources and phone interviews with foreign and Ukrainian analysts and officials.[15]

STAGE 1: UKRAINE'S MILITARY DEVELOPMENT, FEBRUARY 2014–FEBRUARY 2015

In March and April 2014 paramilitary forces backed by Russia began to organize and seize buildings in cities in eastern Ukraine, building on anti-Maidan protests in these cities. By early April these pro-Russian groups had articulated a separatist

TABLE 6.1. Defense Reform in Ukraine

Stage	Threat of Western recommendations	Form of opposition	Resources	Relative success	Quality of institution at the end of the stage (out of 9)
Quality of institutions at highest level of development (effectiveness in 1990, accountability/rule of law in 2013)	—	—	—	—	5
Quality of institution at beginning of reform (February 2014)	—	—	—	—	3
1. Immediate post-Maidan period (February 2014–February 2015)	None	None	Very low	Limited	4
2. Improvement under international assistance (2015–18)	Variable PCNs	Variable private	Low	Moderate	6

Note: PCN = patron-client network.

agenda and announced the formation of the Donetsk People's Republic and, later, the Luhansk People's Republic. During this period approximately forty thousand Russian troops were also stationed near the Russian border.[16]

In mid-April Ukraine deployed what forces it had to fight the separatist movement.[17] Because of the poor state of the military and the urgent need for combat forces, "volunteer" paramilitary units were created, such as the Donbas, Azov, and Dnipro-I battalions.[18] Ukraine restarted obligatory military service, including both conscription (the recruitment of eighteen- to twenty-five-year-olds) and the mobilization of older individuals with previous military service. Drawing primarily on mobilized personnel to staff combat units, Ukraine began to deploy forces to the east and make progress against the separatists in June and July.[19] However, Russia began to arm the separatists with more potent air defenses, leading to the shoot-down of several Ukrainian aircraft and, in July 2014, the downing of civilian Malaysian Airlines Flight 17.[20] By July there were also reports of improvements in Ukraine's military, including in command and control and morale.[21]

By mid-August, Ukrainian government-aligned forces gained territory and were on the verge of defeating the separatists in the key city of Ilovaisk. This progress occurred even as Ukrainian forces were composed of a mix of regular military and volunteer units with few functional armored vehicles and difficulty communicating. At this point Russia escalated, deploying conventional military units over the border to prevent Ukrainian forces from seizing Ilovaisk. By one account, eight Russian army battalion tactical groups crossed the border and engaged the Ukrainian forces. After sustaining significant casualties, the Ukrainian forces were forced to retreat in disarray.[22] Soon thereafter, in early September, Ukraine negotiated a cease-fire at Minsk with Russia, which included the decentralization of power to the regions of Ukraine and the deployment of a monitoring mission by the Organization for Security and Cooperation in Europe. Despite the Minsk Agreement, the conflict continued, and NATO officials began to publicize the Russian presence.[23] The separatists gained ground, leading to a second negotiation and cease-fire agreement, known as Minsk II, on February 12, 2015.[24] Even after the second agreement, fighting continued. Ukrainian forces suffered a major defeat in Debaltseve, which was in part attributed to flaws in Ukraine's command and control, in particular a failure of the military leadership to order a timely retreat or counterattack.[25] After the defeat at Debaltseve, military lines stabilized, but there was continued shelling and sporadic increases in violence.[26]

The battles at Ilovaisk and Debaltseve demonstrated both the continuing weaknesses of the Ukrainian military and its rapid progress. In February 2014 Ukraine was barely able to deploy forces, but by late 2014 and early 2015 it had sufficient combat ability to force Russia to escalate to prevent the defeat of the separatists.[27] Improvements in Ukraine's logistics system mainly seemed to be due to Ukraine reconstructing the Soviet-era systems, with volunteers filling key gaps pending progress in Ukraine's formal institutions.[28] Behind the front, there were other noticeable improvements, such as updating the regulations governing supplying military forces and—in large part thanks to the contribution of volunteers—beginning the development of a transparent e-procurement system called Prozorro.[29] Nevertheless, in many areas, the basic functioning of the Ministry of Defense (MoD) and General Staff did not appear to have dramatically changed since 2014.[30]

Western support played a relatively small role in the improvement of the Ukrainian military from February 2014 to February 2015. By the summer of 2014 the United States, Canada, and other donors had provided nonlethal assistance such as body armor, medical supplies, radios, helmets, and uniforms.[31] Some Western contributions were apparently diverted—for example, there were reports of US "meal, ready-to-eats," commonly known as MREs, being resold online. To the extent Western equipment made its way to the front, it did not appear to impact the supply and equipment problems facing the Ukrainian military.[32] NATO also created trust funds to improve logistics, command and control, and cyber defense, which became operational in December 2014 and supplemented NATO's existing advisory or small-scale training and education programs.[33] The inaugural Ukraine-US Joint Commission—what would become the main organization to provide and coordinate bilateral military support—only happened on October 17, 2014, after the first Minsk cease-fire and some of the most intense fighting.[34] The imperative to improve Ukraine's defense institutions intensified as the Russian presence became publicized in late 2014.

STAGE 2: WESTERN-LED DEFENSE REFORM, FEBRUARY 2015–2018

In late 2014 and early 2015, Ukrainian and Western officials began to develop a somewhat more concrete vision for how Ukraine's defense institution should be reformed. Unlike the reform efforts described in previous chapters, Ukrainian officials had a lead role in determining the goals of reform and articulated the objective that its defense institutions should align with NATO standards.[35] This goal appeared to serve at least two functions: to advance Ukraine's accession to NATO and, with it, further Western support, and to provide a clear set of standards to encourage the recalcitrant Ukrainian bureaucracy to change.[36] However, Ukrainian officials' articulation of the goal of NATO standards was a challenge for Western officials for several reasons. Some in the international community feared that the goal of NATO standards was too ambitious given the poor state of Ukraine's military. Furthermore, if Ukraine did succeed in achieving NATO standards, this would also legitimate Ukraine's efforts to join NATO even though there was little political will within NATO to move forward with Ukraine's accession, especially given the lack of desire of member states to directly come to Ukraine's defense.[37]

Without further specification, the goal of fulfilling NATO standards was also not sufficient to point to a path forward for Ukraine's military. There is no single NATO structure for military organization; instead, there are a wide range of practices across the NATO members. NATO documents did articulate some broad principles, including civilian control, accountability, and transparency, and NATO did work with Ukraine to set specific goals through its advisory programs. But without a specific membership action plan, the specific content of what had to be done remained uncertain.[38]

RAND's report filled this gap by offering an evaluation of what Ukraine had to do to meet NATO standards. The report was supervised by Ukrainian officials and provided in drafts over the course of 2015. A public version was released in 2016.[39] Along with other Western advice, RAND's report informed the Strategic Defense Bulletin (SDB) of 2016 and subsequent reform efforts.[40] In addition to other Western reports and analyses, I use the RAND report as a basis for identifying the main Western recommendations for defense reform. By focusing on the RAND report, I do not mean to imply that it was the single template behind all Western recommendations but rather that it offered an influential and clearly stated template for what Ukraine needed to do to meet European Union and NATO standards. There were Western and Ukrainian critics of RAND's recommendations. Still, many recommendations in the report were echoed by other advisers and reports, and in retrospect advisers noted that it made explicit widely held concerns about Ukraine's institutions.[41]

I identify five categories of recommendations from the RAND report and other sources, which are based on observations of particular problems within Ukraine's structures. Each of these categories threatened Ukrainian patron-client networks to varying degrees (see also table 6.2).

A first category involved changing Ukraine's defense institutional structure to improve defense management and command and control. RAND and other observers noted that there were ambiguities in the Ukrainian constitution about the role of the president and the cabinet of ministers in overseeing particular defense institutions. Further, the RAND report noted that "ministries and agencies operate independently . . . as separate fiefdoms."[42] One concern was the structure of the MoD and General Staff. There was also ambiguity in the roles and responsibilities of the departments within these organizations. The minister of defense and the chief of the General Staff (also referred to as the chief of defense, or CHoD) both reported directly to the president, making it difficult to resolve disputes at lower levels. Two other issues created problems for the command and control of military operations. As of 2015 the command of operations was not separated from the development of forces, as is the case in the United States and other NATO militaries. Ukraine at one time had a Joint Operational Command to exercise command over current operations, but this headquarters had been eliminated under Yanukovych. Relatedly, the mission in eastern Ukraine (known as the Anti-Terror Operation, ATO), was formally overseen by the Security Service of Ukraine (Sluzhba

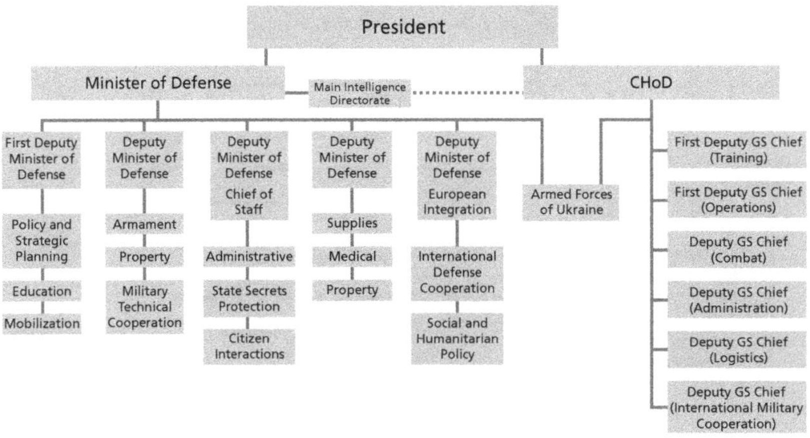

FIGURE 6.1. Prior Structure of the Ukrainian Ministry of Defense and General Staff circa 2015

Source: Reprinted from Oliker et al., *Security Sector Reform in Ukraine*.

Note: CHoD = chief of defense; GS = General Staff.

bezpeky Ukrayiny, SBU), Ukraine's internal security service, even though much of the operation was carried out by the Armed Forces of Ukraine.[43]

To address these structural issues, RAND recommended clarifying the responsibilities of the president and other senior officials and strengthening coordinating bodies such as the National Security and Defense Council. RAND also recommended a major restructuring of the MoD and General Staff. A first step was to subordinate the General Staff and Armed Forces to the MoD. RAND also recommended implementing a numbered, general staffing system (J1 for personnel, J2 for intelligence, etc.) "to align with Euro-Atlantic standards" throughout the Ukrainian military since at the time Ukrainian defense institutions and units operated with a mix of legacy Soviet-era staff systems and a numbered system (see figure 6.2). RAND urged delegation, recommending that "decisions should be made at the lowest level possible."[44] RAND suggested organizing responsibility over all combat operations, including the ATO, within a recreated Joint Operational Command.[45]

The proposed structural reform is shown in figure 6.2. The main threat to elite interests was to the chief of defense and General Staff, who would lose their direct reporting line to the president and would need to delegate authorities. The SBU would also lose its nominal authority over the ATO. The reform left largely intact the extensive authority of the president over national security. To the extent that the restructuring dramatically changed decision-making, as the report urged, it also

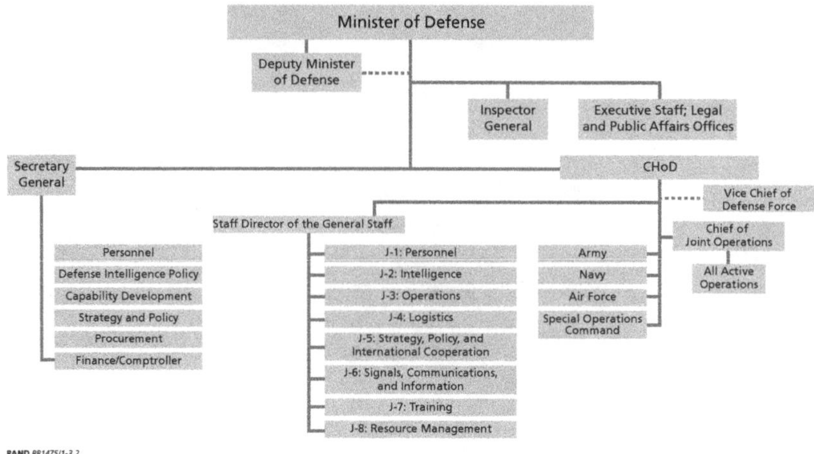

FIGURE 6.2. RAND Recommended Structure for the Ukrainian Ministry of Defense and General Staff

Source: Reprinted from Oliker et al., *Security Sector Reform in Ukraine.*
Note: CHoD = chief of defense.

had the potential to threaten other interests within the MoD and General Staff, but this impact would depend on actual implementation.

A second category of recommendations sought to address gaps in support functions for military operations. Although Ukraine had improved its support functions since the war had begun, these systems remained problematic from a NATO perspective: Ukraine retained some Soviet-era structures, including a separation between the rear (nonlethal supplies) and armaments (weapons and equipment) structures, an inflexible legal framework for the provision of supplies, and paper-based systems that were formally responsible for tracking supplies.[46] Command, control, communications, and intelligence was another major gap, given both a shortage of secure communications equipment and problematic command and control relationships.[47]

To address these issues, RAND recommended restructuring the logistics structure throughout the Ukrainian General Staff and Armed Forces into a single "J-4" structure and implementing an electronic inventory control system to better track supplies. RAND and other donors encouraged and supported acquisition of new communications equipment and systems.[48] These recommendations posed a relatively low threat to elite patron-client networks. The adoption of electronic inventory systems might have made low-level pilfering of military supplies more difficult, but otherwise there was little indication that it would impact the ruling elites.

The third category of recommendations focused on Ukraine's complex and opaque procurement system and its politically connected military industry. Armaments were procured through single-source contracts under a classified annual State Defense Order (SDO), which made acquisition expensive and facilitated corruption. Ukrainian military officers were also frustrated at the inability of Ukroboronprom, Ukraine's state-owned military industrial complex, to supply them with high-quality and necessary equipment, even though Ukroboronprom had extensive advanced equipment available for export. Ukroboronprom was not only the sole legal procurer of foreign equipment but also the main domestic producer, complicating the import of foreign equipment.[49] Nonlethal supplies were procured through separate procedures specified by Ukraine's rules for public procurement and facilitated by the Prozorro e-procurement system.[50] One report also noted the role of the Ministry of Economic Development and Trade on the SDO and links between leaders of this ministry and competing political elites.[51]

To address procurement issues, RAND recommended reorganizing procurement within a single department of the MoD composed of program offices; eliminating the classified SDO; giving the MoD the right to procure foreign equipment; and increasing the transparency surrounding Ukroboronprom as a first step toward eventual privatization.[52] International advisers also strongly encouraged the further application of the Prozorro system.[53] The recommendations surrounding the reform of procurement and Ukroboronprom posed a significant threat to the ruling elites interests' and patron-client networks. As noted earlier, the major factions within the Ukrainian government, including Poroshenko and his allies and the People's Front, a major political party, both appear to have benefited from the existing defense procurement structures. Reform to make procurement more efficient and reduce the power of Ukroboronprom would likely impact their economic interests.

The fourth category of recommendations sought to improve accountability to the population. RAND noted problems of civilian control over defense, especially because the minister of defense was a military officer and there were few empowered civilians within the ministry.[54] Accounts of the Verkhovna Rada, Ukraine's parliament, also reported weaknesses in its ability to oversee government activities, including the defense establishment, especially with regard to budgets.[55] Perceptions of the unfairness of Ukraine's mobilization and conscription policies also undermined accountability to the population.[56]

RAND recommended making the minister of defense a civilian and offered various suggestions to strengthen the civilian presence within the MoD.[57] RAND, among others, also proposed increasing the oversight capacity of the Verkhovna Rada, although, as one adviser noted, absent a constitutional change, given the authority of the president in the Ukrainian constitution, there was little way for the Verkhovna Rada to pose a real counterweight to the executive.[58] To address problems with mobilization and conscription, RAND recommended pursuing an all-volunteer force with an active reserve. These recommendations overall posed little threat to the existing patron-client networks, especially since the report stated that the defense minister, Col. Gen. Stepan Poltorak, could continue in his post. Fostering a more professional civil service within the MoD and moving away from conscription and mobilization could impact some patron-client networks, but the likely impact on the ruling elites would be small or slow to emerge.

Fifth, other foreign analysts expressed concern about the rule of law due to the continued existence of volunteer battalions and illegal activity in Ukraine's east. The volunteer battalions had helped Ukraine avoid military defeat but were concerning since they also received support from oligarchs and could "potentially evolve into private armies," according to one 2015 report.[59] They were also believed to engage in other illegal activity, including a skirmish over smuggling routes in western Ukraine in 2015.[60] Although the volunteer units, with the exception of the Right Sector battalion, were integrated into either the National Guard or Armed Forces of Ukraine by October 2015, the loyalty and control of these organizations remained in question.[61] Foreign analysts recommended disbanding and dispersing the fighters into mainline units. Analysts also pointed to the funding provided by oligarchs to the volunteer battalions and raised the concern that the volunteer units could be used for their private benefit. For example, Kimberly Marten and Olga Oliker note that Ihor Kolomoisky is believed to have encouraged members of the Donbas and Aidar battalions to blockade coal imports from separatist territory, initially in opposition to Ukrainian policy.[62] Disbanding the volunteer units had the potential to weaken the patron-client networks of the oligarchs who supported them.

In June 2016 President Poroshenko enacted an SDB, which set the "main directions" of defense policy and reform through 2020. In particular, the document explained how Ukraine intended to reform its defense institutions to align with NATO standards. One foreign adviser noted that 80–90 percent of the proposals in the RAND report ended up in the SDB in some form. One possible reason that RAND's report was so influential was that it specified a clear framework for moving forward. While NATO officials might have had greater political leverage, they could not propose a framework of what Ukraine's institutions should become. The fact that RAND's work was supervised by Ukrainian officials and not imposed or demanded by Western officials may have also made it easier for Ukraine to more flexibly adapt RAND's recommendations to Ukrainian practices. Still, RAND's report was but one of several influences on the SDB, as US and other NATO advisers also played a strong role in providing separate recommendations for the SDB.[63]

Table 6.2 shows which elements of categories of recommendations described earlier were included in the SDB. In general, the recommendations that posed the least threat to patron-client networks were most implemented in the SDB, with some exceptions. For example, personnel reform, listed under accountability, was only partially included. In particular, the SDB did not insist on a volunteer force, especially since there was a popular view in Ukraine that conscription was essential to the defense of the country against Russia.[64]

In some cases, the threat of a recommendation to entrenched interests led to a delay or watering down of the recommendation. In the case of the proposed structural changes, for example, the overlap between MoD and General Staff departments was intended to be eliminated by 2018, force development and operational control would be separated by 2020, and the integration of the General Staff into the MoD would be achieved "in the future."[65] One Ukrainian official explained that the slowness to incorporate or subordinate General Staff responsibilities and structures under the MoD reflected "the personal ambition of different stakeholders."[66] A former foreign adviser noted that in some cases senior MoD officials lacked an intellectual understanding of how the proposed structures would work but observed at the same time that opposition by these officials was driven by an understanding that "their authorities and usefulness would diminish."[67] The control of volunteer battalions, which the Ukrainian government believed it had already addressed, was not included in either the RAND report or SDB. While procurement reform was included in the SDB, the defense industry reform was not. One official explained that RAND's recommendations for improving the defense industry were not "relevant advice" and "purely [were] not considered."[68] One can hypothesize that the political sensitivity of the defense industry made a major restructuring impractical.

Over the next two years, Ukrainian officials continued to implement the SDB, with mixed success, as detailed in table 6.2. The progress in each of the categories continued to indicate that reform was most likely to progress where it posed the least threat to patron-client networks and that, where reform did occur, it did little to reshape the underlying functioning of Ukrainian defense institutions or existing patron-client networks. At the same time, international assistance increased. A US-led multinational force expanded its training of Ukrainian forces, first providing basic training and later training battalion- and brigade-size formations. In March 2018 the United States announced the first provision of lethal aid to Ukraine since the beginning of the war—210 Javelin antitank missiles and 37 launchers at a cost of $47 million.[69] The US Congress authorized up to $300 million in assistance in FY 2016 and $350 million in both FY 2017 and FY 2018. However, some of this assistance was conditional on the secretary of defense certifying progress on defense institutional reforms. In July 2018 the US released $200 million in security

TABLE 6.2. Recommendations for Defense Reform and Eventual Outcome

Recommendation	Threat to elite interests and network?	Included in SDB?	Outcome as of June 2018
1. Structural changes	Low, except to CHoD and General Staff and maybe SBU	Yes: • Specified roles • Staged integration of General Staff in MoD • Creation of Joint Forces command over operations	Mixed: • ATO renamed, transferred to General Staff • No major General Staff reform • Clarifying roles does not improve coordination
2. Combat support	Low	Yes: • Planned C4ISR improvements • Single "J"-based logistics structure • Automated inventory-control system	Mixed: • Adopted appearance of new logistics structure while improving based on Soviet-era structures • No new inventory-control system • Little progress on comms
3. Procurement and military industry	High	Partially: • Procure weapons via "public defense contract," have "project teams" • No mention of Ukroboronprom or MoD right to procure weapons directly	Low: • Only improvement with greater use of Prozorro for nonlethal supplies • Eventual granting of authority for foreign procurement to MoD

4. Accountability to citizenry	Low	Partially: • Appointment of civilian minister by 2018 • Discussion of parliamentary oversight • Reference to "professionalism" and "fundamental European approaches"	Mixed: • More civilians in MoD, especially in reform offices • Limited parliament improvement • Mobilization is ended, but only temporarily; conscription continues
5. Extralegal units and illegal activity	Mixed	No, but previously claimed to have adopted	Mixed: • Volunteer units integrated but unclear whether still risks

Note: ATO = Anti-Terror Operation; C4ISR = command, control, communications, computers, intelligence, surveillance, and reconnaissance; CHoD = chief of defense; MoD = Ministry of Defense; SBU = Sluzhba bezpeky Ukrayiny (Security Service of Ukraine); SDB = Strategic Defense Bulletin.

assistance after Ukraine passed the Law on National Security.[70] Other NATO members, including the United Kingdom, Canada, and Lithuania, also provided advisers, trainers, and equipment.[71] By late 2017 the NATO staff in Kyiv had tripled since the start of the conflict.[72] Nevertheless, this assistance remained small in scale relative to the challenges facing the Ukrainian armed forces.

After the 2016 SDB, there were significant improvements in Ukrainian military structures, especially the development of a new command structure over the military operation in eastern Ukraine. As mentioned above, RAND proposed placing authority over the operation in the east within the General Staff under a Joint Operational Command—both a headquarters and a command center—to oversee all combat operations. In February 2018 a new law governing Ukraine's policy in eastern Ukraine established a Joint Force Operation under the General Staff to replace the SBU-led ATO.[73] This change effectively resolved the problem of the SBU's nominal authority over the region and clarified responsibility for the operation under the General Staff. A Joint Operational Headquarters was also created, fulfilling the Western recommendation of creating a Joint Operational Command, although one Western observer described the Joint Operational Command as a "building with computers" that did not appear to actually exercise command over forces in the field.[74] Another potential issue was that the commander of the Joint Force Operation was also appointed as the leader of a civilian administration over the territory. This gave the commander a degree of legal authority over governance in the occupied territory, including, for example, administration of a small customs organization. While this arrangement raised democratic accountability concerns among foreign advisers, Ukrainian officials argued it was necessary to ensure coordination in the conflict zone.[75]

Regarding combat support functions, Ukraine implemented some foreign advice while retaining and improving legacy systems.[76] In the case of logistics, for example, one foreign adviser explained that, at the high echelon, "the doorplate now said J-4," following the Western numbered staffing system. At the same time, the adviser noted "otherwise nothing much has changed."[77] Soviet-era approaches to logistics remained, including a "push" system based on providing a predetermined bundle of supplies rather than a Western "pull" system based on individual unit requests.[78] Structures at the tactical and operational level also reportedly continued to vary from unit to unit.[79] The actual provision of supplies reportedly improved, as the MoD was apparently able to take advantage of savings from reduced corruption in the procurement of basic supplies.[80]

International assistance funded new C4ISR (command, control, communications, computers, intelligence, surveillance, and reconnaissance) systems, including more than $20 million for a "joint cybersecurity, command and control, logistical and medical information systems capacity" implemented by the US company

Black Box.[81] The actual impact on combat effectiveness from these investments was hard to judge. For example, one foreign adviser observed that the Western-provided equipment was incompatible with Ukraine's preexisting command and control practices. In particular, Western systems were designed to facilitate "mission command," in which lower echelons have the initiative to make decisions as necessary. Ukraine's existing practices were instead based on having unit commanders exercise more centralized leadership.[82] If indeed Western concepts of mission command facilitate greater military effectiveness, the maintenance of preexisting command practices thus likely diminished the potential improvement in effectiveness that could have arisen thanks to foreign material assistance.[83]

Regarding procurement and the defense industry, there was some progress, but overall these areas remained the least improved. Perhaps the greatest success was the expanded use of the Prozorro e-procurement system for basic supplies, such as food, fuel, and clothing. Improvements related to the purchase of armaments were slower to emerge. Tellingly, Ukraine struggled with giving the MoD the authority to directly procure weapons from foreign countries without going through Ukroboronprom.[84] The United States, for example, could only transfer weapons provided under "foreign military sales" or "excess defense articles" directly to the MoD, not to Ukroboronprom. While the US did transfer the Javelin systems to Ukroboronprom on the basis that it was a foreign military financing transfer, this arrangement limited Ukraine's ability to receive weaponry from the United States in the future.[85] By one account, a presidential decree in June 2018 apparently granted the MoD greater authority to purchase foreign equipment, and in September 2018 two US Coast Guard cutters were transferred to Ukraine as excess defense articles.[86] Even with this change, the more fundamental problems within the procurement and armaments system remained. The July 2018 Law on National Security did not alter the classified SDO system, and frustration with Ukroboronprom's dominance remained. One 2018 article explained that "Ukroboronprom—variously referred to as a 'monster' and a 'parasite'—enjoys a de facto monopoly over Ukraine's defense industry."[87] While Ukroboronprom's inefficiency likely played a role in the inability of Ukraine to field additional modernized equipment and thereby improve military effectiveness, limited funds also played a role.[88]

There was also mixed progress in improving accountability. The passage of the Law on National Security in July 2018, which included measures to improve accountability, was one element of progress. However, with some exceptions, the law was a "framework law" that set time lines and requirements for future legislation and did not in itself impose major changes in governance.[89] One change required by the law was that the minister of defense become a civilian, which was a recommendation that had been included in the RAND report. To meet this requirement, the sitting minister of defense, Poltorak, simply retired from the army and stayed on as a civilian minister. While nominally improving civilian control, this change did not fully meet the substance of the recommendation, especially given that a previously considered version of the law had required that a civilian defense minister be out of uniform for at least five years.[90] Below the minister other civilians who had joined the ministry in various capacities following 2014 remained active and influential after 2016, especially within the office responsible for reform. However, they were often strongly opposed by members of the existing bureaucracy—one adviser, for example, described a "tooth and nail" conflict between the young reformers working on procurement and the preexisting bureaucracy.[91] There were also mixed signs in the improvement of the Verkhovna Rada. One foreign adviser highlighted the improved information exchange between the MoD and the parliament as a key success, although others noted a continuing lack of expertise.[92]

Regarding personnel policy, Ukraine did pursue increased professionalization, and the final, sixth wave of mobilization occurred in 2015. However, the decision to end mobilization appeared to be due mainly to the lower needs of the conflict zone and improved recruitment. Ukrainians seemed to retain a fairly consistent view of overall personnel policy from the beginning of the conflict, including a preference for a mixed system comprising contract personnel, conscripts, and—should the need arise—mobilized personnel.[93]

Assessments of the volunteer battalions and extralegal activities varied. According to those working in the government, the volunteer battalions were a nonissue—they had been fully integrated into the MoI and MoD command structures, and they "cannot be pulled off, new ones created, or recreated."[94] By contrast, Marten and Oliker wrote in September 2017 that some volunteer units' "legal subordination masks their substantial autonomy and political activism."[95] Similarly, one foreign analyst noted in an interview that "volunteer units are integrated but can act independently based on their clan affiliation." He also highlighted corruption in Donbas and other border areas as a major risk to the development of the rule of law in Ukraine.[96]

By mid-late 2018 the Ukrainian military had clearly made substantial improvements, although some gaps remained. I rate the quality of the Ukrainian military in 2018 as a 6 out of 9:

- Effectiveness (2 out of 3): Ukraine was able to maintain its military position in the occupied territories in the face of Russian-backed forces and had achieved notable improvements in support systems and structures. Still, analysts continued to cite problems with its equipment and the military's difficulty adopting Western approaches.
- Accountability (2 out of 3): Civilian control improved, in part through goals set in the SDB and as a result of the greater role of civilians in the MoD, even if the conversation of the defense minister to a civilian may not have made

a major difference. However, defense-management practices remained more in line with those in Russia or the Soviet Union than those in neighboring NATO countries, recognizing the ongoing concern about civilian control of the military in Poland.[97] Recruitment practices also improved, but policies backing conscription and mobilization remained.

- Rule of Law (2 out of 3): Ukraine passed several important laws on defense and retained an overall strong legal framework. However, the Law on National Security remained only a framework for incomplete future legislation.[98] Concerns remained among Western analysts, if not those within the government of Ukraine, about the volunteer units.

CONCLUSION: LESSONS FROM DEFENSE REFORM IN UKRAINE

Overall, from 2014 to 2018 there was a three-point improvement in Ukraine's defense institutions, indicating moderate success. Military effectiveness especially improved during the first stage of reform, while the rule of law and accountability improved more during the second stage. One foreign adviser noted a common belief that "Ukraine achieved more in the last four years than the previous twenty-one," and certainly Ukraine's military was far more able capable against Russia and its proxies in 2018 than it had been when the conflict began in 2014.[99]

In addition to highlighting the improvement in Ukraine's defense institutions, largely due to local initiative, the case study above shows how domestic opposition to foreign-supported reform can occur in cases where there are low international resources and where changes proposed by foreign organizations are framed as optional recommendations rather than obligatory demands. The domestic opposition theory best explains the observed process and outcome of defense reform in Ukraine. Private opposition by Ukrainian officials, likely in response to the threat to their patron-client networks, meant that the most threatening Western recommendations were the least implemented. For example, the General Staff appeared to resist Western structural recommendations based on a fear that reform would diminish their overall power relative to the MoD. Similarly, while Ukroboronprom was generally publicly supportive of defense reform, in practice it appeared to resist any significant substantive changes to procurement practices that might have diminished their authority or financial interests.[100] Avoiding provoking opposition from these powerful stakeholders would likely have facilitated greater reform.

The international resource theory also explains the limited impact of Western assistance, since Western reformers had low resources. Path dependence offers only a partial explanation. It explains the continuing influence of Soviet-era, preexisting institutional structures and practices, but it has difficulty accounting for the rapid improvement in the Ukrainian military that occurred following 2014.

One factor that does provide some explanation for the relative rapid improvement in the Ukrainian military is the impact of an external threat from Russia.[101] There was strong popular support for the defense of the country, demonstrated by examples of private contributions for military equipment. There was also strong political pressure on the government to reform the military.[102] Defense expenditures significantly increased, from 1 percent of gross domestic product in 2013 to 2.5 percent in 2015 and 2016, although they remained low in absolute terms.[103] However, the lack of progress in making reforms despite the threat from Russia is difficult to explain without taking into account the influence of elite opposition to changes that would threaten their patron-client networks.

The next chapter, the conclusion, argues that foreign actors should formulate demands and recommendations to work around elite patron-client networks while still improving state institutions. This was not necessary for RAND in Ukraine, given our mandate to offer recommendations in line with NATO standards, but it could have been more feasible for other foreign advisers. Ultimately, as this book argues, the domestic politicians are in charge of their country, and foreign advisers lack the knowledge and position to contradict their decisions. However, the events in Ukraine show how accommodating certain domestic interests can facilitate the greatest success in achieving reform. Western advisers should make incremental recommendations or demands that do not provoke dramatic opposition, pursue limited improvements where possible, keep in mind their ultimate objectives, and take advantage of support from domestic leaders where possible. This represents the best available path to achieve reform, whatever the available resources.

NOTES

1 For background, see, inter alia, Nick Thompson, "Ukraine: Everything You Need to Know about How We Got Here," *CNN*, February 3, 2017, https://www.cnn.com/2015/02/10/europe/ukraine-war-how-we-got-here/index.html; and Charap and Colton, *Everyone Loses*, chap. 3.

2 Steven Erlanger and David M. Herszenhorn, "I.M.F. Prepares $18 Billion in Loans for Ukraine," *New York Times*, December 20, 2017.

3 See, inter alia, Steven Pifer, "Will Ukraine Join NATO? A Course for Disappointment," *Brookings* (blog), July 25, 2017, https://www.brookings.edu/blog/order-from-chaos/2017/07/25/will-ukraine-join-nato-a-course-for-disappointment/; Charap and Colton, *Everyone Loses*, chap. 3–4; and Paul Belkin, Derek Mix, and Steven Woehrel, "NATO: Response to the Crisis in Ukraine and Security Concerns in Central and Eastern Europe," *Congressional Research Service*, July 31, 2014, 2–3, 13–14.

4 Sergey Denisentsev, "The Soviet Inheritance of Ukrainian Armed Forces," in Howard and Pukhov, *Brothers Armed*, 27–55, quote on 55.

5 Anton Lavrov and Alexey Nikoslky, "Neglect and Rot: Degradation of Ukraine's Military in the Interim Period," in Howard and Pukhov, 65–72.

6 According to a subsequent Ukrainian MoD report. See Lavrov and Nikoslky, 70.

7 Note, for example, similarity between the critiques identified below and those highlighted in prior assessments. See Merle Maigre and Phillipp Fluri, ed. *Almanac on Security Sector Governance in Ukraine, 2010* (Geneva: Geneva Centre for the Democratic Control of Armed Forces, 2010), 55, 68, 76–78, https://www.dcaf.ch/sites/default/files/publications/documents/Ukrainian_SSG_Almanac.pdf; Natalie Mychajlyszyn, "Civil-Military Relations in Post-Soviet Ukraine: Implications for Domestic and Regional Stability," *Armed Forces & Society* 28, no. 3 (April 1, 2002): 455–79; and Oliker et al., *Security Sector Reform in Ukraine*.

8 Kostyantyn Fedorenko, Olena Rybiy, and Andreas Umland, "The Ukrainian Party System before and after the 2013–2014 Euromaidan," *Europe-Asia Studies* 68, no. 4 (April 20, 2016): 612; and David Marples, "Ethnic and Social Composition of Ukraine's Regions and Voting Patterns," *E-International Relations*, March 10, 2015, https://www.e-ir.info/2015/03/10/ethnic-and-social-composition-of-ukraines-regions-and-voting-patterns/.

9 Fedorenko, Rybiy, and Umland, "Ukrainian Party System," 624.

10 Prior to 2014 there were close ties between Ukrainian and Russian military structures—one report explains that under Yanukovich "Ukrainians often say 'the Ministry of Defense was Russian.'" Facon, "Reforming Ukrainian Defense," 14, 22–25.

11 On the role of oligarchs in Ukraine, see Wojciech Konończuk, "Keystone of the System: Old and New Oligarchs in Ukraine," Point of View (Warsaw: Centre for Eastern Studies [OSW], August 2016), https://www.osw.waw.pl/en/publikacje/point-view/2016-08-18/keystone-system-old-and-new-oligarchs-ukraine. On divisions among agencies, see Oliker et al., *Security Sector Reform in Ukraine*, 9–11; and phone interviews with foreign advisers and analysts, June 2018.

12 Oleksiy Bratuschak, "War and Business," *Ukrayins'ka Pravda*, published December 1, 2016, https://antac.org.ua/en/investigations/war-and-business-how-poroshenko-s-friends-control-construction-contracts-for-billons-of-uah-part-1-ukrainska-pravda/.

13 Ivan Verstiuk, "A Company of Two. Secret Orders for Defence Industry Became a Gold Mine for Authorities," April 14, 2018, https://antac.org.ua/en/publications/a-company-of-two-secret-orders-for-defence-industry-became-a-gold-mine-for-authorities/; see also Andrew Higgins, "In Ukraine, Corruption Is Now Undermining the Military," *New York Times*, February 19, 2018.

14 Beronika Melkozerova, "Top Official Allegedly Threatens to 'Tear Up' Magazine over Defense Corruption Story," *Kyiv Post*, April 18, 2018, https://www.kyivpost.com/ukraine-politics/top-official-allegedly-threatens-tear-magazine-defense-corruption-story.html.

15 RAND's report relied on interviews with Ukrainian officials and documents that Ukraine provided to RAND. I do not make use of this proprietary material except insofar as the information has been documented in the publicly available RAND report or

other published documents. Since this chapter relies more heavily on interviews, I also number the interviewees to highlight where there were multiple individuals expressing similar or different points of view.

16 Michael Kofman, Katya Migacheva, Brian Nichiporuk, Andrew Radin, Olesya Tkacheva, and Jenny Oberholtzer, *Lessons from Russia's Operations in Crimea and Eastern Ukraine* (Santa Monica, CA: RAND, 2017), 33–40, 52–60; and Courtney Weaver, "Malofeev, The Russian Billionaire Linking Moscow to the Rebels," *Financial Times*, July 24, 2014.

17 Kofman et al., *Lessons from Russia's Operations*, 42.

18 Marten and Oliker, "Ukraine's Volunteer Militias."

19 Akimenko, "Ukraine's Toughest Fight"; Oliker et al., *Security Sector Reform in Ukraine*, 48–49.

20 Max Fisher, "MH17 Is Third Mysterious Shoot-Down over Ukraine," *Vox*, July 18, 2014, https://www.vox.com/2014/7/18/5914139/ukrainian-rebels-shot-down-two-planes-in-the-last-month; and Michael Birnbaum, "Dutch-Led Investigators Say Russian Missile Shot Down Malaysia Airlines Flight 17 over Ukraine in 2014," *Washington Post*, May 24, 2018.

21 David Herszhenhorn, "Ukraine Military Finds Its Footing against Pro-Russian Rebels," *New York Times*, July 6, 2014.

22 Michael Cohen, "Ukraine's Battle at Ilovaisk, August 2014: The Tyranny of Means," *Army Professional Online Journal*, February 4, 2016, 2–8, http://www.armyupress.army.mil/Portals/7/Army-Press-Online-Journal/documents/16-25-Cohen-10Jun16a.pdf; and Alec Luhn, "Anatomy of a Bloodbath," *Foreign Policy*, September 6, 2014.

23 David Herszenhorn, "NATO Reports Increased Russian Troop Movement," *New York Times*, July 28, 2014.

24 Kofman, *Lessons from Russia's Operations*, 42–45; and "'Little Green Men': A Primer on Modern Unconventional Russian Warfare, Ukraine 2013–2014" (Fort Bragg, NC: US Army Special Operations Command, n.d.) 32–33, https://www.jhuapl.edu/Content/documents/ARIS_LittleGreenMen.pdf.

25 Roland Oliphant, "Defeated Ukrainians Take the 'Road of Life' on Their Retreat from Debaltseve," *Telegraph*, February 18, 2015, https://www.telegraph.co.uk/news/worldnews/europe/ukraine/11421405/Defeated-Ukrainians-take-the-road-of-life-on-their-retreat-from-Debaltseve.html.

26 Charap and Colton, *Everyone Loses*, 142–43.

27 David Herszenhorn, "Fears Rise as Russian Military Units Pour into Ukraine," *New York Times*, November 12, 2014. On Russian forces in Ukraine, see also Igor Sutyagin, "Russian Forces in Ukraine" (London: RUSI, March 9, 2015), https://rusi.org/publication/briefing-papers/russian-forces-ukraine.

28 Oliker et al., *Security Sector Reform in Ukraine*, 64–65.

29 Kateryna Zrembo, "How volunteers both strengthened and weakened the Ukrainian state after Euromaidan," *Euromaidan Press*, February 15, 2018, http://euromaidanpress.com/2018/02/15/how-volunteers-both-strengthened-and-weakened-the-ukrainian-state-after-euromaidan/; and Kyiv School of Economics, "Co-Creation of Prozorro."

30 Oliker et al., *Security Sector Reform in Ukraine*, 65.

31 White House, "Fact Sheet: US Assistance to Ukraine," June 4, 2014, https://obama whitehouse.archives.gov/the-press-office/2014/06/04/fact-sheet-us-security-assistance-ukraine.

32 Simon Shuster, "Corruption Still Plagues Ukraine as West Pumps in Aid," *Time*, April 1, 2014, http://time.com/45253/ukraine-corruption-tymoshenko-kiev/; and Independent Defence Anti-Corruption Committee (NAKO), "Making the System Work: Enhancing Security Assistance for Ukraine," 2017, 18–21, http://ti-defence.org/wp-content/uploads/2017/05/Making-the-system-work-TI-Defence-Security.pdf.

33 NATO, "NATO's Practical Support to Ukraine."

34 US EUCOM, "Readout of Ukraine-US Joint Commission," October 21, 2014, https://www.eucom.mil/media-library/article/28857/readout-of-ukraine-us-joint-commission.

35 See, for example, President of Ukraine, "President's Annual Message to Verkhovna Rada of Ukraine 'On the Internal and External Situation of Ukraine in 2015,'" June 4, 2015, http://www.president.gov.ua/en/news/shorichne-poslannya-prezidenta-ukrayini-do-verhovnoyi-radi-u-35412.

36 Isabelle Facon writes, "The Ukrainian government wants to use adherence to NATO standards as a way of exerting external pressure on the defense sector, to match the internal pressure." "Reforming Ukrainian Defense," 20.

37 Facon, 18–21; and Steven Pifer, "Ukraine Overturns Its Non-Bloc Status. What's Next with NATO?," Brookings Institution, December 26, 2014, https://www.brookings.edu/opinions/ukraine-overturns-its-non-bloc-status-what-next-with-nato/.

38 While each membership plan for a country pursuing accession was different, historically aspirants were required to resolve extant internal disputes, "establish appropriate democratic and civilian control of their armed forces," and be able to contribute militarily to the alliance, among other issues. See NATO, "Membership Action Plan (MAP)," April 24, 1999, https://www.nato.int/cps/en/natohq/official_texts_27444.htm.

39 See Oliker et al., *Security Sector Reform in Ukraine*.

40 Interview with foreign advisors #1, #3, #4, and Ukrainian official #1, May–June 2018.

41 Author phone interview with US advisers, May 2018; Albuquerque and Hedenskog, "Ukraine," 23–37; and Facon, "Reforming Ukrainian Defense," 20–21.

42 Oliker et al., *Security Sector Reform in Ukraine*, 7–10; and Young, *Anatomy of Post-Communist European Defense Institutions*, 79.

43 Oliker et al., *Security Sector Reform in Ukraine*, 23–25, 42–43.

44 Oliker et al., 27.

45 Oliker et al., 38–46.

46 Oliker et al., 64–68.

47 Oliker et al., chap. 4. These areas were also identified for additional attention by NATO Trust Funds, see NATO, "NATO's Practical Support to Ukraine."

48 Oliker et al., *Security Sector Reform in Ukraine*, 43–47.

49 Oliker et al., 91–94. See also Illia Ponomarenko, "Secrecy Blankets Corruption in Ukraine's Defense Sector," *KyivPost*, September 15, 2017, https://www.kyivpost.com/ukraine-politics/secrecy-blankets-corruption-ukraines-defense-sector.html; and Oleg Varfolomeyev, "Ukraine Hopes to Become Arms Exporter to NATO Countries," *Eurasia*

Daily Monitor 14, no. 77, https://jamestown.org/program/ukraine-hopes-become-arms-exporter-nato-countries/.

50 Oliker et al., *Security Sector Reform in Ukraine*, 57–60.

51 Bratuschak, "War and Business."

52 Oliker et al., *Security Sector Reform in Ukraine*, 57–64, 95–101.

53 Kyiv School of Economics, "Co-Creation of Prozorro."

54 Oliker et al., *Security Sector Reform in Ukraine*, 25–27.

55 Young, *Anatomy of Post-Communist European Defense Institutions*, 79; "Proceedings from the First International Conference 'Monitoring Ukraine's Security Governance Challenges—Status and Needs'" (Kyiv: DCAF-Razumkov Centre, 2016), https://www.dcaf.ch/sites/default/files/publications/documents/2016_Conference-Proceedings1_eng.pdf; and European Parliament, "On the Internal Reform and Capacity-Building for the Verkhovna Rada of Ukraine," 2016, http://www.europarl.europa.eu/resources/library/media/20160229RES16408/20160229RES16408.pdf.

56 Oliker et al., *Security Sector Reform in Ukraine*, 49.

57 Oliker et al., 25–27, 53–54.

58 Interview with foreign adviser #2, May 2018.

59 Albuquerque and Hedenskog, "Ukraine."

60 Marten and Oliker, "Ukraine's Volunteer Militias."

61 Albuquerque and Hedenskog, "Ukraine," 22.

62 Marten and Oliker, "Ukraine's Volunteer Militias." Interview with foreign analyst #1, May 2018.

63 Interviews with foreign advisers #1, 2, 3, and 4, May–June 2018.

64 Interview with Ukrainian official #1, June 2018.

65 "Strategic Defense Bulletin of Ukraine," June 6, 2016, 7–8.

66 Interview with Ukrainian official #1, May 2018.

67 Interview with foreign adviser #4, June 2018.

68 Interviews with Ukrainian official #1 and foreign adviser #4, May–June 2018.

69 Cory Welt, "Ukraine: Background and U.S. Policy," *Congressional Research Service*, November 1, 2017, https://fas.org/sgp/crs/row/R45008.pdf; Christopher Miller, "U.S. Confirms Delivery of Javelin Antitank Missiles to Ukraine," *Radio Free Europe / Radio Liberty*, April 30, 2018, https://www.rferl.org/a/javelin-missile-delivery-ukraine-us-confirmed/29200588.html; and interviews with foreign advisors #1, 2, 4, May–June 2018.

70 Welt, "Ukraine: Background and U.S. Policy"; "U.S. House and Senate Armed Service Committees Authorize $350 Million for Ukraine," UNIAN Information Agency, November 9, 2017; and US Department of Defense, "DoD to Provide $200 Million in Security Cooperation Funds to Ukraine," July 20, 2018, https://dod.defense.gov/News/Article/Article/1580565/dod-to-provide-200-million-in-security-cooperation-funds-to-ukraine/.

71 Ukraine Ministry of Defence, "Towards New Armed Forces of Ukraine: Overview of Defence Reforms in Ukraine," 2016, https://defense-reforms.in.ua/en/download?path=%2Ffiles%2FPress%2FGeneral%2FDigests%2FDefenceReformsDigest_2016%2520Summary.pdf; and Welt, "Ukraine: Background and U.S. Policy," 11–17.

72 NATO, "NATO's Practical Support to Ukraine"; and Facon, "Reforming Ukrainian Defense," 18–19.
73 Alya Shandra, "Ukraine's Draft Law on Reintegrating Donbas Finally Says It's under Russian Occupation," *Euromaidan Press*, July 13, 2017, http://euromaidanpress.com/2017/07/13/ukraine-presents-draft-bill-on-reintegrating-donbas/; and Adam Coffey, "Ukraine Declares 'Anti-Terrorist Operation in the Donbas' Officially Over: What Does That Mean?," *RUSI Commentary*, May 16, 2018, https://rusi.org/commentary/ukraine-declares-anti-terrorist-operation-donbas-officially-over-what-does-mean.
74 Interview with foreign adviser #4, June 2018.
75 Interview with foreign adviser #4; and discussion with Ukrainian officials, June and October 2018.
76 Wilk, "Best Army Ukraine Has Ever Had."
77 Interview with foreign adviser #5, June 2018.
78 Interview with foreign adviser #4, June 2018; see also Young, *Anatomy of Post-Communist European Defense Institutions*, 83–84.
79 Interview with foreign adviser #3, June 2018
80 Interview with foreign adviser #3, June 2018.
81 "AGIS Awarded Subcontract by Black Box to Support Ukraine Security Assistance Program," October 2017, https://www.agisinc.com/agis-black-box-ukraine-program/.
82 Interview with foreign adviser #4, June 2018; and interview with Ukrainian analyst #1, August 2018.
83 On the impact of command structures on military effectiveness, see, for example, Talmadge, *Dictator's Army*.
84 Oliker et al., *Security Sector Reform in Ukraine*, 91–92.
85 Interviews with foreign adviser #4; and Ukrainian official #2, June 2018; email correspondence with US official, June 2018.
86 Interviews with foreign adviser #4 and Ukrainian official #2, June 2018; and Illia Ponomarenko, "Ukraine Accepts Two Us Patrol Boats after 4 Years of Bureaucratic Blockades," *Kyiv Post*, September 27, 2018, https://www.kyivpost.com/ukraine-politics/ukraine-accepts-two-us-patrol-boats-after-four-years-of-bureaucratic-blockades.html.
87 Akimenko, "Ukraine's Toughest Fight"; "Ukraine's New Law on National Security: Key Facts to Know," Ukraine Crisis Media Center, June 22, 2018, http://uacrisis.org/67656-ukraine-s-new-law-national-security-key-facts; and interviews with Ukrainian official, foreign advisers #3, #4, and #5, May–June 2018.
88 Wilk, "Best Army Ukraine Has Ever Had," 25–30.
89 "Ukraine's New Law on National Security"; and discussion with Ukrainian officials and analysts, Washington, DC, September 2018.
90 Illia Ponomarenko, "Defense Minister Poltorak Quits Military Service, but Remains in Charge as Civilian," *Kyiv Post*, October 13, 2018, https://www.kyivpost.com/ukraine-politics/defense-minister-poltorak-quits-military-service-to-formally-comply-with-nato-benchmarks.html.
91 Interviews with foreign adviser #4, June 2018.
92 Interviews with foreign advisers #1, #3, and #5, and a foreign analyst, May–June 2018.

93 Wilk, "Best Army Ukraine Has Ever Had," 15–16; and interviews with Ukrainian official and foreign adviser #3 and 5.

94 Interviews with Ukrainian official #1 and foreign adviser #3, June 2018.

95 Marten and Oliker, "Ukraine's Volunteer Militias."

96 Interview with foreign analyst, May 2018.

97 See, for example, Rohr-Garztecki, "Long Shadow of History."

98 Interview with foreign adviser #3, June 2018.

99 Interview with foreign adviser #5, June 2018.

100 As of June 2018 there was a new management team over Ukroboronprom, which was again publicly supportive of reform, although it was unclear whether such support would lead to a major change in policy. Interviews with foreign advisers #1, #2, #4, May–June 2018; and meetings with Ukrainian officials, 2017–18.

101 Note David Edelstein's argument that an external threat facilitates cooperation with occupying authorities. *Occupational Hazards: Success and Failure in Military Occupation* (Ithaca, NY: Cornell University Press, 2010).

102 Charles Ecknagel and Merhat Sharipzhan, "Army in Need: Volunteers Try to Get Supplies to Ukraine's Forces," *RFE/RL*, June 6, 2014, https://www.rferl.org/a/ukraine-army-equipment-donations/25413169.html; and interviews with foreign analyst, foreign adviser #4, May–June 2018.

103 Wilk, "Best Army Ukraine Has Ever Had," 12–14.

CHAPTER SEVEN

CONCLUSION

The United States and the broader international community are constantly engaged in institution building. Institution building is an essential activity to build peace and democracy in postwar countries. It is a recurring and likely unavoidable tool for the United States to enable partners and allies to deter aggressors and defeat terrorism. Building state institutions is also a central means to boost economic development.

This book argues that domestic opposition to foreign-supported reform is an underappreciated and important challenge. As I experienced in Ukraine, foreign reformers commonly seek to replicate Western institutions. Foreign reformers also hope that their mandate and other resources can enable them to overcome opposition if it arises. The seven case studies show how domestic opposition, when it occurred, undermined even the best-resourced efforts and how foreign reformers tended to achieve the greatest success when they were able to avoid opposition.

The case studies also show that domestic opposition often arises because of the threat of reform to nationalist goals and the ruling elites' patron-client networks. Public opposition, including widespread mass demonstrations or elite boycotts, typically emerges due to a threat to nationalist goals and consistently leads to failure. Private opposition, including ignoring foreign requests or covertly blocking reform, typically emerges when reform poses a threat to the ruling elite patron-client networks. I argue that foreign interveners can, to a degree, counter private opposition if given higher resources but that demands or recommendations that threaten elite networks nevertheless tend to be implemented less often.

The key conclusion is that domestic opposition is so damaging for reform that challenging these core interests head-on is foolhardy. Instead, foreign reformers should accommodate nationalist goals and patron-client networks while still finding ways to make state institutions more effective, accountable, and law abiding. Making demands and recommendations that avoid threatening core domestic interests while still improving state institutions is a complex political challenge. It requires a deep knowledge of the society in which foreign institution builders are working and autonomy to adapt reform based on local constraints. The foreign organizations pursuing institution building, however, often do not have sufficient local knowledge or autonomy. Enabling foreign reformers to select demands or recommendations to maximize reform success depends in part on understanding how the current structures and practice of US and international organizations limit local knowledge and autonomy and then changing them accordingly.

The next section presents the results of the case studies and discusses the book's overall conclusions. I then describe the problems that limit the local knowledge and autonomy of foreign institution builders and consider some options to address these issues. The chapter concludes by discussing alternative arguments, the wider applicability of the book, and directions for future research.

FINDINGS AND OVERARCHING RECOMMENDATIONS

In chapter 2, I describe three different theoretical explanations for when and how foreign-supported reform might improve a state institution:

- My own "domestic opposition" theory focuses on how the threat of foreign demands to nationalist goals or patron-client networks can provoke domestic opposition and how different forms of domestic opposition in turn shape the potential for a reform effort to improve a state institution.
- The international resource theory emphasizes the impact of a strong mandate, money, personnel, planning, and coordination. It claims that when high resources are present, foreign reforms have a wide range of available techniques to improve a partner's institution and counter opposition.
- The path dependence theory argues that the preexisting level of development is the greatest determinant of the prospects for foreign-supported reform. It also argues that foreign reform can be counterproductive, as intense foreign assistance can disincentivize domestic actors from pursuing reform.

Each of the seven case studies examines the process and outcome of a given reform effort over multiple stages to determine to what extent the case offers support for the predictions of these theories. While these seven case studies are not necessarily representative of the full range of foreign reform efforts, they do consider a range of regions, varied mandates, and several types of state institutions. By demonstrating that similar dynamics were applied in the best-resourced reform efforts in Kosovo, Iraq, Bosnia, and Timor-Leste and in the lower-resourced case of Ukraine, the case studies indicate that the three theories likely offer insight for a broad range of foreign-supported institution building.

Table 7.1 summarizes the case studies' evaluation of the theories. It indicates whether the process and outcome observed by the case study met the predictions of the theory ("Yes"), whether the case study only partially met the theories' predictions ("Partially"), or whether the case study did not meet the predictions of the theory ("No"). It also notes whether one of the theories offers the "best" explanation of the events I observe.

Table 7.1 indicates that there is substantial support for all three theories. The domestic opposition theory offers the greatest explanatory power, including providing the best available explanation for several reforms in which the other theories provided little or partial explanatory power. The international resources and path dependence theories also helped to explain many cases of reform and offered at least a partial explanation in all but one case study. These results indicate that all three theories can offer at least some insight for improving policymaking in the future.

The international resources theory generally recommends that a foreign mission should have a strong enough mandate and sufficient personnel and money to match the challenges of a given society.[1] The case studies generally show that the strength of the foreign mandate and associated personnel and money enabled greater improvements in state institutions. The resource theory and case studies also emphasize the value of bureaucratic resources, such as planning, unity of effort, and organizational learning. As shown in Iraq and Timor-Leste, addressing bureaucratic gaps offers a ready means to improve institution-building outcomes. Of the techniques suggested by the international resources theory, capacity building (H1A), substituting for local state institutions (H1D), and imposing changes in laws or

TABLE 7.1. Summary of Theoretical Findings of Case Studies

	Does the case study meet the predictions of this theory?		
	Domestic Opposition	**International Resources**	**Path Dependence**
Kosovo Central Government	Yes (Best)	Partially	Partially
Iraq Central Government	Partially (Best)	Partially	Partially
BiH Defense	Yes (Best)	Yes	No
Timor-Leste Defense	Yes	Yes (Best)	Yes
BiH Police	Yes (Best)	No	Yes
Iraq Police	Yes	Yes	Yes (Best)
Ukraine Defense	Yes (Best)	Yes	Partially

Note: BiH = Bosnia and Herzegovina.

regulations (H1F) appear to be generally more effective. Techniques that involve shaping domestic attitudes or political outcomes appear less effective, including persuading domestic actors (H1B), shaping electoral outcomes (H1C), and building support for reform through public campaigns (H1E). Increasing the available international resources can facilitate greater success, but it also increases the costs borne by Western governments.

The path dependence theory, by contrast, argues that foreign reformers should avoid pursuing reform in societies with poor preexisting conditions. There is support for the hypothesis that state institutions follow preexisting structures and practices (H2A), despite foreign efforts to graft on new elements. Preexisting conditions seriously limited the prospects for reform of some institutions, such as the central government and police in Iraq. I find mixed evidence for the hypothesis that state institutions revert to their previous condition after foreign resources decline (H2B). The military in Timor-Leste and the police in Iraq did decline after foreign reformers left, although in Bosnia the quality of the defense institutions persisted after a decline in resources. The case studies do not offer support for the strongest claim of the path dependence theory that foreign-supported reform is counterproductive, because it reduces the incentives for local elites to pursue reform on their own (H2C). Instead, I find that reform failure usually comes about because of low resources or domestic opposition. The implication for Western countries planning reform missions is to be judicious about pursuing ambitious and expensive reform in countries with low-quality preexisting institutions but that the failure of reform in these societies is not inevitable.

While the international resources and path dependence theories do offer insight for future policymaking, two factors limit the utility of the policy implications associated with these theories. First, the politics of domestic opposition often override the expected causal relationship of international resources or preexisting conditions. In the five cases where domestic opposition offered the best explanation, international resources or preexisting conditions could not fully explain the process or outcome of reform. In the case of the BiH police, for example, the threat to Serb nationalist goals had more influence on the behavior of Serb officials than high international resources. In building central governments in both Kosovo and Iraq, UNMIK and the CPA were able to make more rapid progress building central governing institutions than the path dependence theory would expect. Taking account of domestic opposition is therefore essential to understanding why reform succeeds or fails.

Second, foreign demands and recommendations are often easier to change than international resources or the decision of where to intervene. While pursuing reform in societies with poor preexisting institutions may not maximize the potential for success, it may also be necessary for US and international policy objectives. Similarly, while having greater resources may enable greater success, foreign reformers often must work with what they have. Political decisions about where to intervene or what resources to provide may not be negotiable. The challenge for most missions is to figure out how to make the best out of a difficult situation. This book argues that in any reform effort—whatever the available resources or preexisting institutions—it is possible for foreign reformers to achieve greater success by carefully selecting their demands or recommendations to take account of nationalist goals and the ruling elites' patron-client networks.

The case studies show how foreign reforms that threaten nationalist goals are counterproductive. They produce widespread mass protests and elite objections that delegitimize future reform, as in the cases of riots in Kosovo in 2004 and Serb opposition to police restructuring in Bosnia. Avoiding demands that threaten nationalist goals is most straightforward in societies like Timor-Leste, where the dominant group seeks independence and local interests align with those of the international community. It is more difficult for reformers to avoid threatening all major groups' nationalist goals in ethnically divided societies, such as Bosnia and Kosovo. In Bosnia, for example, Bosniaks had the nationalist goal of pursuing a stronger central state, which was often opposed to the Bosnian Serbs' goal of protecting the autonomy of the Republika Srpska. Making an institution more effective and accountable may also contradict the nationalist goals of a particular group. For example, accountability to the broader population may require ethnic integration, which conflicts with a group's desire for autonomy.

In circumstances where desirable reforms have the potential to threaten nationalist goals, foreign reformers must seek clever compromises that thread the needle between groups' competing goals while still improving the quality of institutions. Such compromises often mean slow, incremental reform. Incremental progress can build over time, especially where there are multiple stages of reform. Defense reform in Bosnia offers a good example. Foreign reformers first established a state-level Ministry of Defense supervising the entity-level structures and then in the second stage of reform created a unified BiH military. To recognize Serb political rights, the new military structure effectively, but not officially, established mono-ethnic regiments and infantry battalions. While this compromise did not meet the maximalist goals of the international community or any local group, it did offer a path forward. Deep understanding of the history and political interests in the partner society combined with a wide knowledge of state institutions in other societies appears necessary to formulating such creative compromises.

Foreign reformers can generally achieve the greatest success by avoiding demands or recommendations that threaten the ruling elites' patron-client networks. The domestic opposition theory argues that reforms threatening the ruling elites' patron-client networks are likely to make progress only if there are high resources present. The case studies offer some support for this prediction. In the case of police reform in Iraq and defense reform in Timor-Leste and Ukraine, foreign demands and recommendations that posed the least threat to patron-client networks tended to be more implemented than those that posed a greater threat, and the level of implementation also varied based on available international resources, especially bureaucratic resources. Furthermore, following one of the process predictions of the domestic opposition theory, international resources sometimes enabled foreign reformers to counteract private opposition, such as in Iraq, where US military officers were sometimes able to monitor and limit Shia militia activities.

The case studies suggest that finding creative demands or recommendations that improve state institutions while not threatening ruling elites' patron-client networks is the most efficient approach to improve state institutions. To be sure, there may be cases where challenging some elements of the ruling elites' patron-client networks is necessary and even desirable. There are no clear examples in this book, however, in which international resources enabled foreign reformers to achieve major progress in the face of intense private obstruction. There are several cases in which foreign reformers achieved greater success by formulating their demands to limit the threat to these networks, as in the reform of the BiH military. Indeed, eliminating or fully undermining these networks is beyond the resources of any mission studied in this book, which includes the highest-resourced interventions since 1990. It is also true that the impact of foreign reform efforts on elite networks is more complex than the binary coding suggested by the domestic opposition theory. Further study of the relationship between foreign reform and these networks could be helpful in enabling foreign reformers to improve state institutions.

Increasing the available international resources, especially bureaucratic resources of planning and coordination, may improve the success of reforms that threaten the ruling elites' patron-client networks. But it is equally if not more important for foreign reformers to propose changes in state institutions that navigate the complexities of domestic political constraints, especially in the vast majority of cases where resources are constrained. Understanding the domestic political constraints and having sufficient autonomy are essential for such politically adept maneuvering.

POLICY PROBLEMS AND SPECIFIC RECOMMENDATIONS

My recommendation represents the reverse of the common approach that foreign reformers frequently take to selecting demands and recommendations. Namely, as noted in chapter 2, foreign reformers often begin by identifying the problems with a state institution; proposing changes in structure or practices to address these problems, often drawn from Western countries; and using what resources are available to push these changes forward—over domestic opposition, if necessary.[2] In the case of the development of central government institutions in Kosovo, for example, UNMIK's standards before status policy created a list of reforms and requirements that Kosovo needed to achieve. The United Nations then pressured Kosovo elites to implement these recommendations by drawing on Western consultants and advisers. In the case of police reform in Bosnia, the international community sought to address the ethnocratic control of policing by imposing cross-entity boundary lines. In Ukraine, the RAND report sought to address the separate reporting lines under the MoD and General Staff by subordinating the General Staff to the MoD. This approach does not intentionally threaten nationalist goals or the ruling elites' patron-client networks. But some analysts or officials may believe that threatening these interests is necessary to correct problems in a state institution.

An important policy contribution of the book is to argue that this common approach is flawed. Selecting demands or recommendations based on observed problems leads to destructive opposition that makes reform less effective and often undermines subsequent reform. Instead of designing demands and recommendations based solely on the problems they observe, I argue that foreign reformers should tailor their proposed changes to avoid threatening nationalist goals and the ruling elites' networks and instead ask for smaller but still meaningful improvements to state institutions.

This is not to say that foreign reformers should encourage reforms that would undermine accountability or the rule of law. Reinforcing these flaws would not only harm the target institution but could also undermine efforts to build quality state institutions in other societies. Avoiding threatening nationalist goals and patron-client networks at a minimum typically means that it is necessary to intentionally delay addressing some observed problems, potentially including corruption, ethnic dominance, and inefficiency. Ideally, foreign reformers would pursue incremental reform over the long term, slowly improving an institution, and waiting to exploit a change in local leadership and preferences. However, the length of foreign reform efforts are time limited, and nationalist goals and patron-client networks are generally slow to change. Successful reform therefore often depends on some degree of accommodation for nationalist goals and patron-client networks. Such accommodation is disappointing, especially when nationalist goals of some groups are linked with wartime human rights violations, and corruption undermines economic development and democracy. However, challenging these interests is ineffective and often leaves the society even worse off.

Formulating creative demands and recommendations that make meaningful changes without threatening core interests depends on local knowledge and autonomy. Some missions may already have these attributes and may already be able to follow this book's recommendations. In most cases, however, foreign missions lack these attributes or are not focused on improving state institutions, as discussed below and detailed in other works.[3] The need to enable foreign reformers to select demands or recommendations that maximize the success of reform gives new urgency to addressing these problems.

Problem 1: Insufficient Autonomy for In-Country Foreign Reformers

In many cases the proposed demands or recommendations are predetermined or constrained by political decisions in the Western countries that are funding and supporting a reform effort, as discussed in chapter 2. In Kosovo, for example, the United States and other Western countries did not want to move forward with Kosovo's independence and, hence, delayed status negotiations and maintained the standards before status policy, despite growing Kosovar opposition. In Iraq, US military commanders faced strong pressure to accelerate the departure of US troops out of Iraq, despite the continuing weakness of Iraq's institutions. In both of these cases, the political environment in Western countries limited the autonomy of foreign reformers on the ground and hurt the prospects for reform. Even in cases where political constraints in Western countries pose less of a challenge, bureaucratic structures and procedures may prevent foreign reformers from modulating their proposed changes to local political constraints. While the organization present in the host country has some autonomy, it may not have the ability to determine or change reform demands or recommendations, even though officials on the ground have the greatest understanding of local political constraints.

The case studies in this book also demonstrate how a mission's leadership often determines its autonomy. The most effective leaders seemed to have the greatest autonomy, whether because of the institutional design of the mission or because the individual leaders had a greater ability to shape the political environment. In Bosnia, for example, Paddy Ashdown benefited from his political experience as the leader of the Liberal Democrats in the United Kingdom.[4] Future missions may also benefit from leaders with experience in domestic politics.

The way to resolve the problem of limited autonomy is simple to describe—provide greater authority to missions on the ground. In practice, this recommendation is far more challenging to implement. There is a great diversity in the structure and mandate of the organizations who pursue reform. Other political priorities may also override the benefits of greater autonomy, especially since not all officials on the ground may be as able to achieve success given greater autonomy. Nevertheless, as the case studies above have demonstrated, the success of foreign-supported reform depends on foreign missions having the autonomy to adapt to local circumstances.

Problem 2: Lack of Local Knowledge

It is also essential for foreign reformers to have a deep understanding of the society in which they are working. However, as many works have observed, the existing practices and structures of foreign interveners often do not encourage the development of local knowledge. As noted in chapter 2, Autesserre highlights how several characteristics of foreign missions—a preference for general technical knowledge over local knowledge, a tendency toward one-size-fits-all approaches, and "short deployments and rapid turnover"—can prevent foreign officials from understanding local dynamics.[5] The case studies document several examples of how gaps in local knowledge undermined reform. For example, in Timor-Leste, an internal dispute within UN headquarters led UNTAET to disregard existing knowledge, leading to a failure to recognize the political importance of Falintil. And planning failures in Iraq prior to the 2003 war contributed to the slow recognition by US officials of the importance of Grand Ayatollah al-Sistani for Iraq's future political development.

However, it is possible for foreign reformers to gain sufficient local knowledge to achieve greater success. In Bosnia Ashdown's experience as a politician appeared to enable him to rapidly gain an understanding of Bosnian politics. In Iraq there were examples of Coalition advisers who developed great understanding of the workings of the Ministry of Interior.[6] Prior knowledge of the language, culture, and history of a society can be beneficial. Rory Stewart, for example, highlights the critical contributions of foreign officials with a deep knowledge of Afghanistan, who "had spent long hours sitting on the floor in [Afghans'] houses, listening to their conversation with other Afghans in Dari or Pashto."[7] Still, such individuals are few in number and, given the scale of many Western interventions, insufficient to staff most advisory efforts. Furthermore, individuals without a background as a regional specialist can also gain an understanding of the local context. In general, the longer that officials are deployed, the more that they can learn about the local society and the partner institution. Some of this knowledge may simply come from experience, but establishing networks with a range of individuals in the host country is also likely to be beneficial.

Some of these recommendations are easier to implement than others. Detailed preparation based on existing materials is neither difficult nor especially costly. The case studies in this book are intended in part as a template for a basic evaluation of a state institution that foreign officials can use in the future to gain local knowledge, including tracing the historical context and the interests of the relevant local political actors. Enabling greater interactions between local and foreign officials and longer tenures may be more difficult depending on the situation in the local society. For example, the establishment of fortified US embassies outside the center of capital cities can make it more difficult for US officials to engage with their local counterparts. Longer tenures may also require major changes in the bureaucratic practices of foreign interveners and could undermine organizational cohesion.[8] In the case of war zones or hardship posts, where it is impractical for officials to be accompanied by their families, longer tenures may be dangerous and emotionally exhausting and may reduce the willingness of the best-qualified personnel to serve. Colocating foreign advisers in local state institutions can be beneficial for building trust and understanding but is not always politically or logistically feasible. Recognizing these constraints, foreign missions should take what measures they can to strengthen their local knowledge.

Problem 3: The United States and the International Community May Not Prioritize Institution Building

Scholars and policymakers emphasize the importance of institution building to achieve US and international policy objectives. Nevertheless, in practice not all foreign organizations that have the mission of reforming state institutions are principally focused on this task. Instead, institution building is often seen as a means to an end. Institution building may not always receive priority attention. One indication of the lower prioritization of institution building is that the metrics that organizations adopt to measure their success may not directly assess the quality of partner institutions. The result is that foreign organizations may not design their efforts to maximize the improvement of partner institutions.

Police reform in Iraq offers one example. The US military's mission focused on establishing security in Iraq. Building the police force and the military was a means to that end. US forces were also directly establishing security, including by conducting patrols and killing or capturing members of terrorist groups. Another example is US counterterrorism efforts in the Philippines from 2001 to 2014, which is sometimes cited as a particular success.[9] US forces lacked the legal authority to use lethal force, and, as in other cases, the US military worked "by, with, and through" their local partners, the Philippine Security Forces (PSF), to weaken radical Islamist groups. US forces provided training as well as specific enablers, such as intelligence, surveillance, and reconnaissance assets.[10] At the same time, US forces used measures of success that focused on the strength of adversary groups and the attitudes of the population, while the quality of the partner forces was only qualitatively and anecdotally assessed.[11] After the United States drew down its forces in 2015, lingering problems within the PSF contributed to a worsening security environment. One account attributes the weaknesses of the PSF in large part to corruption, including links with hostage-taking adversary groups.[12] While these patron-client networks might explain the difficulty of achieving reform, the

US military's focus on weakening adversary groups over building sustainable, high-quality institutions may have contributed to the continuing problems with the PSF.

A further challenge is that US security cooperation is not always primarily intended to improve the quality of a partner's institutions. Indeed, security cooperation may be intended to strengthen US forces, gain base access, and increase US sales of military equipment to allies and partners.[13] There are some authorities under 10 USC Section 333 to explicitly build partner capabilities for purposes such as "counterterrorism, counter-weapons of mass destruction operations, ... [and] maritime and border security operations." Operations under these authorities are explicitly required to "promote ... institutional capacity building" as part of their activities.[14] However, such operations are limited in scope and are only one component of the larger range of US security cooperation. How exactly to adapt US structures and institutions to more sustainably strengthen partner institutions is one of several areas for further study discussed below.

ALTERNATIVE ARGUMENTS AND EXTENSIONS

The case studies and other works point to several additional alternative arguments beyond international resources, path dependence, or domestic opposition that may offer insight for the success of institution building. One argument is that some state institutions may have characteristics that make them relatively easier or harder to reform. As proposed in chapter 4, for example, defense institutions may be easier to reform since military officers have a strong sense of professionalism, which makes them relatively more eager to gain respect from their international counterparts. Fukuyama also claims that it is easier to reform state institutions that make fewer decisions, especially when those decisions can be more readily objectively evaluated, such as in central banking.[15] Police forces or educational institutions, by contrast, may be more difficult to reform since they make a large number of decisions that are difficult to evaluate as good or bad. Much of the variation in types of institutions can be explained by the threat to domestic interests, resources, or preexisting institutions. As noted chapter 5, two reasons why the police in particular are more difficult to reform is that patron-client networks are more likely to be embedded in the police, and it is more difficult to have qualified international personnel and, hence, high resources.

A second alternative approach is to explore how other political interests beyond nationalist goals and the ruling elites' patron-client client networks may also explain domestic responses to foreign-supported reform. In Iraq, for example, Sistani achieved more effective opposition by referencing broad democratic standards rather than Shia interests. Louis-Alexandre Berg also argues that the fragmentation or cohesion of domestic parties may determine their incentive and ability to block reform.[16] Another possible extension of the domestic opposition theory would be to explore how nonruling elites may block reform that threatens their patron-client networks. I have focused on the potential threat to nationalist goals and the ruling elites' patron-client networks since these interests appear to be particularly important in motivating and enabling damaging opposition. Nevertheless, other important political interests may motivate domestic behavior.[17] Future study should explore how these other interests also influence domestic responses to foreign reform.

A third approach is suggested by Philippe Leroux-Martin, based on his experience in the later stage of police restructuring in Bosnia. Leroux-Martin describes the competition for power between foreign officials and domestic elites as a complex system that in part adjudicated based on the will of the local population and broader international community.[18] From his perspective, there is no consistently predictable relationship between the content of the reform (e.g., the threat of foreign demands to specific domestic interests) and the effectiveness of domestic opposition. Elites can be expected to oppose reforms that undermine their position, but their power relative to the international community is constantly changing and difficult to evaluate. To be successful, according to this point of view, foreign reformers must have a sufficient understanding of the dynamics of the society to know what reforms they can push for in the face of elite opposition, while still retaining sufficient popular and international support to maintain their legitimacy. Ashdown articulates a similar approach and highlights the importance of public opinion: "Time and again what I had to do was to make assessments about what was tolerable with the public. I was always extremely conscious that if I extended what I did beyond the tolerance of the public my powers would vanish immediately. The point that I thought was difficult and used to cause me to stay awake at night is that the views of the public is not necessarily the views of their political representatives."[19] Ashdown and Leroux-Martin effectively argue that there are not generalizable principles for knowing when foreign reform will be acceptable and when it will not be. The fine-tuned political instincts necessary to predict what type of reform the population will tolerate thereby becomes a critically important international resource—as Ashdown notes, "The ex-politicians are rather better at it than ex-diplomats."[20]

This approach, seeing reform as a broader unpredictable political competition, is certainly more flexible than my domestic opposition theory. There are several problems with it, however. First, it is difficult to falsify. If reform fails, this approach can always claim that foreign officials failed to sufficiently account for domestic political dynamics, whether or not officials had an accurate picture. Second, it is difficult for future missions to replicate. Some lucky missions may have leaders who have an intuitive sense of the local politics, but others may not.

Third, my case studies indicate that even leaders who have a good sense of the local politics sometimes make mistakes. Ashdown argues that the police restructuring effort was largely completed, and subsequent international leaders failed to follow through.[21] Instead, there is indication that Ashdown's assessment of what could be achieved was flawed and that the reform failed because of a threat of foreign demands to nationalist goals. The case studies show how nationalist goals and the ruling elites' patron-client networks indicate where foreign reformers will face strong opposition against which they can achieve little progress. Without discounting the need for political instincts, my domestic opposition theory offers a useful and replicable guide of what demands or recommendations foreign missions should pursue.

APPLICABILITY OF ARGUMENT TO FUTURE INSTITUTION BUILDING

This book has examined seven cases of institution building, but there is good reason to believe that domestic opposition limits reform in other cases as well. One indication of the broader explanatory power of my argument is the example of Ukraine, which shows that domestic opposition can also occur in cases where foreign reformers have relatively little leverage. The key scope condition determining the relevance of my argument is the importance of nationalist goals and the ruling elites' patron-client networks in overall political competition in a society and in a particular state institution. So long as these political interests are important, my theory is likely to offer explanatory power.

Based on this book's focus on central government, military, and police reform, it seems most likely that my argument will apply in other efforts to reform these institutions. The central government and police appear to be particularly important for defining the political rights of groups in a society and for the distribution of political power, so efforts to reform these institutions are also likely to impact nationalist goals or patron-client networks. Foreign reformers working on these issues should be particularly careful to understand how their demands or recommendations interact with these interests.

There is also good reason to believe that the domestic opposition theory could explain the process and outcome of reform in other types of state institutions, such as education, health, and local governance. In Bosnia, for example, local elites appear to have shaped educational institutions to maintain preexisting nationalist ideologies.[22] Opposition to reforms threatening nationalist goals or patron-client networks could similarly slow a wide range of international development efforts seeking to improve democracy, governance, or economic prosperity.

Domestic opposition may be less relevant in societies where nationalist goals or patron-client networks play a smaller role in state institutions or where reform has little chance of impacting these issues. For example, central banking or air traffic control may be less subject to potential domestic opposition. Similarly, US support for the militaries of highly developed European partners and allies has little potential to produce domestic opposition so long as nationalist sentiment supports cooperation with the United States.[23] In such cases international resources likely play a larger role in the outcome of reform, which the domestic opposition theory predicts if there is a low threat.

The domestic opposition theory may also offer insight for reform efforts that do not involve foreign actors. Public and private opposition could occur in the cases where there is no foreign pressure or assistance. For example, one group may try to mobilize large-scale protests in response to a domestically driven reform that threatens their nationalist goals. Elites who feel their patron-client networks threatened could also engage in delay or co-optation to protect their networks. For example, Chris Miller shows how domestic elites within the Soviet Union extracted resources and used delay tactics to block the economic reform proposed by Mikhail Gorbachev in in 1980s.[24] It may be possible for future works to generalize about when and how nationalism and patron-client networks pose a challenge for any reform effort, whether exclusively domestically driven or supported by foreign actors.

DIRECTIONS FOR FUTURE RESEARCH

My theory and case studies suggest several areas for future research. A first area for further study is the applicability of my domestic opposition theory to the wider range of institution-building efforts suggested above. Additional case studies of reform efforts in other countries and regions, including Latin America and Africa or where there are low international resources, could be valuable.

Another challenge that future research could help address is the lack of reliable indicators of the quality of state institutions. This book proposes a system for evaluating the quality of state institutions based on their effectiveness, accountability, and compliance with law. This scoring system facilitates comparisons across the different reform efforts studied in this book, but it is somewhat subjective. Evaluating and improving foreign reform efforts depends on tracing the quality of state institutions over time, but there are not many templates for how to evaluate such progress, nor are there available off-the-shelf measures.[25] One way that future academic work could inform policymaking is to develop more reliable tools for measuring the quality of state institutions over time.

Finally, this book has focused on US, UN, and Western-led institution building. It does not examine institution building by non-Western powers, such as Russia or China, or historical institution-building cases by autocratic states.[26] One possible difference between Western-led institution building and institution building by autocratic powers is that nondemocracies may not take as much account of popular sovereignty and, hence, may be less vulnerable to public opposition. Autocratic institution builders may also have difficulty identifying private opposition, but their recourse to more coercive measures may make it easier to deter such opposition. Nevertheless, contemporary Western institution builders have some important advantages. Many individuals within societies experiencing Western-led institution building recognize that they too stand to benefit from Western efforts. Depending on the specific circumstances, locals may have a greater incentive to assist democratic institution builders than autocratic ones.

The potential for domestic opposition is a major challenge facing foreign reform missions, but it does not mean that Western reformers should abandon institution building or disregard their ultimate objective to build high-quality state institutions. Instead, this book argues that foreign reformers should adopt different tactics. Instead of simply proposing Western models to correct observed problems, foreign reformers should select demands or recommendations that navigate around the core domestic interests—namely, nationalist goals and the ruling elites' patron-client networks. Over time, by carefully proposing new demands or recommendations, foreign reformers can incrementally improve state institutions. Over the long term, foreign missions will ultimately achieve significant progress, building high-quality state institutions that facilitate peace, democracy, and prosperity, even in societies with little prior political development.

NOTES

1 Miller, *Armed State Building.*

2 See also Pritchett and Woolcock, "Solutions When the Solution Is the Problem," 197.

3 See, for example, Autesserre, *Peaceland*; and Autesserre, *Trouble with the Congo.*

4 See Ashdown, *Fortunate Life.*

5 Autesserre, *Peaceland*, 70–93.

6 Andrew Rathmell notes that "one carefully selected, experienced and well-trained advisor is worth several untrained, inexperienced individuals who can actually set back a programme through inappropriate actions." Andrew Rathmell, "Fixing Iraq's Internal Security Forces: Why Is Reform of the Ministry of Interior So Hard?," Center for Strategic and International Studies, November 2007, 12–13, 16.

7 Stewart and Knaus, *Can Intervention Work?*, 83.

8 See, e.g., Harry W. Kopp, *Career Diplomacy: Life and Work in the US Foreign Service, Second Edition* (Washington, DC: Georgetown University Press, 2011).

9 Zachary Abuza, "Where Did the US Go Wrong in the Philippines? A Hard Look at a 'Success' Story," *War on the Rocks*, June 14, 2018, https://warontherocks.com/2018/06/where-did-the-u-s-go-wrong-in-the-philippines-a-hard-look-at-a-success-story/.

10 Robinson, Johnston, and Oak, *US Special Operations Forces in the Philippines, 2001–2014*, 23–31.

11 Robinson, Johnston, and Oak, 91–92.

12 Abuza, "Where Did the US Go Wrong in the Philippines?"

13 For a list of goals, see, for example, Michael Hartmayer and John Hansen, "Security Cooperation in Support of Theater Strategy," *Military Review*, February 2013, 24–29; and Defense Security Cooperation Agency, *Security Assistance Management Manual*, accessed July 2, 2018, http://www.samm.dsca.mil/chapter/chapter-1.

14 10 USC Section 333, accessed at Legal Information Institute, Cornell Law School, https://www.law.cornell.edu/uscode/text/10/333.

15 Fukuyama, *State-Building*, 56–59.

16 Berg, "From Weakness to Strength."

17 As included in the literature on the strategic interaction between foreign and domestic elites. See, e.g., Stedman, "Spoiler Problems in Peace Processes"; and Barnett, Fang, and Zürcher, "Compromised Peacebuilding."

18 Leroux-Martin, *Diplomatic Counterinsurgency*, 194–97.

19 Phone interview with Ashdown, May 2014; see also Ashdown, *Swords and Ploughshares*, 225.

20 Phone interview with Ashdown, May 2014.

21 Phone interview with Ashdown, May 2014; and Ashdown, *Swords and Ploughshares*, appendix B.

22 See, e.g., Valery Perry, "Countering the Cultivation of Extremism in Bosnia and Herzegovina: The Case for Comprehensive Education Reform," Democratization Policy Council, *DC Policy Note*, New Series no. 10, September 2015, https://docs.house.gov/meetings/FA/FA14/20180418/108176/HHRG-115-FA14-20180418-SD009.pdf.

23 See, e.g., Christopher S. Chivvis, Raphael S. Cohen, Bryan Frederick, Daniel S. Hamilton, F. Stephen Larrabee, and Bonny Lin, *NATO's Northeastern Flank: Emerging Opportunities for Engagement* (Santa Monica, CA: RAND, 2017).

24 Chris Miller, *The Struggle to Save the Soviet Economy: Mikhail Gorbachev and the Collapse of the USSR* (Chapel Hill: University of North Carolina Press, 2016). I thank Austin Long for suggesting this example.

25 For one template, for defense institutions, see Schaefer et al., *Developing a Defense Sector Assessment Rating Tool*.

26 For one comparison of different logics of foreign occupation, see Cooley, *Logics of Hierarchy*.

APPENDIX

RESEARCH DESIGN AND METHODOLOGY

This appendix provides additional detail on five methodological issues mentioned in chapter 1. First, the appendix provides additional data demonstrating that Kosovo, Iraq, Bosnia, and Timor-Leste were indeed the highest-resourced interventions with a state-building mandate since 1990. Second, the appendix provides additional details on the three approaches of causal inference used in the case studies: congruence testing, causal process tracing, and within- and across-case comparisons. Third, the appendix discusses the use of interviews and other data sources. Fourth, the appendix offers more detail on the scoring system I use for evaluating the quality of state institutions, including outlining the questions that the case studies use to make assessments. Finally, the appendix offers more detail on the regional comparisons that the case studies use as a benchmark for scoring the quality of state institutions.

CASE SELECTION

Table A.1 lists postwar missions since 1989 and their associated mandate, level of economic assistance, troop presence, and preintervention gross domestic product per capita. This list includes cases of postwar US and UN intervention where there was a significant institution-building mandate since 1990.[1] The highest-resource interventions (shown in bold) occurred in four societies: Bosnia, Kosovo, Iraq, and Timor-Leste. These societies had the strongest mandates: they were transitional administrations in which the foreign actor exercised temporary sovereignty authority, including directly governing the society or maintaining the right to overrule local officials.[2] As part of their mandate, foreign actors in these societies conducted substantial institution building, supported by money and personnel. Bureaucratic

TABLE A.1. Major International Interventions with a State-Building Mandate after 1990

Country	Year	Mission	Mandate, as implemented	Assistance per capita[a]	Peak troops/ 1,000 population	Pre-mission GDP per capita[b]
Namibia	1989–1990	UN Transition Assistance Group	Elections	$132	1.3	$2,798 (1988)
Cambodia	1992–1993	UN Transitional Authority in Cambodia	Executive power to enable free and fair elections	$28	1.5	$302 (1993)
Somalia	1993–1995	UN Operation in Somalia II	Creation of secure environment	$137	5.7	No data
BiH	1995–present	OHR, OSCE, NATO, EU	Various as specified by Dayton Agreement	$277	17.5	$3,116 (1990)
Eastern Slavonia	1996–1998	UN Transitional Administration for Eastern Slavonia	Transitional administration but limited institution building	$290	35.3	$5,887 (1990)
Timor-Leste	1999–2012	UNTAET and successors	Transitional administration	$233	9.8	$490 (1998)
Sierra Leone	1999–present	UN Mission in Sierra Leone	Security sector reform	$25	3.6	$183 (1998)

Kosovo	1999–present	UNMIK	Transitional administration	$526	19.3	$1,125 (1990)
Afghanistan	1999–present	UN Assistance Mission in Afghanistan, International Security Assistance Force	Secure environment, security sector reform	$57	4.7[c]	$117 (2001)
Iraq	2003–present	CPA, UN Assistance Mission in Iraq	Occupation authority under CPA, security sector reform	$206	6.5	$3,022 (2002)

Sources: Dobbins et al., *UN's Role in Nation-Building*, 239; Dobbins et al., *Europe's Role in Nation-Building*, 243–44, 259; World Bank Development Indicators, https://data.worldbank.org/indicator/SP.POP.TOTL?locations=AF; "How Many Foreign Troops Are in Afghanistan," *BBC*, October 15, 2015, https://www.bbc.com/news/world-south-asia-11371138; and Stathis Kalyvas and Nicholas Sambanis, "Bosnia's Civil War: Origins and Violence Dynamics," in *Understanding Civil War*, vol. 2, *Europe, Central Asia, and Other Regions*, ed. Paul Collier and Nicholas Sambanis (Washington, DC: World Bank Publications, 2005), 196.

Note: Bold indicates the highest-resource interventions. CPA = Coalition Provisional Authority; GDP = gross domestic product; NATO = North Atlantic Treaty Organization; OHR = Office of the High Representative; OSCE = Organization for Security and Cooperation in Europe; UNMIK = UN Mission in Kosovo.

[a] In fixed 2000 USD for the first two years after the war.

[b] Prices are in inflation adjusted 2000 dollars. Data is from World Bank, World Development Indicators, drawing from the listed year GDP in USD and then adjusting to 2000 (except for Iraq, where data is from inflation adjusted constant 2010 dollars, then readjusted for inflation to 2000 dollars). I use estimates from Kalyvas and Sambanis for the former Yugoslav regions of Bosnia, Eastern Slavonia (I use data for Croatia), and Kosovo. I use Indonesia data for Timor-Leste. Inflation adjustment using Consumer Price Index Inflation Calculator https://data.bls.gov/cgi-bin/cpicalc.pl.

[c] Based on a population of 29,708,599 and a maximum troop presence of 140,000 in 2011.

resources, including the level of planning and coordination, did vary, as the case studies discuss.

As table A.1 indicates, there is also variation in the level of preintervention socioeconomic development of these four societies. This variation is associated with the quality of state institutions in these societies before foreign intervention. Because of this variation, the case studies drawn from these societies also offer a good opportunity to evaluate the path dependence theory.

CAUSAL INFERENCE

The case studies evaluate the competing hypotheses in three different ways. First, I use congruence testing, meaning determining whether the observed outcome of reform effort reflects the competing outcome predictions of the different theories. Congruence testing involves comparing the change in the quality of the state institution over time to the predicted outcome of the various theories (as provided by the numbered hypotheses, H1–H6). To measure change in outcomes over time, each case study measures the highest historical quality of the state institution, the pre-reform quality of the institution, and the quality after each of stage of reform. To develop a prediction about the outcome of reform for the international resource theory, I measure the level of resources over the course of the reform effort using the guidelines described in chapter 2. To develop predictions based on the domestic opposition theory, I evaluate the threat of foreign demands or recommendations to the nationalist goals and ruling elites' patron-client networks, also discussed in chapter 2. The path dependence theory predicts that the state institution will be below the highest historical level of quality and, if it exceeds this level, will recede to it once foreign resources decline. The conclusion of each case study describes the results of the congruence testing.

Second, the case studies use causal process tracing to evaluate the explanatory power of the process hypotheses (the lettered sub-predictions of the theory, including H1A–E, H2A–D, etc.). Process tracing, as Alexander George and Andrew Bennett write, involves "attempts to trace the links between possible causes and observed outcomes."[3] In the course of telling the story of the reform effort, each case study describes details or data points that offer evidence in support of or opposition to the proposed process hypotheses of the different theories.[4] More formally, this evidence consists of "causal process observations" that indicate that a theory is in fact operating as expected (such as an observation that, when demands threaten nationalist goals, the population opposes the reform effort or opposes the foreign reformer [see H1B]).[5] By identifying and evaluating the causal mechanisms, the theory and case studies can distinguish between the influence of the variables associated with domestic opposition, international resources, or path dependence.[6]

Third, the case studies compare within and across the different case studies using the comparative method. Comparisons are especially useful because there may be many possible reasons why a reform succeeded or failed, and careful comparisons can sometimes eliminate competing explanations. This book uses three main types of comparisons. First, I compare reforms of the same institution in different countries (e.g., defense reform in Bosnia and Timor-Leste). Since the type of institution is the same in both cases, it stands to reason that the type of state institution cannot explain the variation in process or outcome between these cases. Second, I compare different state institutions within the same countries (e.g., reform of the police and military in Bosnia). Similarly, the overall circumstances in a given country cannot explain differences in the development of two reform efforts within the same society. Third, I compare different stages within a particular reform effort. Within-case comparisons can be especially useful for isolating the impact of different factors because many (although not all) factors that influence the success of reform are likely to remain constant over time.[7] The changes over the course of stages of reform outlined in table 1.2 indicate some of the comparisons that I draw from in the case studies.

There are limitations of each of these methods, but by using all three in combination, it is possible to gain confidence about the explanatory power of the different theories. For example, while congruence testing could be biased by measurement challenges and unobserved variables, the comparisons between and within cases can increase confidence that a given variable is associated with a particular outcome. Process tracing shows that a particular variable did lead to a given outcome as expected. While process observations supporting a theory in one or more case studies may not mean that the theory explains other cases, the use of the congruence testing, the comparative method, and examples from other reform efforts can increase confidence that the findings of the case studies are more widely applicable.

SOURCES

The case studies draw on a wide range of primary and secondary source data. For some of the reform efforts studied in chapters 4–7, there is a high-quality existing literature that offers a detailed account of the relevant reforms. In others, especially the more recent cases, there are fewer available sources. To gain a firsthand perspective and provide additional evidence to fill gaps, this book relies on personal interviews that I conducted with international officials, domestic elites, and analysts over the course of 2009–18. These interviews were invaluable for filling gaps in the written record and for understanding the context of the society, the motivation and origin of international demands, and the perspective of domestic actors.

While the interviews provided invaluable insight, there are, however, several constraints on interviews, which lead me to cite written materials to support interview evidence where possible. As noted in chapter 1, in order to protect human subjects, the interviews were conducted on a not-for-attribution basis, with the rare exception where the interviewee explicitly agreed to be identified. There are also written sources that provide more detailed accounts of events in specific countries. Furthermore, in some cases, a great deal of time had passed between the date of the interview and the events in question. Interviewees do not always clearly remember events, or their memories may be influenced by other historical accounts. The case studies therefore draw on a combination of interviews; primary sources, such as official reports or documents and contemporaneous media; and secondary sources, such as academic writing, think tank reports, and books.

SCORING SYSTEM QUESTIONS

Chapter 1 describes a 0–9 scoring system that I use to evaluate the quality of state institutions over the course of the case studies. This scoring system evaluates the three desired dimensions of a state institution: effectiveness, accountability, and the rule of law. This section describes in more detail how I develop scores for each of these three dimensions.

As specified in chapter 1, in each dimension, a score of 0 corresponds to nonexistence or complete dysfunction; 1 means that the institution has some basic framework or structure but little else; 2 means that the state institution has some desired characteristics but does not meet regional standards; and 3 corresponds to an institution that operates at or above the level of comparable institutions in neighboring countries.

Judging the quality of a state institution on these dimensions is not straightforward. There are many possible attributes that could be evaluated. Further, data availability is a major challenge—as noted in chapter 1, the state institutions studied here have not yet been consistently evaluated over time. Because it is necessary to evaluate a state institution across multiple stages of reform, there are also practical limits of how many questions the case studies can realistically answer.

The case studies therefore draw where appropriate from the list of questions below. These questions enable a thorough but flexible approach to incorporate what data is available. I propose different questions for each type of state institution (central representative, military, and police) and each dimension of quality (effectiveness, accountability, and the rule of law).[8] A similar set of questions could be developed for other state institutions, such as education, health, or land management. Where available, I also use other scholars' assessment of the quality of state institutions, such as Elton Skendaj's analysis of Kosovo.[9]

Central Government

Effectiveness

- Is there a constitution or other basic law that specifies the formal rules of government, including the powers of the executive, legislature, and judiciary and the way in which they are selected?
- Are there ministries (or other basic central supervisory and service-providing organizations) in place? Are there ministers (or other leaders) selected to run the ministries?
- Do foreign actors regularly supersede domestic-appointed or elected ruling officials?
- To what extent do outside powers (other than the Western intervener) influence or dictate political outcomes?
- Are there effective and productive negotiations with neighboring countries?
- Does the central government make laws or other rulings? To what extent are the laws enforced?
- In the case of democratic governments, is there a parliament (or other main legislative body)? If so, does it focus on policy discussions and passing legislation or on symbolic (e.g., nationalist) issues?
- For European countries, is there progress toward joining the EU or NATO, or both?

Accountability

- Is the government elected or is there a clear plan for holding elections?
- Are elections free and fair?
- Are ethnic minority parties able to participate in elections, and meaningfully represented?
- Do leading officials or parties express respect for democratic values? Are there "moderates" rather than radical parties in government?
- To what extent is there a framework in place to protect minority rights? This may include minimal ethnic quotas, ethnic autonomy, minority language rights, or other protections.

Rule of Law

- Is there a constitution or other basic law that specifies the formal rules of government, including the powers and means of appointing the executive, legislature, and judiciary?
- To what extent does the legal framework constrain the behavior of the executive?
- To what extent does the judiciary and/or legislature play an oversight role over the executive?
- To what extent is there corruption in the central government, and is corruption investigated and prosecuted?

Defense

Effectiveness

- How effective is the military as a fighting force?
    - Does the military possess capacity and capabilities sufficient to deter or defeat the major internal and external threats facing the country? This may include assessments of doctrine, organization, training, matériel, leadership and education, personnel, and facilities.[10]
    - Can the military support other missions necessary to the country's foreign policy (e.g., deployments to NATO-led missions)?
- Is there a clear and effective chain of command under the government?
- Does the military bureaucracy operate in an efficient manner?

Accountability

- What is the quality of democratic (i.e., linked to the population) oversight of the military within the government?
    - Do parliamentary bodies exist within the government with the authority and ability to oversee defense matters?
- How representative of the overall population is the military?
    - To what extent is the personnel breakdown of the military proportionate to the overall population? Both the enlisted and officer corps?
    - How are minorities represented within the military and leadership? Are they integrated into units?
    - If there is conscription, is it perceived as fair?

Rule of Law

- How well developed is the legal framework ensuring civilian command and control of the military?

  - Is there a legal framework specifying the roles and responsibilities of the military?
  - Is the elected (if country is democratic) leadership in charge of the military?
  - Are civilian officials able to command and make changes in the military?
- How well does the military follow the law?
  - Are there egregious and multiple examples of senior military personnel not following the law? In ways that raise questions about general discipline?
  - Is there a fear of or experience of coups?
  - Does the structure of the military prevent it from initiating a civil war (in ethnically divided/civil war–prone societies)?

Police

Effectiveness

- What are perceptions of security and the police?
  - Do surveys of individuals reveal major concerns about personal security? Do they indicate satisfaction with the police?
  - What is the perception of foreign observers of the quality of the police, its ability to enforce the law, and public security in general?
- How high is the crime rate?
- What police organizations are present in the country? How well staffed or funded?
- Are there known gaps in the functions that the police carry out?

Accountability

- How are minorities represented within the police force and respected by the police?
  - Do the police reflect the ethnic balance of the population? Is the police organization ethnically integrated? Can ethnic minorities serve in the police without fear?
  - Do the police treat ethnic minorities the same as the majority population?
  - Does the structure and function of the police reinforce ethnic segregation or encourage ethnic integration?
  - Is there regular violence or patterns of human rights violations by elements of the police from one group against another?
- How well established are mechanisms for parliamentary accountability of the police?
- Is an elected or representative local official in charge of the police?

Rule of Law

- How developed is the legal framework governing the police?
- Do the police follow the law?
  - Is criminal prosecution believed to be politicized? Are police believed to be under control of the political elite? To what extent is there believed to be corruption in the police?
- Do the police follow international standards, including the prosecution of war crimes?

COUNTRY COMPARISONS

Chapter 1 argues that similar institutions in other countries in the immediate region offer a useful point of comparison for understanding the quality of a state institution experiencing foreign-supported reform. The case studies use such comparisons as a baseline for coding the quality of state institutions before a reform and after a reform effort. The case studies focus on changes in the institution itself, rather than comparisons with other countries, to identify changes across stages. Below I offer additional detail about country comparisons and sourcing for the associated quality measurements in the case studies.[11]

Chapter 3 compares Kosovo's central government to state institutions elsewhere in former Yugoslavia. I rely on discussion of the history of Kosovo prior to 1990 and its institutions from secondary sources, with a particular focus on how Kosovo's institutions compared with the republics within the Yugoslavia (even though Kosovo was not itself a republic, it was an autonomous province of Serbia). For my assessment of the quality of Kosovo's central government after independence in 2008, I use the European Commission 2009 progress reports on both Serbia and Kosovo.[12] While not necessarily the best developed of the former Yugoslav republics, Serbia was the largest and provides a relatively achievable standard of governance. In the progress reports, the European Commission evaluated the progress of both countries to meet the European Union's requirements for membership. I examine the European Commission's assessment of each country separately since the European Commission does not explicitly compare progress in Kosovo and Serbia in these reports. Nevertheless, the extent to where the European Commission identified gaps in each country provides a relatively unbiased comparison of Kosovo's institutions with other institutions in the region.

In analyzing the quality of central government and policing in Iraq, Jordan offers a useful point of comparison as it is generally perceived to be better-governed than nearby Syria.[13] To score the quality of Iraq's central governance and police prior to the Gulf War, I rely on secondary sources describing the Ba'ath regime, some of which offer comparisons to other countries in the region.[14] In the case of the development of the police, I use analysis of the police in Jordan in similar years to offer context for the challenges facing the Iraqi police. In 2011, for example, Iraq's challenges should be seen in the context of the reported abuses by the generally better perceived Jordanian police, which in 2011 reportedly engaged in violence and repression of antigovernment activities, surveillance, torture, and threats against antigovernment groups.[15]

In analyzing the quality of the police and military in BiH, I rely on a range of data and comparisons with the other successor states to Yugoslavia. In the case of defense institutions, a useful comparison is to the Croatian military, given that it also shared its origins in the Yugoslav People's Army and ethnic civil wars that followed.[16] However, the unique challenges facing the BiH military from the original existence of two entity militaries makes direct comparisons more difficult. In the case of the BiH police, I use a 2004 report commissioned by the European Union that specifically sought to compare the quality of the police in BiH to other countries in Europe, not only in the former Yugoslavia.[17] After the end of the reform in 2007, I use as points of comparison homicide data for BiH, Croatia, and Serbia as well as the European Commission progress reports.[18]

In the case of Timor-Leste, Indonesia offers useful point of comparison, albeit with some limitations. To be sure, Timor-Leste seceded from the country and no longer looked to Indonesia as a model. The Indonesian military was also far larger and more developed than the F-FDTL. But Indonesia is a useful comparison because it is the largest country in the region, because of the period of shared history, and because there are few other obvious comparisons available.[19] During Indonesia's occupation, I infer Falintil's military effectiveness based on its engagement with the Indonesian military as well as from a range of secondary sources. To judge the quality of the F-FDTL in 2006, UN reports offer detailed assessments of the problems within F-FDTL, and I use think tank reporting on the Indonesian military to offer additional context.

In the case of the Ukrainian military, I use comparisons with Russia and Poland. The most relevant metric of Ukraine's military effectiveness is the comparison of Ukraine's forces to Russian and Russian-backed forces, especially as demonstrated by Ukraine's ability to fight the separatist forces in eastern Ukraine. Russia does not offer a good comparison regarding accountability and the rule of law, however, given that Ukraine pursued closer integration with NATO. Poland offers a more relevant comparison, although Poland has been a member of NATO since 1999, while Ukraine has consistently pursued NATO membership only since 2014. In addition to my own visits to Ukraine and Poland for prior research, I also rely on several secondary source accounts of the quality of the Polish defense institutions.[20]

NOTES

1 The list draws from Doyle and Sambanis, *Making War and Building Peace*; Dobbins et al., *America's Role in Nation-Building*; Dobbins et al., *UN's Role in Nation-Building*; Dobbins et al., *Europe's Role in Nation-Building*; and Miller, *Armed State Building*. There was a substantial NATO role in Libya, but no significant peace operation or institution-building effort following the conflict. Christopher S. Chivvis, *Toppling Qaddafi: Libya and the Limits of Liberal Intervention* (New York: Cambridge University Press, 2013), 183–87.

2 Tansey, *Regime-Building*; Chesterman, *You, the People*; and Caplan, *International Governance of War-Torn Territories*.

3 George and Bennett, *Case Studies and Theory Development*, 6.

4 As George and Bennett write, "In process-tracing, the researcher examines histories, archival documents, interview transcripts, and other sources to see whether the causal process a theory hypothesizes or implies in a case is in fact evident in the sequence and values of the intervening variables in that case" (6).

5 These causal process observations may include the presence (or absence) of the proposed independent variable, the occurrence of hypothesized mechanisms or intervening variables, or auxiliary outcomes. See Mahoney, "After KKV," 125–29; George and Bennett, *Case Studies and Theory Development*, chap. 10; and Brady and Collier, *Rethinking Social Inquiry*.

6 Oisín Tansey also highlights the utility of process tracing for getting to the root of causality in the case of state building. He notes that many studies of state building conflate "correlation with causation" and assume that the presence of an international intervention indicates that it is responsible for an outcome of interest. Tansey writes, "Many case studies of state-building provide the kind of empirical evidence that is perfectly suited to process tracing" but that they fail because of insufficient specification of causal mechanisms. Tansey, "Evaluating the Legacies of State-Building," 175–77.

7 On within-case comparisons, see George and Bennett, *Case Studies and Theory Development*. See also Staniland, *Networks of Rebellion*, 11–14; and Talmadge, *Dictator's Army*, 37–39.

8 See also the more detailed assessment framework for defense institutions proposed in Schaefer et al., *Developing a Defense Sector Assessment Rating Tool*.

9 Skendaj, *Creating Kosovo*.

10 This is a commonly used template for analyzing military organizations derived from the US Joint Capabilities Integration and Development System. See Chairman of the Joint Chiefs of Staff, "Guidance for Developing and Implementing Joint Concepts," August 17, 2016, CJCSI 3010.02E, http://www.jcs.mil/Portals/36/Documents/Library/Instructions/CJCSI%203010.02E.pdf?ver=2017-02-08-173223-657.

11 Additional citations are included in the case studies.

12 The European Commission Progress Reports for all years are available at https://ec.europa.eu/neighbourhood-enlargement/countries/package_en.

13 See, e.g., the World Bank World Governance Indicators.

14 For example, Ayubi, *Over-Stating the Arab State.*

15 See, e.g., Beverley Milton-Edwards, *Grappling with Islamism: Assessing Jordan's Evolving Approach*, Brookings Doha Center Analysis Paper, no. 19, September 2017, https://www.brookings.edu/wp-content/uploads/2017/09/ap_0930_islamism_in_jordan_milton_edwards.pdf; and Dana Moss, "Repression, Response, and Contained Escalation under 'Liberalized' Authoritarianism in Jordan," *Mobilization: An International Quarterly* 19, no. 3 (September 1, 2014): 261–86.

16 On the Croatian military, see Dreisbach, "Preparing for Peace."

17 ICMPD, "Financial, Organisational and Administrative Assessment of the BiH Police Forces."

18 European Commission, "Bosnia and Herzegovina 2007 Progress Report," November 6, 2007; and European Commission, "Serbia 2007 Progress Report," November 6, 2007. All reports available at https://ec.europa.eu/neighbourhood-enlargement/countries/package_en.

19 For example, there was no military in the Solomon Islands, where Australia also led an intervention. See Dobbins et al., *Europe's Role in Nation-Building*, chap. 8.

20 Rohr-Garztecki, "Long Shadow of History"; and Jeffrey Simon, *Poland and NATO: A Study in Civil-Military Relations* (Lanham, MD: Rowman & Littlefield, 2003).

SELECTED BIBLIOGRAPHY

Acemoglu, Daron, and James A. Robinson. *Economic Origins of Dictatorship and Democracy*. Cambridge: Cambridge University Press, 2006.

———. *Why Nations Fail: The Origins of Power, Prosperity, and Poverty*. New York: Crown, 2013.

Akimenko, Valeriy. "Ukraine's Toughest Fight: The Challenge of Military Reform." Carnegie Endowment for International Peace, February 22, 2018. https://carnegieendowment.org/2018/02/22/ukraine-s-toughest-fight-challenge-of-military-reform-pub-75609.

Albuquerque, Adriana Lins de, and Jakob Hedenskog. "Ukraine: A Defence Sector Reform Assessment." Swedish Defence Research Agency (FOI), December 2015. https://www.foi.se/rapportsammanfattning?reportNo=FOI-R--4157--SE.

Allawi, Ali A. *The Occupation of Iraq: Winning the War, Losing the Peace*. New Haven, CT: Yale University Press, 2007.

Ashdown, Paddy. *A Fortunate Life*. London: Aurum, 2009.

———. *Swords and Ploughshares: Bringing Peace to the 21st Century*. London: Weidenfeld & Nicolson, 2007.

Autesserre, Séverine. *Peaceland: Conflict Resolution and the Everyday Politics of International Intervention*. New York: Cambridge University Press, 2014.

———. *The Trouble with the Congo: Local Violence and the Failure of International Peacebuilding*. Cambridge: Cambridge University Press, 2010.

Aybet, Gülnur. "NATO Conditionality in Bosnia and Herzegovina." *Problems of Post-Communism* 57, no. 5 (September 2010): 20–34. https://doi.org/10.2753/PPC1075-8216570502.

Ayubi, Nazih N. *Over-Stating the Arab State: Politics and Society in the Middle East*. New York: I. B. Tauris, 1996.

Bainter, Ric. "The Elephant in the Room: Defense Reform in Bosnia and Herzegovina." In *Deconstructing the Reconstruction: Human Rights and Rule of Law in Postwar Bosnia and Herzegovina*. Burlington, VT: Ashgate, 2008.

Ball, Desmond. "The Defence of East Timor: A Recipe for Disaster?" *Pacifica Review: Peace, Security & Global Change* 14, no. 3 (2002): 175–89.

Barnett, Michael, Songying Fang, and Christoph Zürcher. "Compromised Peacebuilding." *International Studies Quarterly* 58, no. 3 (September 1, 2014): 608–20.

Barnett, Michael N., and Martha Finnemore. "The Politics, Power, and Pathologies of International Organizations." *International Organization* 53, no. 4 (1999): 699–732.

Bensahel, Nora, Olga Oliker, Keith Crane, and Rick Brennan. *After Saddam: Prewar Planning and the Occupation of Iraq*. Santa Monica, CA: RAND, 2008.

Berg, Louis-Alexandre. "From Weakness to Strength: The Political Roots of Security Sector Reform in Bosnia and Herzegovina." *International Peacekeeping* 21, no. 2 (March 15, 2014): 149–64.

Biddle, Stephen, Jeffrey A. Friedman, and Jacob N. Shapiro. "Testing the Surge: Why Did Violence Decline in Iraq in 2007?" *International Security* 37, no. 1 (July 1, 2012): 7–40.

Bieber, Florian. *Post-War Bosnia: Ethnicity, Inequality and Public Sector Governance*. New York: Palgrave Macmillan, 2006.

Blaydes, Lisa. *State of Repression: Iraq under Saddam Hussein*. Princeton, NJ: Princeton University Press, 2018.

Brady, Henry E., and David Collier, eds. *Rethinking Social Inquiry: Diverse Tools, Shared Standards*. Lanham, MD: Rowman & Littlefield, 2004.

Brand, Marcus. "The Development of Kosovo Institutions and the Transition of Authority from UNMIK to Local Self-Government." Geneva: Centre for Applied Studies in International Negotiations, 2003.

Bratton, Michael, and Nicolas Van de Walle. "Neopatrimonial Regimes and Political Transitions in Africa." *World Politics* 46, no. 4 (July 1, 1994): 453–89.

Bremer, L. Paul. *My Year in Iraq: The Struggle to Build a Future of Hope*. New York: Simon & Schuster, 2006.

Brennan, Rick, Jr., Charles P. Ries, Larry Hanauer, Ben Connable, Terrence Kelly, Michael J. McNerney, Stephanie Young, Jason H. Campbell, and K. Scott McMahon. *Ending the US War in Iraq: The Final Transition, Operational Maneuver, and Disestablishment of United States Forces-Iraq*. Santa Monica, CA: RAND, 2013.

Brownlee, Jason. "Can America Nation-Build?" *World Politics* 59, no. 2 (2007): 314–40.

Call, Charles, and Vanessa Wyeth. *Building States to Build Peace*. Boulder, CO: Lynne Rienner, 2008.

Caplan, Richard. *International Governance of War-Torn Territories: Rule and Reconstruction*. Oxford: Oxford University Press, 2005.

Casey, George W. *Strategic Reflections: Operation Iraqi Freedom, July 2004–February 2007*. Washington, DC: National Defense University Press, 2012.

Chandler, David. "State-Building in Bosnia: The Limits of 'Informal Trusteeship.'" *International Journal of Peace Studies* 11, no. 1 (Spring/Summer 2006): 18–38.

Chandra, Kanchan. *Why Ethnic Parties Succeed: Patronage and Ethnic Headcounts in India*. Cambridge: Cambridge University Press, 2004.

Charap, Samuel, and Timothy J. Colton. *Everyone Loses: The Ukraine Crisis and the Ruinous Contest for Post-Soviet Eurasia*. Abingdon, Oxon: Routledge, 2017.

Chenoweth, Erica, and Maria J. Stephan. *Why Civil Resistance Works: The Strategic Logic of Nonviolent Conflict*. New York: Columbia University Press, 2011.

Chesterman, Simon. *You, the People: The United Nations, Transitional Administration, and State-Building*. Oxford: Oxford University Press, 2004.

Coalition Provisional Authority (CPA). "Agreement of Political Process," November 15, 2003, http://web.archive.org/web/20031121142629/http://www.cpa-iraq.org/audio/20031115_Nov-15-GC-CPA-Final_Agreement-post.htm.

Collantes-Celador, Gemma. "Becoming 'European' through Police Reform: A Successful Strategy in Bosnia and Herzegovina?" *Crime, Law and Social Change* 51, no. 2 (March 2009): 231–42.

Cooley, Alexander. *Logics of Hierarchy: The Organization of Empires, States, and Military Occupations*. Ithaca, NY: Cornell University Press, 2005.

Cousens, Elizabeth M., and Charles K. Cater. *Toward Peace in Bosnia: Implementing the Dayton Accords*. Boulder, CO: Lynne Rienner, 2001.

Daalder, Ivo H., and Michael E. O'Hanlon. *Winning Ugly: NATO's War to Save Kosovo*. Washington, DC: Brookings Institution Press, 2001.

Defense Reform Commission (DRC). "AFBIH: A Single Military Force for the 21st Century." Sarajevo. September 2005. http://www.ohr.int/archive/drc-report/pdf/drc-report-2005-eng.pdf.

———. "The Path to Partnership to Peace." Sarajevo, September 2003. http://www.ohr.int/archive/drc-report/pdf/drc-eng.pdf.

Diamond, Larry. *Squandered Victory: The American Occupation and the Bungled Effort to Bring Democracy to Iraq*. New York: Holt, 2006.

Dobbins, James, Seth G. Jones, Keith Crane, Christopher S. Chivvis, Andrew Radin, F. Stephen Larrabee, Nora Bensahel, Brooke Stearns Lawson, and Benjamin W. Goldsmith. *Europe's Role in Nation-Building: From the Balkans to the Congo*. Santa Monica, CA: RAND, 2008.

Dobbins, James, Seth G. Jones, Keith Crane, and Beth Cole DeGrasse. *The Beginner's Guide to Nation-Building*. Santa Monica, CA: RAND, 2007.

Dobbins, James, Seth G. Jones, Keith Crane, Andrew Rathmell, Brett Steele, Richard Teltschik, and Anga R. Timilsina. *The UN's Role in Nation-Building: From the Congo to Iraq*. Santa Monica, CA: RAND, 2005.

Dobbins, James, Seth G. Jones, Benjamin Runkle, and Siddharth Mohandas. *Occupying Iraq: A History of the Coalition Provisional Authority*. Santa Monica, CA: RAND, 2009.

Dobbins, James, John G. McGinn, Keith Crane, Seth G. Jones, Rollie Lal, Andrew Rathmell, Rachel M. Swanger, and Anga R. Timilsina. *America's Role in Nation-Building: From Germany to Iraq*. Santa Monica, CA: RAND, 2003.

Dodge, Toby. *Iraq—From War to a New Authoritarianism*. London: Routledge, 2013.

Doyle, Michael W., and Nicholas Sambanis. *Making War and Building Peace: United Nations Peace Operations*. Princeton, NJ: Princeton University Press, 2006.

Dreisbach, Tristan. "Preparing for Peace: Croatia Rethinks Defense, 2000–2003." Innovations for Successful Societies, Princeton University, 2016. https://successfulsocieties.princeton.edu/sites/successfulsocieties/files/TD_Military_Croatia_FORMATTED_22Apr2016_ToU_0.pdf.

Dudley, Danijela. "Civil–Military Relations in Bosnia and Herzegovina: State Legitimacy and Defense Institutions." *Armed Forces & Society* 42, no. 1 (January 2016): 119–44.

Easterly, William. *The White Man's Burden: Why the West's Efforts to Aid the Rest Have Done So Much Ill and So Little Good.* New York: Penguin, 2007.

Facon, Isabelle. "Reforming Ukrainian Defense: No Shortage of Challenges." Institut Français des Relations Internationales (IFRI), May 2017. https://www.frstrategie.org/web/documents/publications/autres/2017/2017-facon-ifri-reforming-ukrainian-defense.pdf.

Fedorenko, Kostyantyn, Olena Rybiy, and Andreas Umland. "The Ukrainian Party System before and after the 2013–2014 Euromaidan." *Europe-Asia Studies* 68, no. 4 (2016): 609–30.

Feldman, Noah. "The Democratic Fatwa: Islam and Democracy in the Realm of Constitutional Politics." *Oklahoma Law Review* 58, no. 1 (2005).

Freedom House. "Jordan." Countries at the Crossroads, 2004. https://freedomhouse.org/report/countries-crossroads/2004/jordan.

Fukuyama, Francis. *The Origins of Political Order: From Prehuman Times to the French Revolution.* New York: Farrar, Straus and Giroux, 2011.

———. *Political Order and Political Decay: From the Industrial Revolution to the Globalization of Democracy.* New York: Farrar, Straus and Giroux, 2015.

———. *State-Building: Governance and World Order in the 21st Century.* Ithaca, NY: Cornell University Press, 2004.

Gaub, Florence. *Military Integration after Civil Wars: Multiethnic Armies, Identity and Post-Conflict Reconstruction.* London: Routledge, 2016.

Gellner, Ernest. *Nations and Nationalism.* Oxford: Blackwell, 1983.

George, Alexander L., and Andrew Bennett. *Case Studies and Theory Development in the Social Sciences.* Cambridge, MA: MIT Press, 2005.

Goldstone, Anthony. "UNTAET with Hindsight: The Peculiarities of Politics in an Incomplete State." *Global Governance* 10, no. 1 (January 2004): 83–98.

Gordon, Michael R., and Bernard E. Trainor. *The Endgame: The Inside Story of the Struggle for Iraq, from George W. Bush to Barack Obama.* New York: Random House, 2012.

Government Accountability Office (GAO). "Rebuilding Iraq: Resource, Security, Governance, Essential Services, and Oversight Issues." June 2004, 74–75. https://www.gao.gov/new.items/d05876.pdf.

Guterres, Francisco da Costa. "Elites and Prospects of Democracy in East Timor." PhD diss., Griffith Business School, South-East Queensland, Australia, 2006.

Hendrix, Cullen S. "Measuring State Capacity: Theoretical and Empirical Implications for the Study of Civil Conflict." *Journal of Peace Research* 47, no. 3 (2010): 273–85.

Hohe, Tanja. "'Totem Polls': Indigenous Concepts and 'Free and Fair' Elections in East Timor." *International Peacekeeping* 9, no. 4 (2002): 69–88.

Hood, Ludovic. "Security Sector Reform in East Timor, 1999–2004." *International Peacekeeping* 13, no. 1 (2006): 60–77.

Horowitz, Donald L. *A Democratic South Africa? Constitutional Engineering in a Divided Society.* Berkeley: University of California Press, 1991.

Howard, Colby, and Ruslan Pukhov, eds. *Brothers Armed: Military Aspects of the Crisis in Ukraine.* Minneapolis: East View, 2015.

Howard, Lise Morjé. *UN Peacekeeping in Civil Wars*. Cambridge: Cambridge University Press, 2008.

Hughes, Caroline. *Dependent Communities: Aid and Politics in Cambodia and East Timor*. Ithaca, NY: Cornell University Press, Southeast Asia Publications, 2009.

Huntington, Samuel P. *Political Order in Changing Societies*. New Haven, CT: Yale University Press, 1968.

ICMPD, "Financial, Organisational and Administrative Assessment of the BiH Police Forces and the State Border Service." June 30, 2004, https://www.esiweb.org/pdf/bridges/bosnia/EU_Functional_Review_of_Police.pdf.

Inspectors General U.S. Departments of State and Defense, "Interagency Assessment of Iraq Police Training." July 15, 2015. https://apps.dtic.mil/dtic/tr/fulltext/u2/a596323.pdf.

International Crisis Group (ICG). "Bosnia's Future." *Europe Report*, no. 232 (July 10, 2014). Accessed from http://www.crisisgroup.org.

———. "Bosnia's Incomplete Transition: Between Dayton and Europe." *Europe Report*, no. 198 (March 9, 2009). Accessed from http://www.crisisgroup.org.

———. "Bosnia's Stalled Police Reform: No Progress, No EU." *Europe Report*, no. 164 (September 6, 2005). Accessed from http://www.crisisgroup.org.

———. "Collapse in Kosovo." *Europe Report*, no. 144 (April 22, 2004). Accessed from http://www.crisisgroup.org.

———. "Ensuring Bosnia's Future: A New International Engagement Strategy." *Europe Report*, no. 180, February 15, 2007. Accessed from http://www.crisisgroup.org.

———. "Kosovo Report Card." *Europe Report 100*, August 28, 2000. Accessed from http://www.crisisgroup.org.

———. "Loose Ends: Iraq's Security Forces between US Drawdown and Withdrawal," *Middle East Report*, no. 99 (October 26, 2010). Accessed from http://www.crisisgroup.org.

———. "Resolving Timor-Leste's Crisis," *Asia Report*, no. 120 (October 10, 2006). Accessed from http://www.crisisgroup.org.

———. "Two to Tango: An Agenda for the New Kosovo SRSG." *Europe Report*, no. 148 (September 3, 2003). Accessed from http://www.crisisgroup.org.

Jackson, Colin. "Government in a Box: Counter-Insurgency, State Building, and the Technocratic Conceit." In *The New Counterinsurgency Era in Critical Perspective*, edited by Celeste Ward Gventer, David Martin Jones, and Michael Lawrence Rowan Smith, 82–110. Basingstoke, UK: Palgrave Macmillan, 2014.

Jones, James L., chairman. "The Report of the Independent Commission on the Security Forces of Iraq" (Jones Report), September 6, 2007. https://csis-prod.s3.amazonaws.com/s3fs-public/070906_isf.pdf.

Jones, Seth, Jeremy Wilson, Andrew Rathmell, and Jack Riley. *Establishing Law and Order after Conflict*. Santa Monica, CA: RAND, 2005.

Judah, Tim. *Kosovo: War and Revenge*. New Haven, CT: Yale University Press, 2002.

———. *Kosovo: What Everyone Needs to Know*. Oxford: Oxford University Press, 2008.

Kaufman, Stuart J. "Spiraling to Ethnic War: Elites, Masses, and Moscow in Moldova's Civil War." *International Security* 21, no. 2 (October 1, 1996): 108–38.

Kelmendi, Pellumb, and Andrew Radin. "UNsatisfied? Public Support for Postconflict International Missions." *Journal of Conflict Resolution* 62, no. 5 (May 2018): 983–1011.

King, Iain, and Whit Mason. *Peace at Any Price: How the World Failed Kosovo*. Ithaca, NY: Cornell University Press, 2006.

Kitschelt, Herbert, and Steven Wilkinson. *Patrons, Clients, and Policies: Patterns of Democratic Accountability and Political Competition*. Cambridge: Cambridge University Press, 2007.

Knaus, Gerald, and Felix Martin. "Travails of the European Raj." *Journal of Democracy* 14, no. 3 (2003): 60–74.

Kyiv School of Economics. "Co-Creation of Prozorro: An Account of Process and Actors." Transparency International, September 2016. https://www.transparency.org/whatwedo/publication/co_creation_of_prozorro_an_account_of_the_process_and_actors.

Lake, David A. *The Statebuilder's Dilemma: On the Limits of Foreign Intervention*. Ithaca, NY: Cornell University Press, 2016.

Lawrence, Adria. "Triggering Nationalist Violence: Competition and Conflict in Uprisings against Colonial Rule." *International Security* 35, no. 2 (September 17, 2010): 88–122.

Leroux-Martin, Philippe. *Diplomatic Counterinsurgency: Lesson from Bosnia and Herzegovina*. Cambridge: Cambridge University Press, 2013.

Levitsky, Steven, and Lucan Way. *Competitive Authoritarianism: Hybrid Regimes after the Cold War*. New York: Cambridge University Press, 2010.

Lindvall, Daniel. "The Limits of the European Vision in Bosnia and Herzegovina: An Analysis of the Police Reform Negotiations." PhD thesis, Stockholm University, 2009.

Locher, James, and Michael Donley. "Reforming Bosnia and Herzegovina's Defense Institutions." *NATO Review*, Winter 2004.

Mahoney, James. "After KKV: The New Methodology of Qualitative Research." *World Politics* 62, no. 1 (2010): 120–47.

Makiya, Kanan. *Republic of Fear: The Politics of Modern Iraq, Updated Edition*. Berkeley: University of California Press, 1998.

Manning, Carrie. "Party-Building on the Heels of War: El Salvador, Bosnia, Kosovo and Mozambique." *Democratization* 14, no. 2 (2007): 253–72.

Marten, Kimberly, and Olga Oliker. "Ukraine's Volunteer Militias May Have Saved the Country, but Now They Threaten It." *War on the Rocks,* September 14, 2017, https://warontherocks.com/2017/09/ukraines-volunteer-militias-may-have-saved-the-country-but-now-they-threaten-it/.

Maxwell, Rohan. "Bosnia-Herzegovina: From Three Armies to One." In *New Armies from Old: Merging Competing Military Forces after Civil Wars*. Edited by Roy Licklider. Washington, DC: Georgetown University Press, 2014.

Maxwell, Rohan, and John Andreas Olsen. *Destination NATO: Defence Reform in Bosnia and Herzegovina, 2003–2013*. London: Royal United Services Institute for Defence and Security Studies, 2013.

Miller, Paul D. *Armed State Building: Confronting State Failure, 1898–2012*. Ithaca, NY: Cornell University Press, 2013.

Muehlmann, Thomas. "Police Restructuring in Bosnia-Herzegovina: Problems of Internationally-Led Security Sector Reform." *Journal of Intervention and Statebuilding* 2, no. 1 (2008): 1–22.

NATO. "NATO's Practical Support to Ukraine." December 2015. https://www.nato.int/nato_static_fl2014/assets/pdf/pdf_2015_12/20151130_1512-factsheet-nato-ukraine-supportr_en.pdf.

Niner, Sarah. *Xanana: Leader of the Struggle for Independent Timor-Leste*. North Melbourne, Vic.: Australian Scholarly Publishing, 2009.

North, Douglass C., John Joseph Wallis, and Barry R. Weingast. *Violence and Social Orders: A Conceptual Framework for Interpreting Recorded Human History*. New York: Cambridge University Press, 2009.

Office of the High Representative (OHR). "Statement by the High Representative, Paddy Ashdown at Today's Press Conference," December 16, 2004, http://www.ohr.int/?ohr_archive=statement-by-the-high-representative-paddy-ashdown-at-todays-press-conference.

Oliker, Olga, Lynn E. Davis, Keith Crane, Andrew Radin, Celeste Ward Gventer, Susanne Sondergaard, James T. Quinlivan, Stephan Seabrook, Jacopo Bellasio, Andriy Bega, and Jakub Hlávka. *Security Sector Reform in Ukraine*. Santa Monica, CA: RAND, 2016. https://www.rand.org/pubs/research_reports/RR1475-1.html.

O'Neill, William G. *Kosovo: An Unfinished Peace*. Boulder, CO: Lynne Rienner, 2001.

Ottaway, Marina. "Rebuilding State Institutions in Collapsed States." *Development and Change* 33, no. 5 (November 1, 2002): 1001–23.

Paris, Roland. *At War's End: Building Peace after Civil Conflict*. Cambridge: Cambridge University Press, 2004.

———. "International Peacebuilding and the 'Mission Civilisatrice.'" *Review of International Studies* 28, no. 4 (2002): 637–56.

———. "Saving Liberal Peacebuilding." *Review of International Studies* 36, no. 2 (2010): 337–65.

Paul, Joshua. "An Estimation of the Internal Politics of the Ministry of Interior." March 15, 2007, unpublished manuscript, copy with author.

Perito, Robert. "The Coalition Provisional Authority's Experience with Public Security in Iraq: Lessons Identified." USIP Special Report, April 13, 2005. http://www.usip.org/publications/the-coalition-provisional-authoritys-experience-public-security-in-iraq-lessons.

———. *Where Is the Lone Ranger When We Need Him? America's Search for a Postconflict Stability Force*. 2nd ed. Washington, DC: United States Institute of Peace, 2010.

Perritt, Henry H. *Kosovo Liberation Army: The Inside Story of an Insurgency*. Urbana: University of Illinois Press, 2008.

———. *The Road to Independence for Kosovo: A Chronicle of the Ahtisaari Plan*. Cambridge: Cambridge University Press, 2009.

Petersen, Roger D. *Western Intervention in the Balkans: The Strategic Use of Emotion in Conflict*. Cambridge: Cambridge University Press, 2011.

Phillips, David L. *Liberating Kosovo: Coercive Diplomacy and U.S. Intervention*. Cambridge, MA: MIT Press, 2012.

Power, Samantha. *Chasing the Flame: Sergio Vieira de Mello and the Fight to Save the World.* New York: Penguin Press, 2008.

Pritchett, Lant, and Michael Woolcock. "Solutions When the Solution Is the Problem: Arraying the Disarray in Development." *World Development* 32, no. 2 (2004): 191–212. https://doi.org/10.1016/j.worlddev.2003.08.009.

"Public Opinion in Iraq: First Poll following Abu Ghraib Revelations." June 15, 2004. https://www.globalpolicy.org/images/pdfs/06iiacss.pdf.

Radin, Andrew. "Analysis of Current Events: 'Towards the Rule of Law in Kosovo: EULEX Should Go.'" *Nationalities Papers* 42, no. 2 (2014): 181–94.

———. "Domestic Opposition and the Timing of Democratic Transitions after War." *Security Studies* 26, no. 1 (2017): 93–123.

———. "The Limits of State Building: The Politics of War and the Ideology of Peace." PhD diss., Massachusetts Institute of Technology, 2012.

Ramet, Sabrina P. *The Three Yugoslavias: State-Building and Legitimation, 1918–2005.* Washington, DC: Woodrow Wilson Center Press, 2006.

Rathmell, Andrew, Olga Oliker, Terrence K. Kelly, David Brannan, and Keith Crane. *Developing Iraq's Security Sector: The Coalition Provisional Authority's Experience.* Santa Monica, CA: RAND, 2005.

Rees, Edward. *Under Pressure: FALINTIL-Forças de Defesa de Timor Leste Three Decades of Defence Force Development in Timor Leste, 1975–2004.* Geneva Centre for the Democratic Control of Armed Forces, Working paper no. 139, April 2004.

Reilly, Benjamin. *Democracy in Divided Societies: Electoral Engineering for Conflict Management.* Cambridge: Cambridge University Press, 2001.

———. "Political Engineering and Party Politics in Conflict-Prone Societies." *Democratization* 13, no. 5 (2006): 811–27.

Reveron, Derek S. *Exporting Security: International Engagement, Security Cooperation, and the Changing Face of the US Military.* 2nd ed. Washington, DC: Georgetown University Press, 2016.

Robinson, Linda, Patrick B. Johnston, and Gillian S. Oak. *US Special Operations Forces in the Philippines, 2001–2014.* Santa Monica, CA: RAND, 2016.

Roeder, Philip G., and Donald S. Rothchild. *Sustainable Peace: Power and Democracy after Civil Wars.* Ithaca, NY: Cornell University Press, 2005.

Rohr-Garztecki, Marek. "The Long Shadow of History: Civilian Control and Military Effectiveness in Poland." In *Reforming Civil-Military Relations in New Democracies: Democratic Control and Military Effectiveness in Comparative Perspectives*, edited by Aurel Croissant and David Kuehn, 23–40. Cham, Switzerland: Springer, 2017.

Rosen, Nir. *In the Belly of the Green Bird: The Triumph of the Martyrs in Iraq.* New York: Free Press, 2006.

Sassoon, Joseph. *Saddam Hussein's Ba'th Party: Inside an Authoritarian Regime.* Cambridge: Cambridge University Press, 2011.

Schaefer, Agnes Gereben, Lynn E. Davis, Ely Ratner, Molly Dunigan, Jeremiah Goulka, Heather Peterson, and K. Jack Riley. *Developing a Defense Sector Assessment Rating Tool.* Santa Monica, CA: RAND, 2010. https://www.rand.org/pubs/technical_reports/TR864.html.

Sherman, Matt, and Joshua Paul. "The Role of Police in Counterinsurgency Operations in Iraq, 2003–6." In *Policing Insurgencies: Cops as Counterinsurgents*. Edited by C. Christine Fair and Sumit Ganguly. New Delhi, India: Oxford University Press, 2014.

Short, Elliot. "The Orao Affair: The Key to Military Integration in Post-Dayton Bosnia and Herzegovina." *Journal of Slavic Military Studies* 31, no. 1 (2018): 37–64.

Skendaj, Elton. *Creating Kosovo: International Oversight and the Making of Ethical Institutions*. Ithaca, NY: Cornell University Press, 2014.

Staniland, Paul. *Networks of Rebellion: Explaining Insurgent Cohesion and Collapse*. Ithaca, NY: Cornell University Press, 2014.

Stedman, Stephen John. "Spoiler Problems in Peace Processes." *International Security* 22, no. 2 (1997): 5–53.

Stewart, Rory, and Gerald Knaus. *Can Intervention Work?* New York: Norton, 2011.

Suhrke, Astri. "Peacekeepers as Nation-Builders: Dilemmas of the UN in East Timor." *International Peacekeeping* 8, no. 4 (Winter 2001): 1–20.

Suri, Jeremi. *Liberty's Surest Guardian: Rebuilding Nations after War from the Founders to Obama*. New York: Free Press, 2012.

Talmadge, Caitlin. *The Dictator's Army: Battlefield Effectiveness in Authoritarian Regimes*. Ithaca, NY: Cornell University Press, 2015.

Tansey, Oisín. "Evaluating the Legacies of State-Building: Success, Failure, and the Role of Responsibility." *International Studies Quarterly* 58, no. 1 (March 1, 2014): 174–86. https://doi.org/10.1111/isqu.12094.

———. *Regime-Building: Democratization and International Administration*. Oxford: Oxford University Press, 2009.

Toal, Gerard, and Carl T. Dahlman. *Bosnia Remade: Ethnic Cleansing and Its Reversal*. Oxford: Oxford University Press, 2011.

Toal, Gerard, John O'Loughlin, and Dino Djipa. "Bosnia-Herzegovina Ten Years after Dayton: Constitutional Change and Public Opinion." *Eurasian Geography and Economics* 47, no. 1 (2006): 61–75.

Tolksdorf, Dominik. "Incoherent Peacebuilding: The European Union's Support for the Police Sector in Bosnia and Herzegovina, 2002–8." *International Peacekeeping* 21, no. 1 (2014): 56–73.

Traub, James. "Inventing East Timor." *Foreign Affairs* 79, no. 4 (July 1, 2000): 74–89.

United Nations (UN). "Report of the Secretary-General on United Nations Interim Administrative Mission in Kosovo." July 12, 1999, S/1999/779.

Wilk, Andrzej. "The Best Army Ukraine Has Ever Had: Changes in Ukraine's Armed Forces since the Russian Aggression." Warsaw: Centre for Eastern Studies, July 7, 2017. https://www.osw.waw.pl/en/publikacje/osw-studies/2017-07-07/best-army-ukraine-has-ever-had-changes-ukraines-armed-forces.

Wilson, Bu Vicki Elizabeth. "Smoke and Mirrors: The Development of the East Timorese Police, 1999–2009." PhD thesis, Australian National University, 2010. https://doi.org/10.25911/5d63bdff035fe.

Wisler, Dominique. "The Police Reform in Bosnia and Herzegovina." In *After Intervention. Public Security Management in Post-Conflict Societies—From Intervention to Sustainable*

Local Ownership, edited by Anja Ebnöther and Philipp Fluri, 142–58. Vienna: Bureau for Security Policy, 2005.

Young, Thomas-Durell. *Anatomy of Post-Communist European Defense Institutions: The Mirage of Military Modernity*. New York: Bloomsbury Academic, 2017.

Zürcher, Christoph, Carrie Manning, Kristie Evenson, Rachel Hayman, Sarah Riese, and Nora Roehner. *Costly Democracy: Peacebuilding and Democratization after War*. Stanford, CA: Stanford University Press, 2013.

INDEX

Information in figures and tables is indicated by *f* and *t*, respectively.

ABOUT THE AUTHOR

Andrew Radin is a political scientist at the RAND Corporation. His work at RAND has focused on European security and building partner state institutions. In a 2015 project, he worked with the government of Ukraine to offer recommendations on security sector reform. He has also written and contributed to RAND reports on topics including the threat of "hybrid" warfare in the Baltics; Russian views of the international order; and the political, economic, and military vulnerabilities of Europe. His academic and policy research on intervention and state building has been published in *Security Studies*, the *Journal of Conflict Resolution*, *Washington Quarterly*, and *Survival*, among other venues. He has taught at Georgetown University's Walsh School of Foreign Service. He was a postdoctoral fellow at the Harvard Kennedy School and the University of Southern California. He earned a PhD in political science from the Massachusetts Institute of Technology.

CPSIA information can be obtained
at www.ICGtesting.com
Printed in the USA
BVHW030920270520
580207BV00036B/50

9 781626 167940